Macro Magic

in

Microsoft Word 6 & 7

A Kid's Only Guide to Writing Macros

Learn to Write Programs in WordBasic

Laura Bufano Edge

Rhache Publishers, Ltd.
9 Orchard Drive • Gardiner, NY • 12525–5710

Macro Magic in Microsoft Word 6 & 7—A Kids Only Guide to Writing Macros
 by Laura Bufano Edge
Cover Design by Carolyn Hutchings Edlund
Wizards designed and created by Carolyn Hutchings Edlund
Book Design by Richard H. Adin Freelance Editorial Services
Production Services provided by Richard H. Adin, Freelance Editorial Services,
 9 Orchard Drive, Gardiner, NY 12525 (914–883–5884)
Editor: Paul R. Edlund

Published in the United States of America

Printed in the United States of America. 0 9 8 7 6 5 4 3 2 1

Rhache Publishers, Ltd.
9 Orchard Drive
Gardiner, NY 12525–5710
(914) 883–5884 / 7169 • (888) 643–0302 / 849–5257

Microsoft®, Windows 3.1®, and Windows 95® are the registered trademarks of Microsoft Corporation. Word® is the registered trademark of the Microsoft Corporation. Other trademarks of products mentioned in this book are held by the companies that produce them. Trademarks are used in this book for purposes of identification only.

ISBN 1–887288–02–3 (print edition) & ISBN 1–887288–04–X (disk edition)

Library of Congress Cataloging-in-Publication Data

Edge, Laura Bufano, 1953–

 Macro magic in Microsoft Word 6 & 7 : a kid's only guide to writing macros : learn to write programs in WordBasic / Laura Bufano Edge.

  p. cm.

 Summary: Provides an introduction to macroprogramming and WordBasic language, with a number of projects to help build and reinforce skills.

 ISBN 1-887288-02-3 (pbk.). — ISBN 1-887288-04-X (disk)

 1. WordBasic (Computer program language)—Juvenile literature. 2. Microsoft Word—Juvenile literature. 3. Word processing—Juvenile literature. 4. Macroprogramming—Juvenile literature. [1. Macroprogramming. 2. WordBasic (Computer program language) 3. Microsoft Word. 4. Word Processing.] I. Title.

Z52.5.W52E34 1997
652.5'536—dc21   97–26408
                 CIP
                 AC

What You Need to Use this Book

Besides imagination and the desire to have fun, you will need the following software:

1. Microsoft Windows (3.1 or 95)
2. Microsoft Word for Windows version 6 or 7

Surprise! Nothing special is needed. Just what you already have.

Why Both Word 6.1 & 7 in One Book?

The answer is really pretty simple, at least I think so ☺ ! A lot of kids have one of these programs on their home computer and the other program on their school computer. With both programs covered in one book, that's all you need to buy — just one book. And, if you get a summer job using a computer and it has a different word processing program than what you use at home, well, we've got two of the most popular ones covered here.

Now that you've got the lowdown on what you need and the why's, let's have some fun learning the fundamentals of programming and writing macros.

Laura Edge

P.S. If you get confused or want to ask a question, I'll try to help. If you have access to the Internet, you can send me e-mail at bufanoedge@aol.com. If you can't send me e-mail, you can write me in care of Rhache Publishers, Ltd., 9 Orchard Drive, Gardiner, NY 12525–5710. They will make sure I get your letter.

Meet Laura Edge

Laura is the author of over 45 computer-related manuals and a regular contributor to her local newspaper of computer-related articles. She has a lot of experience with both kids and computers. Laura has taught over 400 computer classes and more than 2,500 students. She has 7 years experience as a computer programmer along with 5 years experience teaching 7th and 8th grade math. Laura graduated from the University of Texas with high honors.

A Special Note!

If you use WordPerfect 6.1 or 7 at home or school, you can learn to write macros in WordPerfect, just as you are learning to do it in WordBasic 6 or 7. **Macro Magic in WordPerfect 6.1 & 7** (ISBN 1-887288-03-1), the companion to this book, is available at your local bookstore.

If you would like the on-line version of either **Macro Magic in Microsoft Word 6 & 7** or **Macro Magic in WordPerfect 6.1 & 7**, write or call us:

Rhache Publishers, Ltd.
9 Orchard Drive, Gardiner, NY 12525–5710
(914) 883-5884 or 883-7169

If you have any suggestions for macros that you would like to learn in future editions of this book, drop us a line. Your suggestions are welcome.

Dedication

For the guys,
Gerry, Jeremy, and Jonathan

What's Coming Up
(What Other Books Call the Table of Contents)

Let the Magic Begin...

CHAPTER 1

The Basics

How in the world did people get along without computers in the old days? You can certainly write something without using a word processor, but using a word processor makes it so, SO, SO much easier!

You've probably been using Microsoft Word to type stuff. The program works great for that, but it can do a whole lot more than type words. In this book, we're going to look at some of the incredibly cool features that come with Microsoft Word. We're going to find ways to make your life easier by getting the most out of your word processor.

First, let's go over the basics—just so we're talking the same language.

What's on the Screen

When you start Microsoft Word, you'll see a blank document window waiting for you to fill it up with anything you want. The screen is like a clean sheet of paper with margins and spacing already set.

Each new document window contains four key elements: a title bar, a menu bar, toolbars and a status bar.

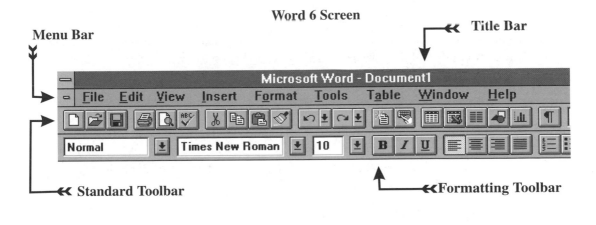

Word 6 Screen

Title Bar

Menu Bar

Standard Toolbar

Formatting Toolbar

Word 6 Status Bar

Word 7 Screen

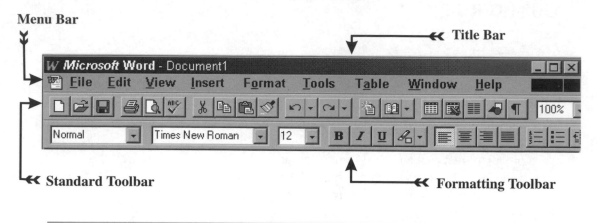

Menu Bar

Title Bar

Standard Toolbar

Formatting Toolbar

Word 7 Status Bar

Above the document window, at the very top of the screen, is the title bar. The title bar displays "Microsoft Word" and the name of the active document.

Immediately below the title bar is the menu bar.

The menus on the menu bar are used to give Microsoft Word commands. A command is an instruction that tells the computer to do something. Commands are grouped in menus. For example, the File menu contains the commands related to files, such as opening a file, closing a file or saving a file.

Below the menu bar are the toolbars. Menu items that are used a lot are listed on toolbars. In Microsoft Word, two toolbars are displayed automatically when you start the program: the standard toolbar and the formatting toolbar.

The Status bar is at the very bottom of the screen. Word uses it to show information about your document, and to show prompts and messages when you use certain commands. When you make macros, you'll need to look at the status bar from time to time.

Choosing Commands

There are several ways to choose commands in Microsoft Word. You can choose selections from the menu bar, click a toolbar button or press a shortcut key on your keyboard. Each method works great, so use the method that seems the easiest to you. There is no ONE way to use Microsoft Word!

CHOOSING COMMANDS FROM THE MENU BAR

The menus on the menu bar contain all of the commands for Microsoft Word. Each of the first level menus offer its own set of related commands.

To choose a command from a menu, use the mouse to point to that menu and then click the left mouse button once. When the list of available commands appears below the menu name, point to and click on the command you want.

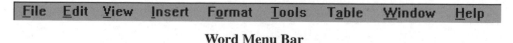

Word Menu Bar

In this book whenever I want you to make a menu selection, the menu name will be printed in bold type, like

Click on **Tools**.

"Click" lets you know that you need to press the left mouse button once, and **Tools** tells you which menu to choose.

Another way to access the menu bar is by pressing the **Alt** key and then the underlined letter on the menu. The underlined letter is a hot key that will let you get to the command quickly. So, to use this method,

Tools	
<u>S</u>pelling...	F7
<u>G</u>rammar...	
<u>T</u>hesaurus...	Shift+F7
<u>H</u>yphenation...	
<u>L</u>anguage...	
<u>W</u>ord Count...	
<u>A</u>utoCorrect...	
Mail Me<u>r</u>ge...	
<u>E</u>nvelopes and Labels...	
<u>P</u>rotect Document...	
Re<u>v</u>isions...	
<u>M</u>acro...	
<u>C</u>ustomize...	
<u>O</u>ptions...	

1. Press the **Alt** key.
2. Press the letter "**F**"
   The letter "F" is the underlined letter for the File menu. When you press the letter "F" the drop down menu for File commands will appear.
3. Press the letter "**S**" to choose the Save command from the File menu. You are taken to the Save file dialog box.
4. Press **Esc** to close a menu without giving a command. If you change your mind and don't want to give a command, press the Esc key to "Escape" from giving the command.
5. Click on **Cancel** to close a dialog box without giving a command. When a dialog box is displayed on the screen and you decide not to issue a command, click on Cancel to "Cancel" the command.

CHOOSING COMMANDS WITH KEYBOARD SHORTCUT KEYS

As you check out the different menus, you'll notice that on some of the menus there are shortcut keys (like F7, or Ctrl + O) listed beside the menu selection. These shortcut keys tell you a quick way to give the command through the keyboard.

Click on **File**. The shortcut key Ctrl + O appears next to the menu selection "Open..." That means that you can open a document by clicking on File, Open or by pressing Ctrl + O on your keyboard.

The sequence for pressing shortcut keys is important. Microsoft Word needs to know exactly what you're asking it to do. To give a command using a keyboard shortcut key,

1. Press and *hold down* the first key listed.
2. Press and release the second key.
3. Release the first key.

In this book when I say,

Press **Ctrl + O**

I'll be asking you to press a keyboard shortcut key. "Press" means that these are keys on your keyboard. Press and hold down the Ctrl key, then press and release the letter

"O," then release the Ctrl key. As you use shortcut keys more and more, the sequence for pressing the keys will seem automatic. You won't even have to think about it. Click on Cancel to close the Open dialog box.

CHOOSING COMMANDS USING TOOLBAR BUTTONS

Below the menu bar are the toolbars.

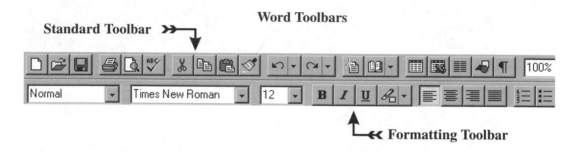

Menu items that are used a lot are listed on toolbars. Choosing a command from a toolbar saves you time. You can give the command by clicking on one button rather than making two menu selections.

When you move the mouse pointer to a toolbar button, the name of the command will show in a little box called a quick tip. If you can't remember where a command is located, you can move the mouse pointer to each icon (picture) and Microsoft Word will tell you what the button does.

When you need to select a command from a toolbar in this book, I'll tell you the command name in bold type, and which toolbar holds the button. For example,

Click on **Save** on the Standard toolbar.

"Click" lets you know that you need to press the left mouse button once. **Save** tells you the command name, and "Standard toolbar" tells you which toolbar holds the button.

So, you can use menus, keyboard shortcut keys, or toolbar buttons to give commands. For example, to save a file you can,

Click on **File**;
Click on **Save**.
   or
Press **Alt**;
Press **F** to issue the File command;
Press **S** to issue the Save command.
   or
Press **Ctrl + S**.
   or
Click on **Save** on the Standard toolbar

All of these methods will take you to the same place. Use whichever method is most comfortable for you.

Macro Basics

WHAT'S A MACRO?

Macros were invented to make life easier. You know how in the morning you have to do the same boring stuff every day—eat breakfast, brush your teeth, figure out what to wear, get dressed, comb your hair, make your bed, and go to school. If you had a macro to do those things, you could sleep a whole lot longer. You'd just get up, run the macro and presto, you'd be at school. A macro lets you do what needs to be done once, and then whenever you need to do it again, you run the macro and the program does it for you.

Well, that's the idea anyway. Macros can't make your bed for you, but they can do anything you can think of to do in Microsoft Word.

HOW DO YOU MAKE A MACRO?

Macros range from very short, simple commands to very elaborate programs. You can make a macro by recording it with the macro recorder, writing it with the macro programming language, WordBasic, or both.

The macro recorder is like a tape recorder. You turn it on, press the keys to be recorded, and turn it off. Then, you run the macro and the recorded instructions are performed automatically by Microsoft Word. For example, if you need to type your name in a document, that task might take sixteen keystrokes. If typing your name was a macro, the task would take one keystroke, running the macro.

Sometimes you need a macro to perform tasks that cannot be recorded. That's when WordBasic comes into the picture. WordBasic is a macro programming language that allows you to create macros that go beyond what the macro recorder can handle. For example, a macro to practice your multiplication facts could pick random numbers, ask you to multiply them, tell you if you got the answer right, and keep score. Using WordBasic turns you into a real live, totally brilliant, extremely impressive, computer programmer.

So, start thinking of things you do over and over again with your word processor. Macros to do those things can make your life a lot easier. Plus, they're fun to make!

GETTING READY TO RECORD — THE PLANNING

When you make a macro, record as much as you can, and write the rest.

The first step in recording a macro is planning — lots of planning.

Think about the go and the flow, which is illustrated on the next page.

The "go" is what the macro will do when it is going, or running. Think about each task you want the macro to perform. Exactly what is it suppose to accomplish?

The "flow" is the order in which the tasks are performed. When you run your macro, does each task have to be carried out in a certain order? For example, does your macro select options from Microsoft Word menus? If so, does it make all related selections at the same time? You don't want to open the same menu several times when you could open it just once.

Another thing to think about when you are planning a macro is where the insertion point needs to be when you start the macro recorder. When the macro

The Go and The Flow

Planning

What will this macro do?
What is on the screen?
Where is the insertion point?
What should be done first?

Task 1

Task 2

Task 3

recorder is on, your word processor is recording your every move. It is also performing the task you are recording. So, if you tell the recorder to change your margins, your margins will be changed in the current document too. This may not be what you want.

A good rule to follow when you're making a macro is: unless your macro contains editing commands that require a document to be active in the document window, start the macro recorder with a blank screen.

The goal in all of this planning is to make the macro recording session go smoothly so you can start using your macros. But don't worry. If you mess up while recording a macro, there is always a way to fix it. Yes, I did say *always*. As you learn more about macros, you'll see examples of things that can cause problems in macros, and lots of ways to fix those problems. So relax, have fun and record to your heart's content.

How Will You Run the Macro?

After you're done planning the recording session, think about how you will run the macro. You can run any macro by clicking on the Macro command on the Tools menu. Or, you can save time by having each macro assigned to a button on a toolbar, a menu, or a shortcut key on your keyboard, as illustrated on the next page.

For simple, quick macros that you use all the time, assigning them to a shortcut key is the best method. When you need to run the macro, simply press the shortcut key and the macro runs immediately. For more complex macros, assigning them to a

Assign to a toolbar

Assign to a menu

Assign to the keyboard

**Three ways to run a macro: from a toolbar; from a menu; or from
a shortcut key on the keyboard**

button on a toolbar or a menu makes them easy to find and remember. So before you
begin recording, choose the best way to run the macro.

Well, we're ready. Let's start recording!

If your computer is not up and running, turn it on. Then start Microsoft Word in
version 6 or version 7 as shown below.

In Microsoft Word version 6:

1. Double-click on the **Word for Windows** group icon in the Windows Program
    Manager.
2. Double-click on **Word for Windows**.

In Microsoft Word version 7:

1. Click on **Start**.
2. Click on **Programs**.

3.   Click on **Microsoft Word**.

     A blank document window appears, waiting for your instructions.

Let's get started!
Your first macro recording
session begins in Chapter 2.

CHAPTER 2

Recording Macros

You've planned it. You've decided how you want to run it. Now it's time to record your macro.

To **record** a macro is to tell Word what actions you want to put into the macro.

To **run** a macro is to have those actions "played back."

Keyboard Macros

RECORDING A KEYBOARD MACRO

The first macro you're going to record will do some typing for you. If you have to do reports on a regular basis, the name of the report will change each time. But the other heading information will not change. So, this macro will type the word "by" in the center of a line, move the insertion point down to the next line by pressing Enter for you, and then type your name in the center of a line. You can use it any time you want a quick way to type your name on a paper or report.

1. Double-click on **REC** on the Status Bar at the bottom of the screen.

Record »———▶

The Record Macro Dialog Box appears on your screen.

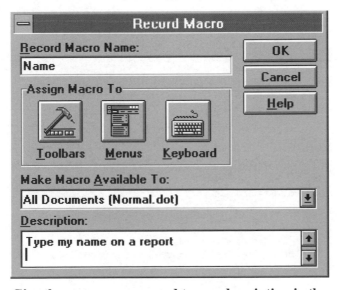

**Give the macro a name and type a description in the
Record Macro Dialog Box**

2. Type **Name** in the Record Macro Name box.

   A macro name can contain any combination of upper and lowercase letters, but cannot include spaces, commas, semicolons, colons, dashes or periods. Macro names should be descriptive. You want to be able to remember what your macros do when you need them. Use a combination of upper and lowercase letters to make your macros easy to read. For example, a macro that deletes a line of text might be called DeleteLine. A macro that averages your grades could be called AverageGrades.

3. Click once in the description box to position the insertion point.

4. Type: "**Type my name on a report**" in the description box.

   A macro description can be up to 255 characters in length. It's a good idea to write a short description for your macros, because over time, as you accumulate lots of macros, you may not be able to remember what each one does. The description will give you a helpful reminder.

5. Click on **Keyboard**.

   After you fill in the name and description text boxes, you need to tell Word how you want to run the macro. The Name macro will be run by pressing a shortcut key on the keyboard. The Customize dialog box appears on your screen.

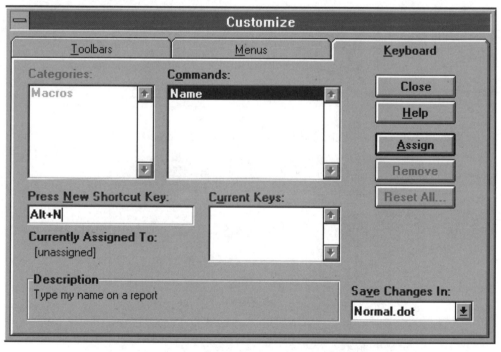

Press a shortcut key to assign a macro to the keyboard

The name you entered for the macro appears in the "Commands" section of the dialog box. The description appears in the "Description" area.

6. Press **Alt + N**.

   This is where you tell Word which shortcut key you want to use for the macro. Press the shortcut key you want to use in the Press New Shortcut Key box.

Make sure the shortcut key is not already assigned to some other function. Word will tell you this under the "Currently Assigned To" section of the dialog box. Make sure it says (unassigned). You don't want to accidentally wipe out something that comes with Word. You might need it later!

7. Click on **Assign**. Notice in the "Current Keys" text box, **Alt + N** appears as the shortcut key.

8. Click on **Close**. The Macro Record toolbar is displayed on your screen.

Stop Button **Pause Button**

The left button is the stop button and the right button is the pause button. To stop a macro recording session, click on the stop button. The pause button turns off the recorder temporarily so that you can do things that you don't want recorded. When you are ready to turn the recorder back on, click on the pause button again.

9. Press **Ctrl + E** to turn on centering.

Type: **by**

Press **Enter**.

Type: *your name.*

Press **Enter** three times.

Press **Ctrl + L** to turn on left justification (so you can begin typing your report at the left margin).

The macro recorder does not record mouse movements in the document window, so use the keyboard for moving the insertion point and selecting text. You can select menu choices with the mouse and Word will record those choices.

10. Click on **Stop** on the Macro Record Toolbar to turn off the macro recorder (the left button). You can also stop a macro recording session by double-clicking on REC on the Status Bar.

That's it! You've made your first macro. Now, let's run that baby!

RUNNING A KEYBOARD MACRO

Make sure before you run a macro that the document window is clear or the insertion point is where it needs to be for the macro to work properly. In other words, don't have the insertion point in the middle of a document and run a macro that will type a bunch of stuff and mess it up.

Let's clear the document window so that you can see exactly what the macro does.

1. Press **Ctrl + Home** to move the insertion point to the top of the document.

2. Press **Shift + Ctrl + End** to highlight the entire document window.

3. Press the **Delete** key on the keyboard

Now to run the Name macro,

1. Press **Ctrl + E** to turn on centering.

2. Type: **Macro Mania** as the name of your report.

3.   Press **Enter**.

4.   Press **Alt + N** to run the Name macro. Presto! Word types "by" and your name. The insertion point is at the left margin, ready for you to begin typing your report.

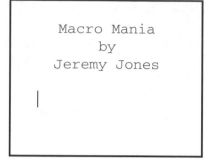

```
          Macro Mania
               by
          Jeremy Jones


          |
```

The Name Macro

THE ERASESCREEN MACRO

When you begin a macro recording session, you need to start from a blank screen. Wouldn't it be handy to have a macro that would erase the screen for you? If you record the keystrokes you pressed just a second ago when you erased the screen yourself, you'll be able to press one keystroke to erase the screen from now on. Let's record the EraseScreen macro.

1.   Double-click on **REC** on the Status Bar.

2.   Type **EraseScreen** in the Record Macro Name box.

3.   Click once in the description box to position the insertion point.

4.   Type: "**Erase the screen**" in the description box.

5.   Click on **Keyboard**.
      This is a macro that you'll run all the time. To make it quick and easy, assign it to a shortcut key on your keyboard. The Customize dialog box appears on your screen.

6.   Press **Alt + E**.
      Check to make sure that the shortcut key is not already assigned to some other function. Word will tell you this under the "Currently Assigned To" section of the dialog box. Make sure it says (unassigned).

7.   Click on **Assign**.

8.   Click on **Close**. The Macro Record toolbar is displayed on your screen.

9.   Press **Ctrl + Home** to move the insertion point to the top of the document.
      Press **Shift + Ctrl + End** to highlight the entire document window.
      Press the **Delete** key on the keyboard.

10.   Click on **Stop** on the Macro Record Toolbar to turn off the macro recorder.

When you record a macro, you are also performing the tasks that are being recorded. So, the screen is now blank because recording the EraseScreen macro performed the steps in the macro and erased your screen. Let's run the Name macro again, and then erase the screen with the EraseScreen macro.

1. Press **Ctrl + E** to turn on centering.
2. Type: **Michael and Shaq** as the name of your report.
3. Press **Enter**.
4. Press **Alt + N** to run the Name macro. The Name macro finishes typing the heading of your report.
5. Press **Alt + E** to run the EraseScreen macro. The EraseScreen macro erases the screen faster than you can say "Erase!"

One of the benefits of using macros is that you can run them in any Word document. You can run the Name macro any time you need to type a report. Type the name of the report first, then run the macro to add the rest of the heading information. Or at the end of a report, run the macro to add your name to the bottom. Experiment with that for a few minutes. Use any kind of crazy name for the name of your report. Run the EraseScreen macro to erase the screen after each report.

KEEPING TRACK OF YOUR KEYBOARD MACROS

As you accumulate more and more keyboard macros, it's easy to forget the shortcut key for each one. There's nothing worse than trying to use a quick little macro and not being able to remember the shortcut key. That drives me crazy! So, since macros are designed to make life easier, let's make a macro that will let us add each keyboard macro and its shortcut key to a master list.

1. Click on **New** on the Standard toolbar (first button on the left).
   First, you need an empty file.
2. Press **Ctrl + E** to turn on centering.
   Type: "**Shortcut Key Macros**" as the title.
   Press **Enter** three times.
   Press **Ctrl + L** to turn on left justification.
   Type: "**Shortcut Key**"
   Press the **Tab** key 4 times.
   Type: "**What the Macro Does**"
   Press **Enter** two times.

This sets up the layout of the file that will hold the list of shortcut keys. The screen should look like this example.

Shortcut Key Macros	
Shortcut Key	What the Macro Does

Your screen may look a bit different from the example if the default font for your computer is different from the Times font shown above. That's okay. Your font will work just fine.

3.   Click on **Save** on the Standard toolbar (third button from the left) to save the file.
4.   Type **shortcut** as the file name.
5.   Press **Enter** to save the file.
6.   Click on **File**.
7.   Click on **Close**.
8.   Click on **New** on the Standard toolbar.

Now let's make the shortcut key macro.

1.   Double-click on **REC** on the Status Bar to turn on the macro recorder.
2.   Type: "**Shortcut**" for the macro name.
3.   Click once in the description box to position the insertion point.
4.   Type: "**Add macro shortcut keys to a master list**" for the description.
5.   Click on **Keyboard**.
6.   Press **Alt + S** for the shortcut key to run this macro ("S" for shortcut of course).
7.   Click on **Assign**.
8.   Click on **Close**.
9.   Click on **Open** on the Standard toolbar (second button from the left).
     Click on **shortcut.doc** (Word 6) or **shortcut** (Word 7) as the document to open.
     Press **Enter** to open the document.
     Press **Ctrl + End** to position the insertion point at the bottom of the document.
10. Click on **Stop** on the Macro Record Toolbar (the square).

RUNNING THE SHORTCUT MACRO

When you run the Shortcut macro, it will retrieve the Shortcut file and position the insertion point at the bottom of the document. You can then add your macros to the list. Try it for the three macros we've done so far, the Name macro, the EraseScreen macro and the Shortcut macro.

1.   Click on **File**.
2.   Click on **Close**.
3.   Click on **New** on the Standard toolbar (first button on the left).
4.   Press **Alt + S** to run the Shortcut macro.
5.   Type: **Alt + N**.
6.   Press the **Tab** key 4 or 5 times.
     The insertion point should be lined up under the words "What the Macro Does." If it's not, press the Tab key again.
7.   Type: **Types my name on a report**
8.   Press **Enter**.
9.   Type: **Alt + E**.
10. Press the **Tab** key 4 or 5 times.
11. Type: **Erases the screen**
12. Press **Enter**.
13. Type: **Alt + S**.
14. Press the **Tab** key 4 or 5 times.
15. Type: **Adds shortcut keys to this list**

16. Press **Enter** (so the insertion point will be in the right spot the next time you run this macro).
17. Click on **Save** on the Standard toolbar to save the file.

Shortcut Key Macros

Shortcut Key   What the Macro Does
Alt + N   Types my name on a report
Alt + E   Erases the screen
Alt + sincerely   Adds shortcut keys to this list

18. Click on **File**.
19. Click on **Close** to close the file.

Pretty cool isn't it? Macros can even retrieve files for you. Now, anytime you need to check which shortcut key runs a macro, press Alt + S to see the list. Go ahead and check it out.

FILES IN WORD 7

When you recorded the Shortcut macro, Word 6 typed the file name (Shortcut.doc) and the exact location of where to find the file (C:\WINWORD) in the macro. Word 7 typed the file name in the macro, but not the exact location of where to find it inside your computer. Because of this change in Word 7, when you're running macros that open files, you may encounter an error message stating that Word could not find the file.

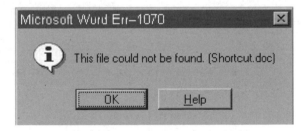

There is an easy way to fix this problem. In the next chapter, you'll learn how to edit macros, and modify the statement that Word created so that it knows exactly where to find the Shortcut file. For now, if you get this error message on your screen, click on **OK** to remove the message box from the screen. Then click on **Open** on the Standard toolbar to establish the document folder as the active folder. Click on **Cancel** to close the Open dialog box. Press **Alt + S** to run the Shortcut macro again.

You may never see this error message, but now you know how to handle it if you do.

Menu Macros

RECORDING A MENU MACRO

Let's record a macro that does some formatting for a History report and types some information for us. We'll assign it to a menu.

1. Press **Alt + E** to erase the document window if it is not blank.
2. Double-click on **REC** on the Status Bar to start the macro recorder.
3. Type **HistoryReportFormat** in the Record Macro Name box.
4. Type **History report formatting** for the description.
5. Click on **Menus** to assign this macro to a menu.

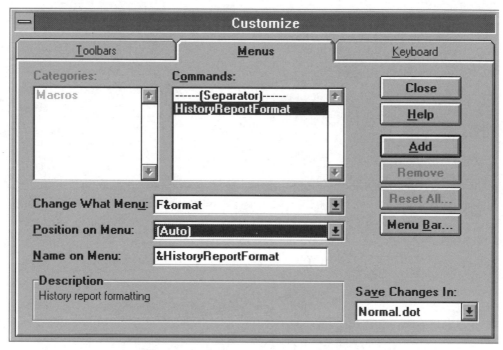

Assign the HistoryReportFormat macro to the format menu

The name you entered for the macro appears in the Commands section of the dialog box. The description appears in the Description area.

6. Click on ↓ to the right of the "Change What Menu" box to select the menu you want to change.
7. Click on **F&ormat** in the "Change What Menu" box.
    The "Change What Menu" box is where you tell Word which menu will contain the macro. The default is the Tools menu. Since this macro does formatting for a History report, we'll assign it to the Format menu. The & in a menu selection means that the next letter is underlined on the menu. Underlined letters are the shortcut keys for the selection. So on the Format menu, the letter "o" is the shortcut key for selecting the Format menu.
    Choose the menu that most closely relates to what your macro does.
8. Select **(Auto)** in the "Position on Menu" box.

"Position on Menu" tells Word where the macro will appear on the menu. Auto means that Word will automatically position similar menu items together, all macros together, for example. You can position your macro at the top (At Top) of the menu or at the bottom of the menu (At Bottom). You can also specify an exact position on the list of menu choices.

9. Name on Menu: **&HistoryReportFormat**. "Name on Menu" is the name that will appear on the menu. Word automatically displays the name of the macro as the name on the menu. It's a good idea to leave it at that, so that if you need to edit the macro, the name on the edit screen will be the same as the name on the menu to run the macro.

10. Click on **Add**.

11. Click on **Close**. The Macro Record toolbar is displayed on your screen.

12. Perform the actions you want to record.

- Click on **File**, **Page Setup...**
- Set the Top and Bottom margins to 1.5"
- Click on **OK**.
- Click on **Format**, **Font...**
- Select Font = **Courier New**, Font Style = **Regular**, Size = **10**
- Click on **OK**.
- Type "**Name:**"
- Press the **spacebar** two times.
- Type your name.
- Press the **Tab** key 4 or 5 times (If your name or your teacher's name is long, pressing the tab key 4 times will work best. If the names are short, press the tab key 5 times.)
- Type "**Teacher:**"
- Press the **spacebar** two times.
- Type **Mrs. Hanson** (or your teacher's name)
- Press **Enter**.
- Type "**Date:**"
- Press the **spacebar** two times.
- Click on **Insert, Date and Time. . .**
- Click on **mm/dd/yy** (like **9/21/97**) as the date format
- Click on **OK**.
- Press the **Tab** key 4 or 5 times (Line up the insertion point with the teacher's name above.)
- Type "**Subject:**"
- Press the **spacebar** two times.
- Type "**History**"
- Press **Enter** three times.

◆ Press **Ctrl + 2** to turn on double spacing.

13. Click on **Stop** on the macro record toolbar to turn off the macro recorder.

Now, let's try it!

1.   Press **Alt + E** to clear the document window.
2.   Click on **Format**.
3.   Click on **HistoryReportFormat**.

```
Name: Sue Smothers          Teacher: Mrs. Hanson
Date: 9/21/97               Subject: History

|
```

The HistoryReportFormat Macro

The date is inserted automatically, so whenever you run this macro, the correct date will appear on the report.

So, that's a menu macro. Now let's learn about toolbar macros. They are really cool!

Toolbar Macros

Let's record a macro that creates custom made stationery for us. We'll assign it to a toolbar so it will be easy to use.

Before creating a toolbar macro, you need to decide which toolbar you want to assign it to and display that toolbar on the screen. There are eight toolbars that come with Word 6 and nine toolbars that come with Word 7. You can assign a macro to any of those toolbars, or create your own custom toolbar to hold your macros. If other people will be sharing your computer, it's a good idea to create your own custom toolbar rather than adding things to the toolbars that come with Word. That way, the toolbars that come with Word will look the same every time someone uses the computer. So, before we record the Stationery macro, let's create a new toolbar.

CREATING A TOOLBAR

1.   Press **Alt + E** to erase the screen.
2.   Click on **View**.
3.   Click on **Toolbars...** The "Toolbars" dialog box, shown on the next page, appears on your screen.
4.   Click on **New...** The "New Toolbar" dialog box appears on your screen.

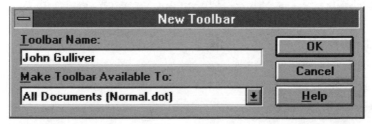

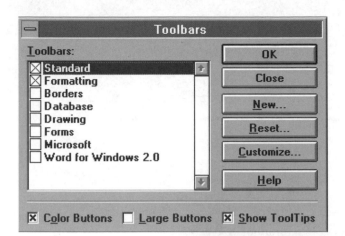

Word 6 Toolbars

Word 7 Toolbars

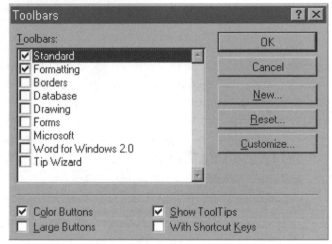

5. Type *your name* as the name for the toolbar.
    If you are sharing a computer, type *your name* as the toolbar name. If you have
    your own version of Word, type "**Macros**" for the toolbar name so that you can
    keep all of your macros together.
6. Click on **OK**.
7. Click on **Close**.

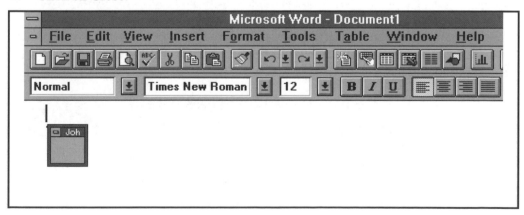

A new toolbar in Word 6

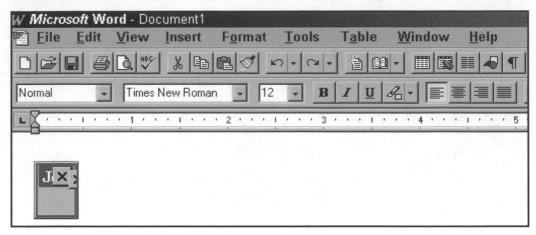

A new toolbar in Word 7

An empty toolbar appears on the screen. You can move it up so that it just touches the bottom of the formatting toolbar and looks more like a regular Word toolbar. To do this, position the mouse pointer on the title bar of the new toolbar, then click the left mouse button and drag the toolbar up to where you want it to appear on the screen (so it's just touching the bottom of the formatting toolbar).

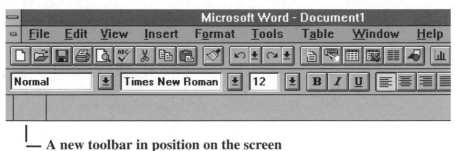

A new toolbar in position on the screen

The Stationery macro inserts a picture into a document, along with your name in big fancy print. Clipart pictures are automatically loaded onto your computer when you install Word version 6, but they are not automatically installed in Word version 7. If you're using Word 7, let's make sure your computer has pictures before we begin the macro recording session. If you're using Word 6, you're ready to begin recording the Stationery macro. Go to page 22 and follow the instructions labeled, "Recording a Toolbar Macro."

INSTALLING CLIPART IN WORD 7

1. Click on **Insert**.
2. Click on **Picture…**
    If your Insert Picture dialog box shows a bunch of file names on the screen, and the folder "Clipart" then you've got everything you need. If there are no file names listed on the screen, they you'll need to install the clipart images before you go any further.

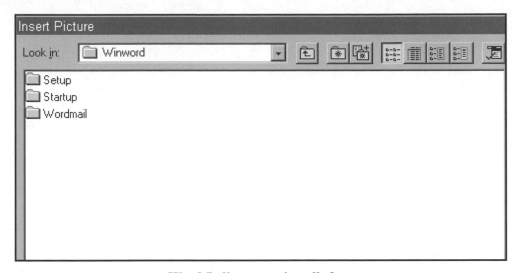

Word 7 clipart not installed

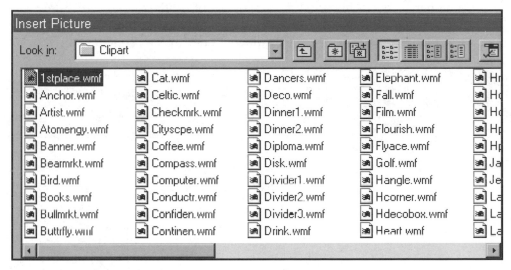

Word 7 clipart installed

3. Click on **Cancel** to close the Insert Picture dialog box.

4. If your computer already has clipart, then begin recording the Stationery macro by following the instructions labeled "Recording a Toolbar Macro."

5. If your computer does not have clipart, you can add the clipart files to your computer by running the Microsoft Word installation program and installing just the clipart files. Make sure you have the original program disks handy before you start this process.

6. Click on **File, Exit** to exit Word.

7. Click on **Start, Run...**

8. Insert the Microsoft Word for Windows setup disk 1 into the disk drive.

9. Type: **a:\setup** and press **Enter** or click on **OK**.

10. Click on **Add/Remove...**

Look at the option "Word Clip Art." If there isn't a check in the box in front of "Word Clip Art" it means that the clipart files are not loaded on your computer.

11.   Click on **Word Clip Art** to place a check mark in the box.
12.   Click on **Continue**.
13.   Follow the instructions on your screen for loading the files onto your computer.
14.   When the installation is complete, start Word by clicking on **Start, Programs, Microsoft Word**.

Okay, now we're ready to record the Stationery macro.

RECORDING A TOOLBAR MACRO

1.   Double-click on **REC** on the Status Bar to start the macro recorder.
2.   Type "**Stationery**" in the Record Macro Name box.
3.   Type "**Personal Stationery**" for the description.
4.   Click on **Toolbars** to assign this macro to a toolbar. The name of the macro, Stationery, appears highlighted in the center of the dialog box. This name will appear when you point to the toolbar button after the macro has been assigned. The description shows in the description section of the dialog box.

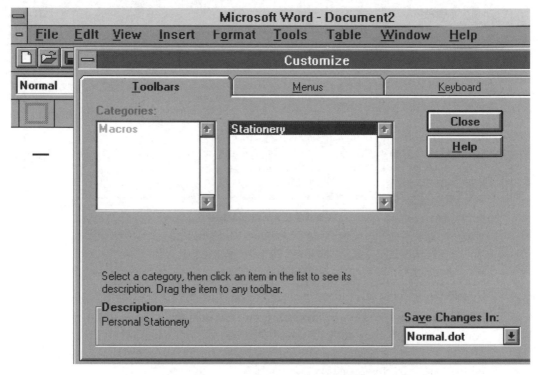

Assign a macro to a toolbar with a click and drag

5.   Click and hold down the left mouse button on the word "Stationery" and drag it up to the toolbar. Then release the mouse button. A button with a blank face appears on the toolbar, and the "Custom Button" dialog box appears. Word now lets you add a picture to the button.

6. Click on the picture that looks like a letter (bottom row, third picture from the left). Since this macro creates stationery, click on the picture that looks like a letter. Try to make each button face remind you of what the macro does.

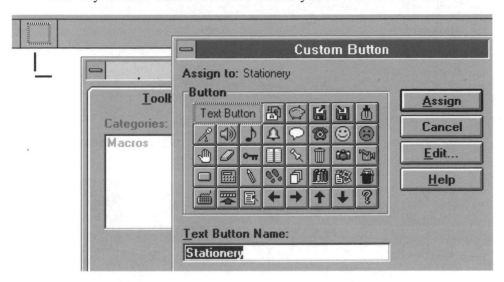

7. Click on **Assign**.
8. Click on **Close**.
9. Perform the actions you want to record.

    ◆ Click on **Format**

    ◆ Click on **Font…**

    ◆ Click on Font = *Matura MT Script Capitals*, Font Style = **Bold**, Size = **14**
    If your computer doesn't show this font listed in the Font dialog box, choose one that looks kind of fancy like this: *Matura MT Script Capitals.*
    As you click on the different font names, look in the preview window to see an example of what each font looks like.

    ◆ Click on **OK**.

    ◆ Press **Ctrl + E** to turn on centering.

    ◆ Click on **Insert**.

    ◆ Click on **Picture…**

    ◆ Click on "**deco.wmf**" as the picture name. If you can't find deco.wmf, pick another picture that you like.
    In Word 6, clipart is generally found in the directory C:\Winword\Clipart
    In Word 7, clipart is generally found in the folder C:\MSOffice\Winword\Clipart

    ◆ Click on **OK**.

    ◆ Press **Enter**.

    ◆ Type your name.

    ◆ Press **Enter** two times.

    ◆ Press **Ctrl + L** to turn on left justification.

- ◆ Click on **Format**
- ◆ Click on **Font. . .**
- ◆ Click on Font = **Courier New**, Font Style = **Regular**, Size = **10**
- ◆ Click on **OK**.
- ◆ Click on **Stop** to turn off the macro recorder.

RUNNING A TOOLBAR MACRO

1.   Press **Alt + E** to erase the document window.
2.   Click on the Stationery button on your personal toolbar.
      Voilà! Your own personal stationary. Go ahead and write that letter to grandma
      now.

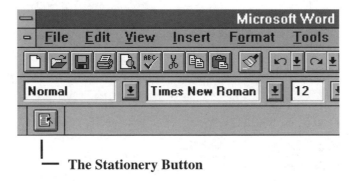

The Stationery Button

The Stationery Macro

If you get an error message on your screen stating that the file could not be
found, it means that Word 7 couldn't find the picture file. Click on **OK** to remove the
message box from the screen. Then click on **Insert, Picture, Cancel** to establish the

picture folder as the active folder. Click on the Stationery button on your toolbar and run the macro again.

DISPLAYING AND HIDING TOOLBARS

You can keep your new toolbar displayed all the time, or just when you are working with the macros held there. If you think the toolbar takes up too much screen space, you can hide it until you need it.

To display or hide toolbars:

✔	Standard
✔	Formatting
	Borders
	Database
	Drawing
	Forms
	Microsoft
✔	Tip Wizard
✔	John Gulliver
	More Toolbars...
	Toolbars...
	Customize...

1. Click the right mouse button on any blank space on a displayed toolbar.
    A list of possible toolbars is shown on the screen with a check mark beside the toolbars that are currently being displayed.
2. Click on your toolbar name.
    If a toolbar is displayed, a check mark will appear next to the toolbar name. To hide a displayed toolbar, click on the toolbar name and the check mark disappears. To display a hidden toolbar, click on the toolbar name and the check mark appears.

    or

You can also display and hide toolbars by clicking on **View, Toolbars...** Toolbars that have a check in the box beside the toolbar name are the toolbars that are displayed on the screen. If you want to hide a toolbar, click on the toolbar name and the check mark disappears. To display a hidden toolbar, click on the toolbar name and a check mark appears in the box.

Congratulations! You've recorded keyboard, menu, and toolbar macros. Here is a recap of the really good stuff.

Chapter Review — Absolutely, Positively the Most Important Stuff

To record a macro

1. Plan it carefully.
2. Decide if you will assign it to a toolbar, menu or keyboard shortcut key.
3. Double-click on **REC** on the status bar to turn on the macro recorder.
4. Type a name for the macro that reminds you what the macro does.
5. Type a description for the macro.
6. Assign the macro to a toolbar, menu or keyboard shortcut key.
7. Perform the action you want the macro to record.

8.   Click on **Stop** on the Macro Record toolbar to turn off the macro recorder.

To run a macro

1.   Position the insertion point or clear the document window.
2.   Run a macro by:
    ◆ Pressing the macro shortcut key or
    ◆ Selecting the macro from the assigned menu or
    ◆ Clicking on the macro button from the assigned toolbar or
    ◆ Clicking on Tools, Macro, Run

Projects for Practice

Now for some fun! Here are four recorded macro projects for you to experiment with. You can do them by yourself, or follow me.

The BoldUnderline Macro

1.   BoldUnderline is a keyboard macro that will turn on the bold and underline commands. Assign it to the shortcut key (Alt + B). This macro comes in handy when you need to jazz up reports.

    ◆ Double-click on **REC**.
    ◆ Type "**BoldUnderline**" as the macro name.
    ◆ Type "**Turn on bold and underline**" for the description.
    ◆ Click on **Keyboard**.
    ◆ Press **Alt + B** for the shortcut key.
    ◆ Click on **Assign**.
    ◆ Click on **Close**.
    ◆ Press **Ctrl + B** to turn on bolding.
    ◆ Press **Ctrl + U** to turn on underlining.
    ◆ Click on **Stop** on the Macro Record Toolbar.

2.   Running the BoldUnderline macro
    The BoldUnderline macro will work if you are typing new text in a document window, or if you have already typed something and you want to come back later and make the text bolded and underlined. Let's run the macro both ways and check it out.

    ◆ Press **Alt + E** to erase the screen. I know the screen looks blank now, but it's not. When you recorded the macro, bold and underline were turned on in your document window. Those two little hidden codes could mess you up if you're not looking, so it's best to get rid of the little rascals.

    To run the BoldUnderline macro on new text:

◆ Press **Alt + B** to turn on bold and underlining.

◆ Type: **Macros are the coolest invention since video games.**

◆ Press **Alt + B** to turn off bold and underlining.

So, when you're typing something new in a document, press Alt + B once to turn on bold and underlining and press Alt + B again to turn them off.

To run the BoldUnderline macro on existing text:

◆ Type: Macro maniacs are people who love making macros.

◆ Move the insertion point to the beginning of the word "love."

◆ Press **Shift +** → to highlight the word "love."

◆ Press **Alt + B** to run the BoldUnderline macro.

◆ Click the mouse once to remove the highlighting from the word. The macro adds bold and underlining to the word "love."

Macro maniacs are people who **love** making macros.

To add bold and underlining to something you've already typed, highlight the text, then press Alt + B. Try it yourself on the word "maniacs."

The DeleteLine Macro

3.   DeleteLine is a keyboard macro that will delete a line of text from the insertion point to the end of the line. Assign it to the shortcut key (Alt + D). You must have a document in the document window when you record this macro since you will need some text to delete during the recording session. You can use the existing document on your screen. Add to it by typing some more stuff on the screen.

◆ Position the insertion point at the beginning of the text you want to delete.

When you turn on the macro recorder, the insertion point needs to be at the beginning of the text you want to delete. If you move the insertion point after the macro recorder has been turned on, then the movements of the insertion point will be recorded too.

◆ Double-click on **REC**.

◆ Type "**DeleteLine**" as the macro name.

◆ Type "**Delete from the insertion point to the end of a line**" for the description.

◆ Click on **Keyboard**.

◆ Press **Alt + D** for the shortcut key.

◆ Click on **Assign**.

◆ Click on **Close**.

◆ Press **Shift + End** to highlight the text to be deleted.

◆ Press the **Delete** key on your keyboard.

◆ Click on **Stop** to turn off the macro recorder.

This macro comes in handy when you're writing or editing reports. Test it by positioning the insertion point in the middle of a line of text and pressing **Alt + D**. The macro deletes to the end of a line, not the end of a sentence. If there is text on the next line, Word will bring it up to fill in the gap. So, test this macro by running it on lines in the middle of a paragraph as well as the last line of a paragraph.

4.   Now, add the two new shortcut key macros to your list of macros.

   ◆ Press **Alt + E** to erase the screen.

   ◆ Press **Alt + S** to run the Shortcut macro.

If you get that old error message in Word 7 that says it can't find the Shortcut file, click on **OK** to remove the message box from the screen. Then click on **Open** on the Standard toolbar to establish the document folder as the active folder. Click on **Cancel** to close the Open dialog box, and press **Alt + S** to run the Shortcut macro again. Hang in there! We'll fix this once and for all in the next chapter.

   ◆ Type: **Alt + B**

   ◆ Press the **Tab** key 4 or 5 times.

   ◆ Type: **Turn on bold and underlining**

   ◆ Press **Enter**.

   ◆ Type: **Alt + D**.

   ◆ Press the **Tab** key 4 or 5 times.

   ◆ Type: **Deletes a line of text**.

   ◆ Press **Enter**.

   ◆ Click on **Save** on the Standard toolbar to save the file.

   ◆ Click on **File**.

   ◆ Click on **Close** to close the file.

The Homework Macro

Here's a macro to help you out at school. With this macro you'll be the most organized kid in class!

5.   Homework macro is a menu macro that will make a homework planner, as shown on the next page. Assign the macro to the Tools menu. You'll use the table commands to make this macro.

   ◆ Press **Alt + E** to erase the screen if it is not blank.

   ◆ Double-click on **REC** on the Status bar.

   ◆ Type "**Homework**" as the macro name.

   ◆ Type "**Make a homework planner**" for the description.

   ◆ Click on **Menus**.

   ◆ Click on **Add** to add the homework macro to the Tools menu.

   ◆ Click on **Close**.

   ◆ Click on **File, Page Setup...**

   ◆ Set the left and right margins at **0.5 inches**.

Homework Assignments for Bobby Brown

Week of: _____

	Monday	Tuesday	Wednesday	Thursday	Friday
Language Arts					
Reading					
Spelling					
Math					
Social Studies					
Science					
Study Skills					

- ◆ Click on **OK**.
- ◆ Press **Ctrl + E** to turn on centering.
- ◆ Type "**Homework Assignments for Bobby Brown**" (Use your name instead of Bobby's).
- ◆ Press **Enter** two times.
- ◆ Type "**Week of:**"
- ◆ Press **Ctrl + U** to turn on underlining.
- ◆ Press the **Tab** key several times to create a blank line.
- ◆ Press **Ctrl + U** to turn off underlining.
- ◆ Press **Enter** three times.
- ◆ Press **Ctrl + L** to turn on left justification.
- ◆ Click on **Table, Insert Table…**
- ◆ Set the number of columns = **6**, number of rows = **12**
- ◆ Click on **AutoFormat…**
- ◆ Click on **Grid 5** to format the table.

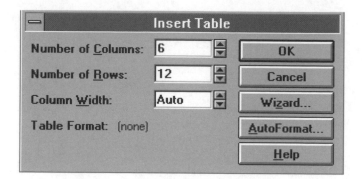

**Click on AutoFormat
to format your table**

◆ Click on **OK**.

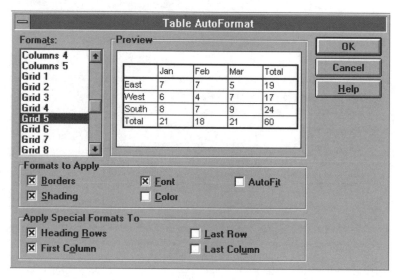

◆ Click on **OK** again.
◆ Click on **Table, Select Table** (the table now looks completely black)
◆ Click on **Table**.
◆ Click on **Cell Height and Width...**
◆ Set the row height at **Exactly 40 pt**
◆ Click on **Column**.

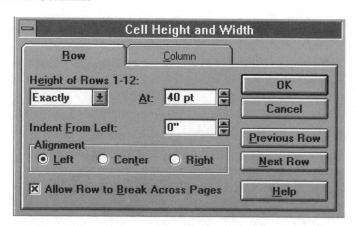

◆ Set the column width at **1.2,** space between columns = **0**

◆ Click on **OK**.

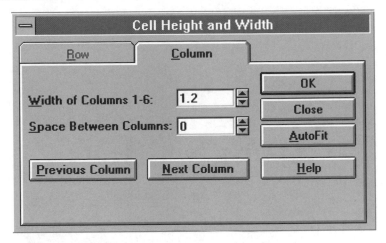

◆ Press the **Tab** key to clear the highlighting from the table.

◆ Type the column and row headings as shown below. Use the tab key to move from column to column. Use ↓ to move from row to row.

	Monday	Tuesday	Wednesday	Thursday	Friday
Language Arts					
Reading					
Spelling					
Math					
Social Studies					
Science					
Study Skills					

Headings for the Homework macro

◆ Click on **Stop** to turn off the macro recorder.

Now, let's try it out.

◆ Press **Alt + E** to erase the screen.

◆ Click on **Tools**.

◆ Click on **Homework**.

◆ Click on **Print** on the Standard toolbar to print a copy of the study planner.

The blank squares at the bottom of the table are for other assignments you may need to write in once in a while. Now, don't you feel organized?

The GiftCertificate Macro

6.   GiftCertificate macro is a toolbar macro that you can use all year long—a macro that creates custom gift certificates. Use it for parents, teachers, friends, little brothers. It's a good way to get on someone's good side. Assign this macro to your toolbar.

- ◆ Press **Alt + E** to erase the screen.
- ◆ Click on **View, Toolbars...**
- ◆ Check four toolbars: **Standard**, **Formatting**, **Drawing** and *your toolbar*.
- ◆ Click on **OK**.
- ◆ Double-click on **REC** on the Status Bar to turn on the macro recorder.
- ◆ Type "**GiftCertificate**" for the macro name.
- ◆ Type "**Fill in the blanks gift certificate**" for the description.
- ◆ Click on **Toolbars** to assign the macro to your toolbar.
- ◆ Assign the macro to your personal macro toolbar by dragging the macro name to the toolbar. Make sure you overlap the new box with the Stationery box a little. If the buttons don't overlap, Word will think you want to create a brand new toolbar.
- ◆ Click on the happy face button (since a gift certificate will make someone very happy).
- ◆ Click on **Assign**.
- ◆ Click on **Close**.
- ◆ Your toolbar with the stationery macro and the gift certificate macro
- ◆ Click on **File**, **Page Setup...**
- ◆ Click on the **Paper Size** tab.
- ◆ Click on **Landscape** (to make the paper go across instead of up and down).

◆ Click on **OK**.

◆ Click on **View, Page Layout**

◆ Click on **Whole Page**

◆ Display the whole page when recording the
GiftCertificate macro.

◆ Click on **Insert, Frame**

◆ Click on **Format, Frame…**

◆ Set the size of the frame as:

Width = Exactly **9**

Height = Exactly **6.5**

Horizontal Position = **Center**, Relative to **Page**

Vertical Position = **Center**, Relative to **Page**

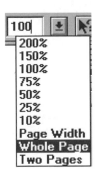

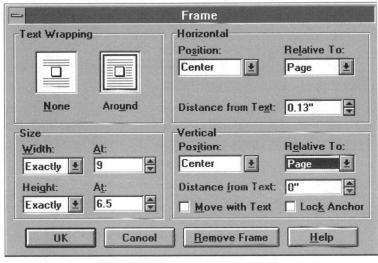

Position the frame on the paper with the Frame Dialog Box

◆ Click on **OK**.

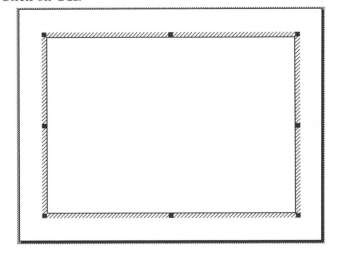

**The blank frame
centered on the
page**

◆ Click on **Insert, Picture…**

◆ Click on **hplaque.wmf** as the picture name.

The graphics file
hplaque.wmf

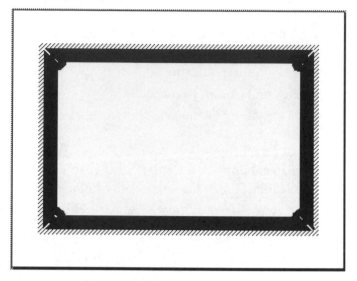

◆ Click on **OK**.

◆ Click on **Text Box** on the Drawing toolbar (6th button from the left on the Drawing toolbar). The Drawing toolbar may be hiding at the bottom of your screen, just above the status bar.

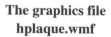 **Text Box**

The Drawing Toolbar

◆ Click on **Format, Drawing Object…**

◆ Click on **Size and Position**

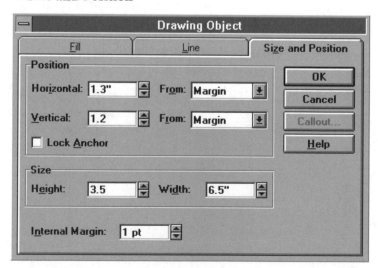

◆ Set the size of the text box as:
Horizontal Position = **1.3"**, From:
Margin
Vertical Position = **1.2"**, From
Margin
Height = **3.5"**
Width = **6.5"**

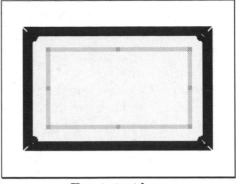

Empty text box

◆ Click on **Line**.

◆ Click on **None**.

◆ Click on **OK**.

◆ Click on **Format, Font…**

◆ Select Font = **Matura MT Script Capitals**, Font Style = **Bold**, Size = **36**
If your computer doesn't show this font listed in the Font dialog box, choose one that looks kind of fancy. *Matura MT Script looks good. Brush Script looks good, too.*

◆ Click on **OK**.

◆ Press **Ctrl + E** to turn on centering.

◆ Type: **Gift Certificate**

◆ Press **Enter**

◆ Click on **Format, Font…**

◆ Select Font = **Times,** Font Style = **Regular**, Size = **24**
If your computer doesn't show the Times font listed, choose another font that looks sort of like the example on the gift certificate.

◆ Click on **OK**.

◆ Press **Enter**.

◆ Type: **from** *your name* **to**

◆ Press the **spacebar**.

◆ Click on **Stop** on the Macro Record toolbar to turn off the macro recorder.

Make a gift certificate for someone special.

◆ Press **Alt + E** to erase the screen.

◆ Click on the smiling face on your personal toolbar. When you run the macro, the insertion point will be in the correct spot for you to type the name of the person you're giving the gift certificate to. Type the name of a special friend, then press Enter two times to add the other information.

◆ Click on **Print** on the standard toolbar to print the gift certificate. If you get an error message on your screen stating that the file could not be found, it means that Word 7 couldn't find the picture file. Click on **OK** to remove the message box from the screen. Then click on **Insert, Picture, Cancel** to establish the picture folder as the active folder. Press **Alt + E** to erase the screen, then click on the GiftCertificate button on your toolbar and run the macro again.

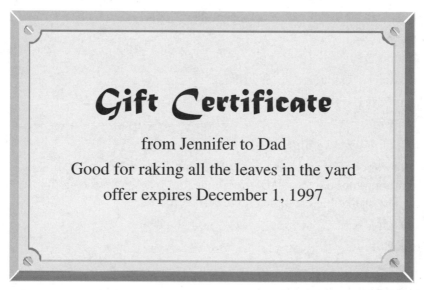

Gift Certificate

from Jennifer to Dad

Good for raking all the leaves in the yard

offer expires December 1, 1997

As you can see, recorded macros are powerful programs. WordBasic can add even more magic to the marvel of macros. Don't believe it? Well, just go to Chapter 3.

CHAPTER 3

Editing Macros

After you've recorded a macro and run it a few times, you may find yourself wishing the macro did things just a little bit differently. A few small changes is all the macro would need to make it awesome, but you don't feel like going through the whole process of recording the macro from scratch. Good news—you don't have to. You can edit a recorded macro and make changes to part of the program without having to record the whole thing all over again. Here's how.

To edit a macro:

1. Click on **Tools**.
2. Click on **Macro...** The Macro dialog box appears on your screen.
3. Click on **BoldUnderline**.

Click on the name of the macro you want to modify. If you can't remember which macro does what, look at the description box at the bottom of the dialog box. When you click on a macro name, the description you entered when you recorded the macro is displayed.

Click on the macro name, then edit to modify a macro

4. Click on **Edit**. The macro-editing window is displayed.

The Macro-Editing Window

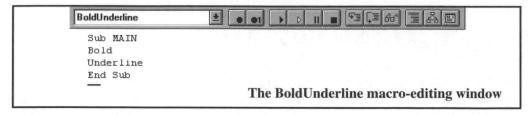

```
Sub MAIN
Bold
Underline
End Sub
```

The BoldUnderline macro-editing window

The top line of the macro-editing window is the macro toolbar. This toolbar is displayed whenever you edit a macro. Notice the macro name, BoldUnderline, on the left side of the toolbar. Below the toolbar are the WordBasic statements that make up the macro.

When you record a macro each keystroke you press is translated into a WordBasic statement. These statements tell the macro what to do. Every Word macro begins with the statement **Sub MAIN**, and ends with the statement **End Sub**. "Sub" stands for subroutine. A subroutine is a subset of a larger program. In macro language, the larger program is the entire Word program. In Word's mind, macros are smaller tasks within the larger task of running Word. They are a program within a program.

Between the Sub MAIN and End Sub statements are the WordBasic instructions that make up the macro. Think of Sub MAIN and End Sub as the bread, and the statements in between as the meat of the macro.

When the macro runs, Word starts at the Sub MAIN statement and performs each instruction, line by line, down the program until it reaches the End Sub statement. End Sub is Word's signal to stop.

In the BoldUnderline macro, there are two statements: Bold and Underline.

What if you found out after you recorded this macro that your teacher won't accept underlining on a report (she thinks it looks lame). She wants all important stuff in bold and italic type instead. You could edit the BoldUnderline macro and turn it into the BoldItalic macro.

To modify the BoldUnderline macro, all you have to do is change the WordBasic instruction for underlining to the WordBasic instruction for italics. Treat a macro in the macro-editing window the same way you would treat a regular document in a regular document window. You can press "Enter" to insert blank lines, add instructions, delete instructions, or change instructions.

In the BoldUnderline macro, delete the word **Underline** and type the word **Italic** in its place. The edited macro should look like this:

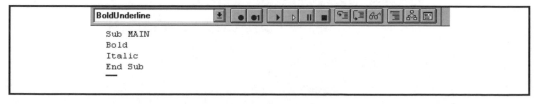

```
Sub MAIN
Bold
Italic
End Sub
```

Saving a Macro

After you've made changes to a macro in the macro-editing window, you need to save the macro. Saving a macro is just as easy as saving a Word document file.

1. Click on **Save** on the Standard toolbar.

   A message box appears asking if you want to save the macro changes.

2. Click on **Yes**.

3. Click on **File, Close** to close the macro-editing window.

   Now, let's test the edited macro.

1. Type: I am a

2. Press the **spacebar**.

3. Press **Alt + B** to turn on bold and italic type.

4. Type: *macro maniac*.

5. Press **Alt + B** to turn off bold and italic type.

   The macro typed, "I am a ***macro maniac***." The shortcut key still works, only now instead of turning on bold and underlining, the macro turns on bold and italics.

Editing the macro was no big deal, but now we've got a problem. BoldUnderline is a pretty crummy name for a macro that turns on bold and italics. We'd better change the name of the macro to BoldItalic.

Changing a Macro Name

Sometimes after you've modified a macro, the original name of the macro doesn't fit anymore. It's an easy process to change the name. Changing the name of a macro will not affect the way the program runs, or its assignment to a shortcut key, menu or toolbar.

1. Click on **Tools, Macro...**

2. Click on the macro name, **BoldUnderline**

3. Click in the description box to position the insertion point.

4. Change the description in the description box to "Turn on bold and **italics**"

5. Click on **Organizer...**

6. Click on **BoldUnderline** as the macro you want to rename.

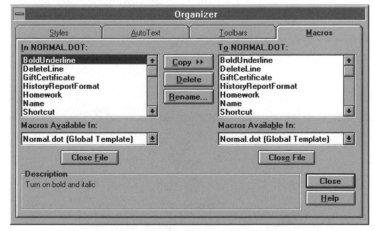

The Macro Organizer dialog box

7. Click on **Rename...**
    The Rename dialog box appears on your screen.

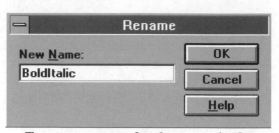

8. Type "**BoldItalic**" as the new name for the macro.

9. Click on **OK**.
    You can also delete macros from the Organizer dialog box by highlighting the macro name and clicking on Delete.

Type a new name for the macro in the Rename dialog box.

10. Click on **Close** at the lower right corner of the dialog box (Close, not Close File).

Let's check out the new macro name.

1. Click on **Tools**.

2. Click on **Macro...**
    The first name on your list of macros is now BoldItalic. When you click on BoldItalic, the description is correct too.

3. Click on **Cancel** to clear the Macro dialog box from the screen.

4. Type: Something

5. Press the **spacebar**.

6. Press **Alt + B** to run the BoldItalic macro.

7. Type: *strange*

8. Press **Alt + B** to turn off bold and italic type.

9. Press the **spacebar**.

10. Type: is going on!
    The macro typed, "Something *strange* is going on!" Changing the name of the macro did not affect the shortcut key assignment (Alt + B) or the way the macro works.

WordBasic Statements

Macros are made up of WordBasic statements. A statement is an instruction that tells the macro to do something. Every action you can do in Word has an equivalent WordBasic statement. We have already seen a few WordBasic statements in the BoldItalic macro. Here are some more:

Bold	Turns on bold type
Underline	Turns on underlining
Italic	Turns on italics
SpacePara2	Turns on doublespacing
	There is logic here. "Space" is the abbreviation for spacing. "Para" is short for paragraph and "2" means double. Doublespacing.
CenterPara	Turns on centering (like pressing Ctrl + E)
	"Para" stands for paragraph, so this command is the abbreviation for "center a paragraph"

LeftPara	Turns on left justification (like pressing Ctrl + L)
RightPara	Turns on right justification (like pressing Ctrl + R)
InsertPara	Inserts a blank line in the document (like pressing Enter)
Insert	This statement types information in the document window for you. The information that is typed is placed in quotation marks.

Insert "*whatever you want typed on the screen*"

Insert "Jeremy Jones" types the words Jeremy Jones (without the quotation marks) on the screen.

Insert "History" types the word History on the screen

Each statement name is a single word, or a couple of words abbreviated and stuck together. Notice the capitalization of the statements. Macro statements must be capitalized as shown above. In fact, if you type a statement with the wrong capitalization (insert instead of Insert) Word will change the capitalization when you save the macro. Each statement is placed on a separate line in the macro.

EDITING THE NAME MACRO

Let's take a look at the Name macro you created in Chapter 2.

1. Click on **Tools, Macro...**
2. Click on **Name**.
3. Click on **Edit**. The Name macro appears in the macro-editing window.

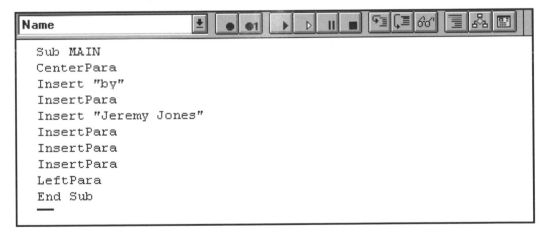

When you recorded this macro, Word built WordBasic statements for every key you pressed and wrote them in order between the Sub MAIN and End Sub statements. Let's look at those statements.

CenterPara	Turns on centering
Insert "by"	Types the word "by"
InsertPara	Types a blank line
Insert "Jeremy Jones"	Types your name
InsertPara	Types three blank lines
LeftPara	Turns on left justification

When you run the macro, Word starts with the Sub MAIN statement and performs each instruction in order down the list.

4. Position the insertion point on the End Sub statement at the bottom of the macro.

5. Press **Enter** to insert a blank line into the macro.

6. Type: **SpacePara2** in the blank line. This statement will turn on doublespacing after the macro types your name.

The Name macro should now look like this:

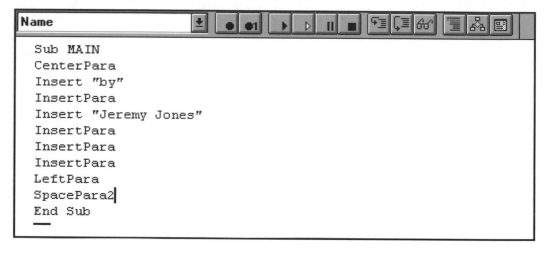

```
Sub MAIN
CenterPara
Insert "by"
InsertPara
Insert "Jeremy Jones"
InsertPara
InsertPara
InsertPara
LeftPara
SpacePara2
End Sub
```

7. Click on **Save** on the Standard toolbar.

8. Click on **Yes**.

9. Click on **File**.

10. Click on **Close**.

11. Press **Alt + E** to erase the screen if it is not blank.

12. Press **Ctrl + E** to turn on centering.

13. Type: **Computers** as name of your report.

14. Press **Enter**.

15. Press **Alt + N** to run the edited Name macro.

16. Type: **A computer program is a set of instructions that tells the computer to perform a task. A computer programmer is the person who writes those instructions.**

Pretty cool! You can now type your report with doublespacing.

Arguments and Values

The WordBasic statements we've looked at so far are simple one word statements that were created by pressing one or two keys when a macro was recorded. When Word menus or dialog boxes are used in recording a macro, WordBasic statements get a little longer.

Each Word dialog box has a corresponding WordBasic statement. These statement names look like the menu or dialog box name. For example:

Statement Name	Menu Names
FormatFont	Click on Format, Click on Font
FilePageSetup	Click on File, Click on Page Setup
TableInsertTable	Click on Table, Click on Insert Table
InsertPicture	Click on Insert, Click on Picture
FileOpen	Click on File, Click on Open

Each option in a Word dialog box has a corresponding argument in a WordBasic statement. No, these are not like the arguments you have with your brother. WordBasic arguments show the settings for the stuff in the dialog box. Arguments always begin with a period followed by the argument name. Multiple arguments are separated from each other by commas.

Point size, font name and strikethrough are all options on the Font dialog box. So, they appear as arguments in the FormatFont statement.

```
FormatFont .Points, .Font, .Strikethrough
```

Each WordBasic argument has a value, shown to the right of an equal sign. Values are the setting for the option. Values can be either a number or text enclosed in quotation marks.

.Points = "36"

> .Points is the argument, "36" is the value

.Font = "Matura MT Script Capitals"

> .Font is the argument, "Matura MT Script Capitals" is the value

.Strikethrough = 0

> .Strikethrough is the argument, 0 is the value
>
> If the option on the dialog box is a check box, values are shown as 1 or 0
>
> in the WordBasic statement. "1" means the check box was selected, "0"
>
> means it was not. In this example the strikethrough option was turned off.

The FormatFont statement with three arguments and their values looks like this:

```
FormatFont .Points = "36", .Font = "Matura MT
Script Capitals", .Strikethrough = 0
```

This WordBasic statement changes the font to 36-point Matura MT Script Capitals. The strikethrough option is not turned on.

That's pretty easy, but the Font dialog box has lots of options—17 to be exact. Let's look at the Font dialog box, shown on the next page, and see how it compares to the complete FormatFont statement.

Click on **Format, Font...**

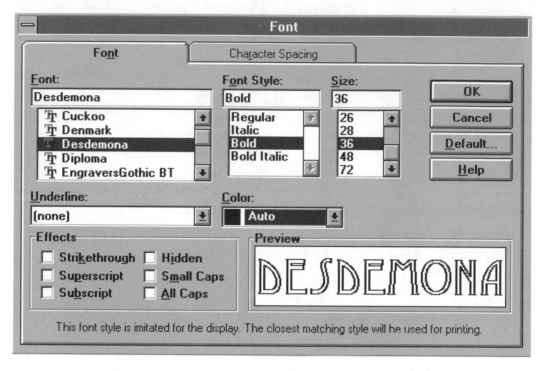

This is the dialog box you used when you recorded the Stationery macro. In it, you set the font to Matura MT Script Capitals, bold type and 36 points. You didn't change anything else in the dialog box, but notice how many other options there are (underline, color, strikethrough, hidden, superscript, etc.).

Now, let's take a look at the FormatFont statement that was created when you recorded the Stationery macro.

Click on **Cancel** to close the Font dialog box.

Click on **Tools, Macro, Stationery, Edit**

```
Sub MAIN
```

```
CenterPara
InsertPicture .Name = "C:\WINWORD\CLIPART\DECO.WMF",
LinkToFile = "0"
InsertPara
Insert "John Gulliver"
InsertPara
```

```
InsertPara
LeftPara
FormatFont .Points = "10", .Underline = 0, .Color = 0,
.Strikethrough = 0, .Superscript = 0, .Subscript = 0,
.Hidden = 0, .SmallCaps = 0, .AllCaps = 0, .Spacing = "0
pt", .Position = "0 pt", .Kerning = 0, .KerningMin = "",
.Tab = "0", .Font = "Courier New", .Bold = 0, .Italic = 0
End Sub
```

The Stationery Macro Statements

Look at the FormatFont statement that was created when you recorded the Stationery macro. The name of the statement is **FormatFont**. The arguments all begin with a period, and correspond to the various options on the dialog box. Multiple arguments are separated with commas. Each argument has a value, which is shown after the equal sign.

The arguments we changed are:

.Points, which stands for font size in the dialog box
.Font, which stands for the font name
.Bold which stands for font style in the dialog box

Even though we didn't change any of the other options in the dialog box, WordBasic included their arguments with values of zero. The zero means the option was not selected.

When you record a macro, WordBasic puts all the arguments into the statement even when they're turned off. That makes editing macros easy because all you have to do to turn an option on is change the value of the corresponding argument to one. But having all of the arguments shown can make some WordBasic statements look long and scary. Don't worry about all the junk you see in some statements. If the value equals zero, ignore the argument.

Click on **File, Close** to close the Stationery macro-editing window.

The Record Next Button

Let's edit the Name macro to include a font change. To do this, you could type the FormatFont statement in the macro. That would work. But the FormatFont statement is kind of long. I don't know about you, but I don't trust my typing well enough to type the whole thing without messing up any periods, commas or quotation marks.

Instead of typing the command, you can use the Record Next button on the macro toolbar to record the statement for you.

The Record Next button turns on the macro recorder and records the next command you choose. What's so great about this button is that if Word is doing the recording, you know the WordBasic statement it creates will be perfect.

Using the Record Next Button

1. Click on **Tools, Macro...**
2. Click on **Name**.
3. Click on **Edit**. The Name macro appears in the macro-editing window.
4. Position the insertion point at the beginning of the CenterPara line so the Font statement will be placed on the line above the CenterPara statement when it is inserted into the macro.
5. Click on **Record Next**

The Macro Toolbar

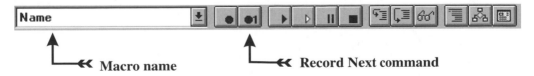

◄◄ **Macro name**   ◄◄ **Record Next command**

6.   Click on **Format, Font...**

Hold on, there's a problem. (Don't worry, I set you up.) When you have a macro in the macro-editing window a lot of the menu selections are not available. Word does that on purpose to protect you from accidentally messing up the macro in the macro-editing window.

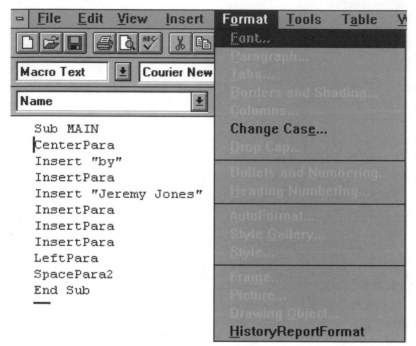

When the macro-editing window is displayed, some menus are not available

Menu selections that are not available are shown as light gray. When you click on them, nothing happens.

There is an easy solution to this problem. All you have to do is create a document window and you'll be able to access any Word menu. The macro-editing window can stay open while you do this.

7.   Click in the macro-editing window to remove the Format menu from the screen.

8.   Click on **Record Next** to turn off the recorder for a minute.

9.   Make sure the insertion point is still at the beginning of the CenterPara statement.

10.   Click on **Window**.

11.   Click on **Document1** (or whatever document window is listed, Document2, Document3) to make it the active window. If there is not a document window listed when you click on Window, click on **New** on the Standard toolbar (the first button on the left) to create a new document window.

Word takes you to the document window screen. There are now two windows open at the same time, the macro-editing window and a document window.

12. Press **Alt + E** to erase the screen if it is not blank.
13. Click on **Record Next**.
14. Click on **Format, Font…**
15. Click on **Arial, 14 point**.
16. Click on **OK**.

    What happened? The document window looks empty and the Record Next button is no longer depressed. You need to look at the macro-editing window to see what happened.

17. Click on **Window**. There are two windows listed, the document window and the Name macro-editing window.
18. Click on **Global: Name**

    The Name macro-editing window is displayed. A FormatFont statement for a 14-point Arial font was inserted into the macro, right before the CenterPara statement. Amazing, isn't it!

19. Click on **Save** on the Standard toolbar to save the macro.
20. Click on **Yes**.
21. Click on **File**.
22. Click on **Close** to close the macro-editing window.

    Now, try out the Name macro by pressing **Alt + N**. Arial is a good font for titles.

EDITING THE STATIONERY MACRO

Let's look at another macro you recorded in Chapter 2, the Stationery macro. In this example, we want to change the font that is used in the macro and choose a different picture. We don't need new FormatFont and InsertPicture statements. We just need to change the name of the font and the name of the picture that are already in the macro. We can do that easily with a copy and paste.

1. Press **Alt + E** to erase the screen.
2. Click on **Tools, Macro…**
3. Click on **Stationery**.
4. Click on **Edit**. The Stationery macro appears in the macro-editing window.

```
Sub MAIN
FormatFont .Points = "36", .Underline = 0, .Color = 0,
.Strikethrough = 0, .Superscript = 0, .Subscript = 0, .Hidden
= 0, .SmallCaps = 0, .AllCaps = 0, .Spacing = "0 pt",
.Position = "0 pt", .Kerning = 0, .KerningMin = "", .Tab =
"0", .Font = "Matura MT Script Capitals", .Bold = 1, .Italic =
0
CenterPara
InsertPicture .Name = "C:\WINWORD\CLIPART\DECO.WMF",
.LinkToFile = "0"
InsertPara
Insert "John Gulliver"
InsertPara
InsertPara
LeftPara
```

```
FormatFont .Points = "10", .Underline = 0, .Color = 0,
.Strikethrough = 0, .Superscript = 0, .Subscript = 0, .Hidden
= 0, .SmallCaps = 0, .AllCaps = 0, .Spacing = "0 pt",
.Position = "0 pt", .Kerning = 0, .KerningMin = "", .Tab =
"0", .Font = "Courier New", .Bold = 0, .Italic = 0
End Sub
```

Take a look at the WordBasic statements that make up this macro. They are in the exact order you gave the commands when you recorded the macro. Change the font, turn on centering, insert the picture, insert a blank line, type your name, insert two blank lines, turn on left justification and select another font.

5. Type a new font name in the FormatFont statement and a new picture name in the InsertPicture statement.

That sounds easy enough, but what if you don't know any font and picture names off the top of your head? I know I sure don't. Well, good old Word has a solution. You can click on Format, Font and look at the examples of each font in the preview screen. When you find one you like, you can copy its name onto the clipboard, and then paste it into the macro. The same method can be used for finding another picture.

6. Click on **Window**.
7. Click on **Document1** or whatever document window is listed.
8. Click on **Format**, **Font...**
9. Click on the **Algerian** fon t.

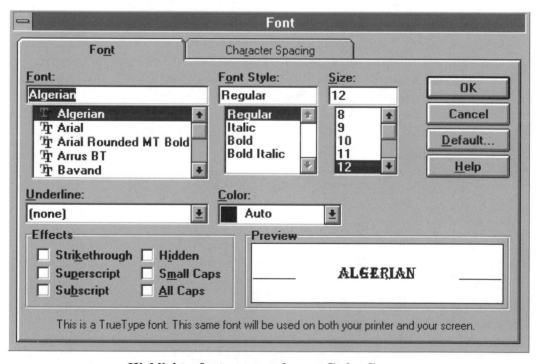

Highlight a font name and press Ctrl + C

If you don't have this font on your computer, scroll through the fonts until you find one you like. To see what each font looks like, click on its name. An

example of the font will be shown in the Preview box at the bottom of the dialog
box.

10. Press **Ctrl + C** to copy the name of the font onto the clipboard.
11. Click on **Cancel** to dismiss the Font dialog box.
12. Click on **Window**.
13. Click on **Global: Stationery**.
14. Find and delete the old font name "Matura MT Script Capitals" in the
    FormatFont statement, and with the insertion point in the same spot (between
    the empty quotation marks), press **Ctrl + V** to paste the new font name from
    the clipboard.

```
FormatFont .Points = "36", .Underline = 0, .Color = 0,
.Strikethrough = 0, .Superscript = 0, .Subscript = 0, .Hidden
= 0, .SmallCaps = 0, .AllCaps = 0, .Spacing = "0 pt",
.Position = "0 pt", .Kerning = 0, .KerningMin = "", .Tab =
"0", .Font = "Algerian", .Bold = 1, .Italic = 0
```

Doublecheck to make sure that the new font name is enclosed in quotation
marks.

Now, let's find a new picture.

15. Click on **Window**.
16. Click on **Document1** or whatever document window is listed.
17. Click on **Insert, Picture...**
18. Click on **horse.wmf**.

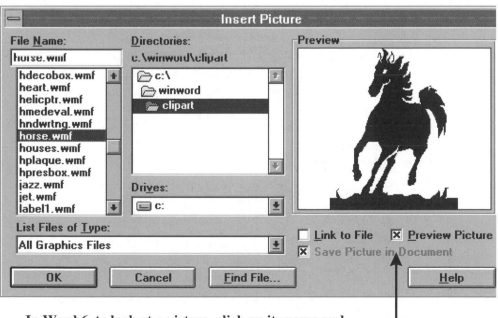

**In Word 6, to look at a picture, click on its name and
click on "Preview Picture"** ≫

**In Word 7, to look at a picture, click on its name
and click on "Preview"** ➤➤

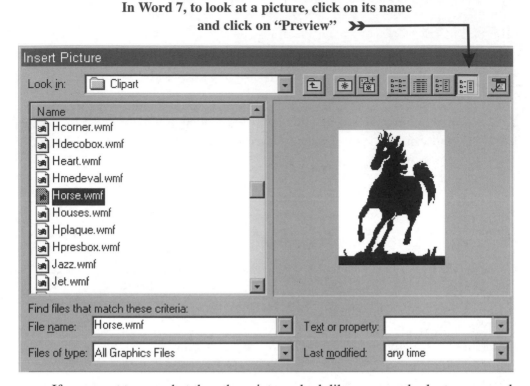

If you want to see what the other pictures look like, you can look at an example of each one in the preview section of the screen. To see what each picture looks like, click on its name in the File Name section of the dialog box, then click on "Preview." A sample of the picture will appear in the preview box.

19. In Word 6,   Position the insertion point before the first character of the name "horse.wmf" in the File Name text box at the top of the dialog box. Not the horse.wmf in the list of files, the horse.wmf at the *top* of the dialog box.

In Word 7,   Type: **Horse.wmf** in the File name box.
Press **Home**.

20. Press **Shift + End** to highlight the file name.

In Word 6
Highlight the file name by pressing **Shift + End**

In Word 7
Type: **Horse.wmf**
Press **Home**
Press **Shift + End**

21. Press **Ctrl + C** to copy the picture name onto the clipboard.
22. Click on **Cancel** to dismiss the Insert Picture dialog box.
23. Click on **Window**.
24. Click on **Global: Stationery**.
25. Position the insertion point on the InsertPicture statement.
    Delete the old picture name "DECO.WMF" and with the insertion point in the same spot, press **Ctrl + V** to paste the new picture name from the clipboard.
    Word 6

```
InsertPicture .Name = "C:\WINWORD\CLIPART\horse.wmf",
.LinkToFile = "0"
```

   Word 7

```
InsertPicture .Name = "Horse.wmf", .LinkToFile = "0"
```

   If you're using Word 7, notice how Microsoft Word did not write the location of the file in the macro statement. Because of this change in Word 7, an error message stating that the file could not be found sometimes appears when you run this macro. Let's add the path name to the InsertPicture statement so that the macro will always be able to find the Horse.wmf file.

26. Modify the InsertPicture statement to include the exact location of the file.
    Type: InsertPicture .Name ="**C:\MSOffice\Winword\Clipart\horse.wmf**"
27. Click on **Save** on the Standard toolbar.
28. Click on **Yes**.
29. Click on **File**.
30. Click on **Close**.

You are so good! Press **Alt + E** to erase the screen. Then run the macro and check out your new stationery. Remember, this macro was the first macro assigned to your personal toolbar. If the toolbar is not currently displayed on the screen, click the right mouse button on any blank space on the Standard toolbar, then click on your toolbar name to display it.

Click on **Print** on the Standard toolbar to print a copy of your cool-looking stationery.

Press **Alt + E** to erase the screen.

Printing Your Macros

It's helpful to keep a printed copy of all of your macros. As you learn more and more about WordBasic, you'll find that you can mix and match statements to make new macros. Take a few commands from here, a few others from there, and Voila! You have a whole new and incredible wonderful macro.

To print the Stationery macro:

1. Click on **Tools, Macro...**
2. Click on **Stationery**.
3. Click on **Edit**.
4. Click on **Print** on the Standard toolbar (fourth button from the left).

```
Sub MAIN
FormatFont .Points = "36", .Underline = 0, .Color = 0,
.Strikethrough = 0, .Superscript = 0, .Subscript = 0, .Hidden
```

```
= 0, .SmallCaps = 0, .AllCaps = 0, .Spacing = "0 pt",
.Position = "0 pt", .Kerning = 0, .KerningMin = "", .Tab =
"0", .Font = "Algerian", .Bold = 1, .Italic = 0
CenterPara
InsertPicture .Name = "C:\WINWORD\CLIPART\horse.wmf",
.LinkToFile = "0"
InsertPara
Insert "John Gulliver"
InsertPara
InsertPara
LeftPara
FormatFont .Points = "10", .Underline = 0, .Color = 0,
.Strikethrough = 0, .Superscript = 0, .Subscript = 0, .Hidden
= 0, .SmallCaps = 0, .AllCaps = 0, .Spacing = "0 pt",
.Position = "0 pt", .Kerning = 0, .KerningMin = "", .Tab =
"0", .Font = "Courier New", .Bold = 0, .Italic = 0
End Sub
```

Pretty neat! You can read this macro and understand what it does. Give the macro to your mom and ask her to read it. She'll think you're a genius!

Even though we can read macros to figure out what they do, it bothers me that we don't immediately know the name of a printed macro or its purpose. Of course, WordBasic has a solution for this.

Documenting Your Macros

When you have a macro in the macro-editing window, the name of the macro is displayed in the toolbar at the top of the screen. That's helpful when you're working on the macro, but it doesn't help at all when you've printed the macro and have no record of its name or what it does. You can insert comments into a macro to explain the macro and remind you of the purpose of the macro or a particular instruction. When the macro runs, WordBasic totally ignores all comments. You can use the REM statement or an apostrophe to insert comments into a macro.

THE REM STATEMENT

"REM" stands for remark, or comment, and tells the macro to ignore whatever it finds on that line after the letters "REM."

Let's add comments to some of our macros.

1. The Stationery macro should already be in the macro-editing window. If it's not, put it there by clicking on Tools, Macro, Stationery, Edit.

2. Add comments to the macro. Comments begin with the letters "REM" and a space. If you type the letters "rem" in lowercase letters, Word will convert them to uppercase when you save the macro.

    Comments should be easy to see. Enclose the comments at the beginning of the macro in a row of asterisks or some other symbol to make them really stand out. Always include the name of the macro, and its author. When you start sharing macros with other macro maniacs, you may need to talk to the people who wrote them. Also include the purpose of the macro and how to run it. That way, if you have a printed copy of a macro that you haven't run in a long time, you'll know how to find it. You can put blank lines in your macros to make them easier to read. WordBasic won't mind a bit.

```
Sub MAIN
REM********************************************************
REM Macro:      Stationery
REM Author:     John Gulliver
REM Purpose:    Create custom made stationery
REM Toolbar:    Located on personal toolbar
REM********************************************************
FormatFont .Points = "36", .Underline = 0, .Color = 0,
.Strikethrough = 0, .Superscript = 0, .Subscript = 0, .Hidden
= 0, .SmallCaps = 0, .AllCaps = 0, .Spacing = "0 pt",
.Position = "0 pt", .Kerning = 0, .KerningMin = "", .Tab =
"0", .Font = "Algerian", .Bold = 1, .Italic = 0
CenterPara
InsertPicture .Name = "C:\WINWORD\CLIPART\HORSE.WMF",
.LinkToFile = "0"
InsertPara
```

3. Click on **Save** on the Standard toolbar to save the macro.
4. Click on **Yes**.
5. Click on **Print** on the Standard toolbar to print the macro.
   6. Click on **File**.
7. Click on **Close** to close the macro-editing window.
8. Click on the Stationery toolbar button to test the macro and make sure it still works.

   It works the same as it always did. That's because any line that begins with REM is ignored by WordBasic when the program runs.

There's another way to add REM statements to a macro, the REM button on the macro toolbar. Let's add comments to the Homework macro using the REM toolbar button.

1. Click on **Tools**.
2. Click on **Macro...**
3. Click on **Homework**.
4. Click on **Edit**. The Homework macro is shown in the macro-editing window.
5. Position the insertion point at the beginning of the *FilePageSetup* statement.
6. Press **Enter** to insert a blank line into the macro.

```
Sub MAIN

FilePageSetup .Tab = "0", .PaperSize = "0", .TopMargin = "1" +
Chr$(34), .BottomMargin = "1" + Chr$(34), .LeftMargin = "0.5"
+ Chr$(34), .RightMargin = "0.5" + Chr$(34), .Gutter = "0" +
Chr$(34), .PageWidth = "8.5" + Chr$(34), .PageHeight = "11" +
Chr$(34), .Orientation = 0, .FirstPage = 0, .OtherPages = 0,
.VertAlign = 0, .ApplyPropsTo = 4, .FacingPages = 0,
.HeaderDistance = "0.5" + Chr$(34), .FooterDistance =
```

Type the comments beginning at the blank line.

7.   Click on **REM** on the macro toolbar.

Word types REM and places the insertion point at the beginning of the line. You just need to add the rest.

8.   Press **End** to move the insertion point to the end of the line (after the REM statement).
9.   Type first line of comments.
      REM**
10.   Press **Enter** to move down to the next line.
11.   Click on the **REM** button for each line of comments.
12.   Click on **End** to position the insertion point at the end of the line.
13.   Type the comments.
14.   Press **Enter** to move down to the next line.
      REM Macro: **Homework**
      REM Author: **Bobby Brown**
      REM Purpose: **Create a study guide for homework assignments**
      REM Menu Macro: **Tools, Homework**
      REM**
15.   Click on **Save** on the Standard toolbar.
16.   Click on **Yes**.
17.   Click on **Print** on the Standard toolbar to print the macro.
18.   Click on **File**.
19.   Click on **Close** to close the macro-editing window.
20.   Press **Alt + E** to erase the screen if it is not blank.
21.   Click on **Tools**.
22.   Click on **Homework** to run the macro and make sure it still works.
23.   Press **Alt + E** to erase the screen.

COMMENTS WITH APOSTROPHES

As you start creating more complex macros, you may find it helpful to add comments to individual statements in the macro. A statement might be crystal clear to you today, but three months from now you may not remember what the statement does. You can use an apostrophe (') to explain a macro instruction. When you add a comment to a line with a WordBasic statement, make the comment short. The whole comment must fit on the line with the WordBasic statement. If the comment won't fit on the same line as the WordBasic statement, use a REM statement to put the entire comment on a separate line in the macro instead.

Commenting the DeleteLine macro.

1.   Click on **Tools**.
2.   Click on **Macro...**
3.   Click on **DeleteLine**.

4. Click on **Edit**. The DeleteLine macro is shown in the macro-editing window.
5. Position the insertion point at the beginning of the *EndOfLine* statement.
6. Press **Enter** to insert a blank line into the macro. Type the comments beginning at the blank line.
7. Click on **REM** on the macro toolbar.
8. Press **End** to move the insertion point to the end of the line (after the REM statement).
9. Type the comments.
10. Press **Enter** to move down to the next line.

REM***

REM Macro: DeleteLine

REM Author: *Your name*

REM Purpose: Delete a line of typing (Alt + D)

REM***

11. Position the insertion point on the *EndOfLine* statement.
12. Press **End** to move the insertion point to the end of the line.
13. Press the **Tab** key 4 times.
14. Type: **'Highlights to the end of the line**
15. Position the insertion point on the EditClear statement.
16. Press **End** to move the insertion point to the end of the line.
17. Press the **Tab** key 4 times.
18. Type: **'Deletes highlighted text**

The DeleteLine macro should look like this:

```
Sub MAIN
REM*******************************************************
REM Macro:     DeleteLine
REM Author:    Joyce Banks
REM Purpose:   Delete a line of typing (Alt + D)
REM*******************************************************

EndOfLine 1        'Highlights to the end of the line
EditClear          'Deletes highlighted text
End Sub
```

19. Click on **Save** on the Standard toolbar.
20. Click on **Yes**.
21. Click on **Print** on the Standard toolbar to print the macro.
22. Click on **File**.
23. Click on **Close** to close the macro-editing window.

Let's check it out. When you make even the smallest change to a macro, test it to make sure it still works like you want it to.

1. Type: **I am going to test this macro and it will be perfect.**
2. Position the insertion point on the "m" in macro.
3. Press **Alt + D** to delete the line.

The comments were ignored by the macro and the line was deleted.

Chapter Review — Absolutely, Positively the Most Important Stuff

1. To edit a macro, click on Tools, Macro, Edit.
2. Every macro must begin with the statement "Sub MAIN" and end with the statement "End Sub."
3. Place each macro statement on a separate line.
4. Begin argument names with a period, like .Points
5. Make sure each argument has a value, like .Points = "36"
6. Separate arguments with commas.
7. Use the Record Next button to record one command into an existing macro.
8. When you have a macro in a macro-editing window and find that certain Word menus are not available, open a document window.
9. Document your macros with REM statements or apostrophes.
10. Save a macro by clicking on Save on the Standard toolbar, then Yes.
11. Change the name of a macro by clicking on Tools, Macro, Organizer, Rename.
12. Delete a macro by clicking on Tools, Macro, Organizer, Delete.

Projects for Practice

The Comments Macro

1. Record a macro that will automate adding comments to a macro. Place the Name macro in the macro-editing window to use during the recording of the Comments macro.

◆ Click on **Tools**.

◆ Click on **Macro…**.

◆ Click on **Name**.

◆ Click on **Edit**.

Now, record the Comments macro.

◆ Double-click on **REC** on the status bar to turn on the macro recorder.

◆ Type: **Comments** as the macro name.

◆ Click in the description box to position the insertion point.

◆ Type: **Add comments to macros** as the description

◆ Click on **Keyboard** to assign the macro to a keyboard shortcut key.

◆ Click in the **Press New Shortcut Key** box to position the insertion point.

◆ Press **Alt + C** as the shortcut key.

◆ Click on **Assign**.

◆ Click on **Close**.

◆ Press ↓ to move the insertion point down one line.

◆ Press **Enter** to insert a blank line into the macro.

◆ Press ↑ to move the insertion point to the blank line.

◆ Type: **REM***

You must type the letters "REM" during this recording session. The REM button on the macro toolbar will not create the correct WordBasic statement if you press it while the macro recorder is on.

Type as many asterisks as you need to make the remark line extend as far as the macro statement lines.

◆ Press **Enter** to move down to the next line.

◆ Type: **REM Macro:**

◆ Press the **Tab** key two times.

◆ Press **Enter** to move down to the next line.

◆ Type: **REM Author:**

◆ Press the **Tab** key two times.

◆ Press **Enter** to move down to the next line.

◆ Type: **REM Purpose:**

◆ Press the **Tab** key.

◆ Press **Enter** to move down to the next line

◆ Type: **REM***

◆ Press **Enter** to move down to the next line.

◆ Press ↑ four times to move the insertion point up four lines.

◆ Press **End** to move the insertion point to the end of the line.

◆ Click on **Stop** on the Macro Record Toolbar to turn off the recorder.

2. Add comments to the Name macro.

◆ Type the following comments. Press ↓ to move down to the next line.
    REM Macro: **Name**
    REM Author: **Jeremy Jones**
    REM Purpose: **Type my name on a report (Alt + N)**

◆ Click on **Save** on the Standard toolbar to save the comments.

◆ Click on **Yes**.

◆ Click on **Print** on the Standard toolbar to print a copy of the macro.

◆ Click on **File**.

◆ Click on **Close**.

◆ Press **Alt + E** to erase the screen if it is not blank.

◆ Press **Alt + N** to run the Name macro to make sure it still works.

3. Run the Comments macro and add comments to the Shortcut macro.

◆ Click on **Tools**.

◆ Click on **Macro...**

◆ Click on **Shortcut**.

◆ Click on **Edit**.

◆ Press **Alt + C** to run the comments macro.

◆ Type the following comments. Press ↓ to move down to the next line.

    REM Macro: **Shortcut**

    REM Author: **Kathy Foster**

    REM Purpose: **Add shortcut key macros to a master list (Alt + S)**

◆ For those of you who are using Word 7, let's add the path name to the FileOpen statement so that the macro will always be able to find the Shortcut file.

◆ Position the insertion point on the FileOpen statement.

◆ Type: FileOpen .Name = **"C:\ My Documents\shortcut.doc"**,
There is a space between "My" and "Documents."

◆ Click on **Save** on the Standard toolbar to save the comments.

◆ Click on **Yes**.

◆ Click on **Print** on the Standard toolbar to print a copy of the macro.

◆ Click on **File**.

◆ Click on **Close**.

◆ Press **Alt + E** to erase the screen.

◆ Press **Alt + S** to run the Shortcut macro.

◆ Type: **Alt + C** to add the Comments macro to the shortcut key list.

◆ Press the **Tab** key 4 or 5 times (to line up the insertion point with the second column)

◆ Type: **Add comments to macros**

◆ Press **Enter**.

◆ Click on **Save** on the Standard toolbar.

◆ Click on **File, Close** to close the Shortcut file.

4.   Run the Comments macro and add comments to the HistoryReportFormat macro.

    ◆ Click on **Tools**.

    ◆ Click on **Macro...**

    ◆ Click on **HistoryReportFormat**.

    ◆ Click on **Edit**.

    ◆ Press **Alt + C** to run the Comments macro.

    ◆ Type the following comments. Press ↓ to move down to the next line.

        REM Macro: **HistoryReportFormat**

        REM Author: **Sue Smothers**

> **REM Purpose:**   **Do all the formatting for History reports**

◆ Press **Enter** after typing the purpose to add a blank line for another line of comments. This blank line will contain a remark explaining where to find the HistoryReportFormat macro. Type the following remark.

> **REM Menu Macro:**   **Format, HistoryReportFormat**

◆ Click on **Save** on the Standard toolbar to save the comments.

◆ Click on **Yes**.

◆ Click on **Print** on the Standard toolbar to print a copy of the macro.

◆ Click on **File**.

◆ Click on **Close**.

◆ Click on **Format, HistoryReportFormat** to run the macro.

Editing the Homework Macro

5.   You've started a new semester at school and have added two new classes to your schedule. Edit the Homework macro to include "Computer Lab" and "Band" at the bottom of the list of classes. The "Study Skills" class is over, so you can delete the heading for it.

◆ Press **Alt + E** to erase the screen if it is not blank.

◆ Click on **Tools, Homework** to run the Homework macro.
See how the insertion point is at the bottom of the study planner. It would be easier if the insertion point were at the top of the document. That way, you could start filling in the homework assignments without having to scroll to the top. We'll fix that.

◆ Click on **Print** on the Standard toolbar to print a copy of the study planner.

```
Homework Assignments for Bobby Brown
     Week of:   _____
```

	Monday	Tuesday	Wednesday	Thursday	Friday
Language Arts					
Reading					
Spelling					
Math					
Social Studies					
Science					
Study Skills					

◆ Press **Alt + E** to erase the screen.

◆ Click on **Tools, Macro…**

◆ Click on **Homework**.

◆ Click on **Edit**.

◆ Click on **Print** on the Standard toolbar to print the macro statements.

```
Sub MAIN
REM*********************************************************
REM Macro:       Homework
REM Author:      Bobby Brown
REM Purpose:     Create a study guide for homework assignments
REM Menu Macro: Tools, Homework
REM*********************************************************
FilePageSetup .Tab = "0", .PaperSize = "0", .TopMargin = "1" +
Chr$(34), .BottomMargin = "1" + Chr$(34), .LeftMargin = "0.5" +
Chr$(34), .RightMargin = "0.5" + Chr$(34), .Gutter = "0" +
Chr$(34), .PageWidth = "8.5" + Chr$(34), .PageHeight = "11" +
Chr$(34), .Orientation = 0, .FirstPage = 0, .OtherPages = 0,
.VertAlign = 0, .ApplyPropsTo = 4, .FacingPages = 0,
.HeaderDistance = "0.5" + Chr$(34), .FooterDistance = "0.5" +
Chr$(34), .SectionStart = 2, .OddAndEvenPages = 0,
.DifferentFirstPage = 0, .Endnotes = 0, .LineNum = 0,
.StartingNum = "", .FromText = "", .CountBy = "0", .NumMode = - 1
CenterPara
Insert "Homework Assignments for Bobby Brown"
InsertPara
InsertPara
Insert "Week of:"
Underline
Insert Chr$(9) + Chr$(9) + Chr$(9) + Chr$(9) + Chr$(9)
Underline
InsertPara
InsertPara
InsertPara
LeftPara
TableInsertTable .ConvertFrom = "", .NumColumns = "6",
.NumRows = "12", .InitialColWidth = "Auto", .Format = "20",
.Apply = "167"
TableSelectTable
TableRowHeight .RulerStyle = "0", .LineSpacingRule = 2,
.LineSpacing = "40 pt", .LeftIndent = "0" + Chr$(34),
.Alignment = 0, .AllowRowSplit = 1
TableColumnWidth .ColumnWidth = "1.2" + Chr$(34),
.SpaceBetweenCols = "0" + Chr$(34), .RulerStyle = "0"
NextCell
NextCell
Insert "Monday"
NextCell
Insert "Tuesday"
NextCell
```

```
Insert "Wednesday"
NextCell
Insert "Thursday"
NextCell
Insert "Friday"
NextCell
Insert "Language Arts"
LineDown 1
Insert "Reading"
LineDown 1
Insert "Spelling"
LineDown 1
Insert "Math"
LineDown 1
Insert "Social Studies"
LineDown 1
Insert "Science"
LineDown 1
Insert "Study Skills"
End Sub
```

◆ Look over the WordBasic statements that make up the Homework macro and compare them with the study planner you just printed. Comparing the finished product with the WordBasic statements that make up a macro is the easiest way to figure out what a macro is doing. Remember, ignore arguments with values of zero.

✻ **FilePageSetup** sets the left and right margins to 0.5 inches.

✻ **CenterPara** turns on centering.

✻ **Insert** statements type the heading information

✻ **InsertPara** statements type some blank lines

✻ **LeftPara** turns on left justification

✻ **TableInsertTable** makes a table of six columns and twelve rows

✻ **TableSelectTable** highlights the entire table

✻ **TableRowHeight** sets the height of the rows

✻ **TableColumnWidth** sets the width of the columns

✻ **Insert** statements type the days of the week across the columns

✻ **NextCell** moves the insertion point to the next column

✻ **Insert** statements type the subjects down the rows

✻ **LineDown 1** moves the insertion point down the rows

◆ Press **Ctrl + End** to move the insertion point to the end of the macro.

◆ Delete "Study Skills" and replace it with "**Computer Lab**"

◆ On the next line, type **LineDown 1**

◆ On the next line, type **Insert "Band"**

One last little fix and this macro will be perfect. Let's put the insertion point at the top of the study planner so that you can start filling in the homework assignments right away. One WordBasic statement is all we need to perform this magic.

◆ On the next line, type **StartOfDocument**
This WordBasic command is just like pressing Ctrl + Home in a regular Word document.

◆ Press the **Tab** key three times to add a comment to this line.

◆ Type: **'Moves the insertion point to the top**

◆ This is how your new macro should look.

```
Sub MAIN
REM********************************************************
REM Macro:      Homework
REM Author:     Bobby Brown
REM Purpose:    Create a study guide for homework assignments
REM Menu Macro: Tools, Homework
REM********************************************************
FilePageSetup .Tab = "0", .PaperSize = "0", .TopMargin = "1" +
Chr$(34), .BottomMargin = "1" + Chr$(34), .LeftMargin = "0.5" +
Chr$(34), .RightMargin = "0.5" + Chr$(34), .Gutter = "0" +
Chr$(34), .PageWidth = "8.5" + Chr$(34), .PageHeight = "11" +
Chr$(34), .Orientation = 0, .FirstPage = 0, .OtherPages = 0,
.VertAlign = 0, .ApplyPropsTo = 4, .FacingPages = 0,
.HeaderDistance = "0.5" + Chr$(34), .FooterDistance = "0.5" +
Chr$(34), .SectionStart = 2, .OddAndEvenPages = 0,
.DifferentFirstPage = 0, .Endnotes = 0, .LineNum = 0,
.StartingNum = "", .FromText = "", .CountBy = "0", .NumMode = - 1
CenterPara
Insert "Homework Assignments for Bobby Brown"
InsertPara
InsertPara
Insert "Week of:"
Underline
Insert Chr$(9) + Chr$(9) + Chr$(9) + Chr$(9) + Chr$(9)
Underline
InsertPara
InsertPara
InsertPara
LeftPara
TableInsertTable .ConvertFrom = "", .NumColumns = "6",
.NumRows = "12", .InitialColWidth = "Auto", .Format = "20",
.Apply = "167"
TableSelectTable
TableRowHeight .RulerStyle = "0", .LineSpacingRule = 2,
.LineSpacing = "40 pt", .LeftIndent = "0" + Chr$(34),
.Alignment = 0, .AllowRowSplit = 1
TableColumnWidth .ColumnWidth = "1.2" + Chr$(34),
.SpaceBetweenCols = "0" + Chr$(34), .RulerStyle = "0"
NextCell
NextCell
```

```
Insert "Monday"
NextCell
Insert "Tuesday"
NextCell
Insert "Wednesday"
NextCell
Insert "Thursday"
NextCell
Insert "Friday"
NextCell
Insert "Language Arts"
LineDown 1
Insert "Reading"
LineDown 1
Insert "Spelling"
LineDown 1
Insert "Math"
LineDown 1
Insert "Social Studies"
LineDown 1
Insert "Science"
LineDown 1
Insert "Computer Lab"
LineDown 1
Insert "Band"
StartOfDocument            'Moves the insertion point to the top
End Sub
```

- ◆ Click on **Save** on the Standard toolbar.
- ◆ Click on **Yes**.
- ◆ Click on **Print** on the Standard toolbar.
- ◆ Click on **File**.
- ◆ Click on **Close** to close the macro-editing window.
- ◆ Press **Alt + E** to erase the screen if it is not blank.
- ◆ Click on **Tools, Homework** to run the Homework macro.
  Your new homework assignment planner is illustrated on the next page.
- ◆ Click on **Print** on the Standard toolbar to print a copy of the Homework planner.
- ◆ Press **Alt + E** to erase the screen.

```
Homework Assignments for Bobby Brown
    Week of:    _____
```

	Monday	Tuesday	Wednesday	Thursday	Friday
Language Arts					
Reading					
Spelling					
Math					
Social Studies					
Science					
Computer Lab					
Band					

Editing the HistoryReportFormat Macro

6.   Your History teacher has gone crazy! She wants you to read a book every month about a famous person in history and write a report about it. She even wants you to give the book a rating or a grade. Let's add some stuff to the HistoryReportFormat macro to make this a little easier.

◆ Click on **Format, HistoryReportFormat** to run the HistoryReportFormat macro.

```
Name:  Sue Smothers      Teacher:  Mrs. Hanson
Date:  9/21/97           Subject:  History


|
```

The original History report

◆ Click on **Print** on the Standard toolbar to print a copy of the report.

◆ Press **Alt + E** to erase the screen.

◆ Click on **Tools, Macro…**

◆ Click on **HistoryReportFormat**.

◆ Click on **Edit.**

◆ Compare the WordBasic statements for the HistoryReportFormat macro to the printed report.

    ✳ **FilePageSetup** sets the top and bottom margins to 1.5 inches.

    ✳ **FormatFont** selects a font

    ✳ **Insert** statements type your name, teacher's name, date and subject

    ✳ **InsertPara** statements insert blank lines

    ✳ **SpacePara2** turns on double spacing

◆ This is how the report will look after you add the information for the book report to the HistoryReportFormat macro.

```
Name: Sue Smothers        Teacher: Mrs. Hanson
Date: 9/21/97             Subject: History

Book Title:
Author:
Rating:
```

◆ Position the insertion point near the end of the macro on the **InsertPara** statement just before the SpacePara2 statement.

◆ Press **Enter** to add a blank line to the macro.

```
InsertPara
InsertPara
|
InsertPara
SpacePara2
End Sub
```

◆ Type the following WordBasic Statements, starting at the blank line:

Insert "Book Title:"
InsertPara
Insert "Author:"
InsertPara
Insert "Rating:"
InsertPara
InsertPara

Before you save the macro, check a couple of things. "InsertPara" should be one word. Each left quotation mark must have a matching right quotation mark.

◆ Click on **Save** on the Standard toolbar.

◆ Click on **Yes**.

◆ Click on **File**.

◆ Click on **Close**.

◆ Click on **Format, HistoryReportFormat** to run the macro.

Now the macro has the book report information your teacher needs. You could improve it even more by having the insertion point end up on the "Book Title" line so that you can begin typing immediately. How can you get the insertion point to the "Book Title" line? Well, how would you do it in Word? First, move the insertion point to the top of the document (Ctrl + Home). Then move down three lines to the "Book Title" line (↓ three times). Then move to the end of the line (End). All you have to do is translate what you just did into WordBasic statements and the macro can make sure the insertion point is in the right spot every time you do a History report.

◆ Press **Alt + E** to erase the screen.

◆ Click on **Tools, Macro...**

◆ Click on **HistoryReportFormat**.

◆ Click on **Edit**.

◆ Press **Ctrl + End** to move the insertion point to the end of the macro.

◆ Add these WordBasic statements after the SpacePara2 statement.

StartOfDocument   **'Moves the insertion point to the top**
LineDown 3   **'Moves down three lines**
EndOfLine   **'Moves to the end of the line**

◆ This is how your macro should look.

```
Sub MAIN
REM*******************************************************
REM Macro:      HistoryReportFormat
REM Author:     Sue Smothers
REM Purpose:    Do all the formatting for History reports
REM Menu Macro:  Format, HistoryReportFormat
REM*******************************************************
FilePageSetup .Tab = "0", .PaperSize = "0", .TopMargin = "1.5" +
Chr$(34), .BottomMargin = "1.5" + Chr$(34), .LeftMargin = "1.25"
+ Chr$(34), .RightMargin = "1.25" + Chr$(34), .Gutter = "0" +
Chr$(34), .PageWidth = "8.5" + Chr$(34), .PageHeight = "11" +
Chr$(34), .Orientation = 0, .FirstPage = 0, .OtherPages = 0,
.VertAlign = 0, .ApplyPropsTo = 4, .FacingPages = 0,
.HeaderDistance = "0.5" + Chr$(34), .FooterDistance = "0.5" +
Chr$(34), .SectionStart = 2, .OddAndEvenPages = 0,
.DifferentFirstPage = 0, .Endnotes = 0, .LineNum = 0,
.StartingNum = "", .FromText = "", .CountBy = "0", .NumMode = -1
FormatFont .Points = "10", .Underline = 0, .Color = 0,
.Strikethrough = 0, .Superscript = 0, .Subscript = 0, .Hidden
= 0, .SmallCaps = 0, .AllCaps = 0, .Spacing = "0 pt",
```

```
.Position = "0 pt", .Kerning = 0, .KerningMin = "", .Tab =
"0", .Font = "Courier New", .Bold = 0, .Italic = 0
Insert "Name: Sue Smothers" + Chr$(9) + Chr$(9) + Chr$(9) +
Chr$(9) + Chr$(9) + "Teacher: Mrs. Hanson"
InsertPara
Insert "Date: "
InsertDateTime .DateTimePic = "MMMM d, yyyy", .InsertAsField = 0
Insert Chr$(9) + Chr$(9) + Chr$(9) + Chr$(9) + Chr$(9) +
"Subject: History"
InsertPara
InsertPara
Insert "Book Title:"
InsertPara
Insert "Author:"
InsertPara
Insert "Rating:"
InsertPara
InsertPara
InsertPara
SpacePara2
StartOfDocument    'Moves the insertion point to the top
LineDown 3         'Moves down three lines
EndOfLine          'Moves to the end of the line
End Sub
```

◆ Click on **Save** on the Standard toolbar.

◆ Click on **Yes**.

◆ Click on **File**.

◆ Click on **Close**.

◆ Click on **Format, HistoryReportFormat** to run the macro.
Your History report is ready for you to fill in the book title.

＊ Press **Tab**, and type the name of the book.

＊ Press ↓ and **Tab** to move down to the author line.

＊ Press ↓ and **Tab** to move down to the rating line.

＊ Press **Ctrl + End** to move down to the bottom of the document and begin typing the report. Pressing Ctrl + End will move the insertion point past the doublespacing command.

The File Fixer — Word 7 Only

7. Let's modify the GiftCertificate macro to include the path name in the InsertPicture statement so that the macro will always be able to find the picture it needs for the gift certificate.

◆ Click on **Tools, Macro…**

◆ Click on **GiftCertificate**

◆ Click on **Edit**.

◆ Position the insertion point on the InsertPicture statement.

◆ Modify the InsertPicture statement to include the exact location of the picture file.

◆ InsertPicture .Name = "**C:\MSOffice\Winword\Clipart\Hplaque.wmf**", .LinkToFile = "0"

◆ Click on **Save** on the Standard toolbar.

◆ Click on **Yes**.

◆ Click on **File, Close**.

◆ Run the Shortcut, Stationery, and GiftCertificate macros. They will work now in whatever order you choose to run them.

Are you hooked on macros yet? Good, because in the next chapter we're going to look at some of the ways to fix problems that may occur when you're writing and editing macros. Anything that gets broken in a macro can be fixed!

CHAPTER 4

Getting Rid of Bugs

There's an old story, passed down from programmer to programmer that tells of a computer pioneer named Grace Hopper. (Grace Hopper was a brilliant inventor whose contribution to the computer age will always be remembered. She invented the first computer compiler and the first easy to use computer programming language, COBOL, which is still in use today. She retired as a Rear Admiral from the Navy.) Grace couldn't get her program to run one day and discovered that a moth had gotten caught in one of the computer's switches. When the moth was removed, Grace told everybody that she had "debugged" the computer. That's how we get the term "bug," which means any error in a computer program.

This chapter is going to describe the kinds of errors you may see in macros, and the steps you can take to fix those errors and "remove the bugs."

Messed Up Macros

An error occurs in a macro whenever an instruction breaks one of the rules of WordBasic. Those rules are called syntax rules. In Language Arts class, your teacher takes off for misspelled words and sentences without periods. In macro land, Word takes off for misspelled statement names and arguments without periods. Word also checks to make sure that there are commas between arguments and that each argument has an acceptable value. If your macro breaks a syntax rule Word displays a message box on the screen telling you that the macro is messed up. It does this when you try to run the macro. You won't know about any errors when you save the macro. Let's look at several causes of errors and see how to "debug" each.

SYNTAX ERROR

Syntax error is by far the most common WordBasic error. It is caused by the following conditions:

- ◆ A missing period in an argument (like .Font)
- ◆ A missing, misplaced or extra comma
- ◆ A missing quotation mark
- ◆ A missing parenthesis

As you learn more about WordBasic statements, you'll see a few more conditions that can cause syntax errors.

Word 6 syntax error

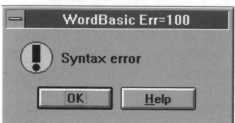

Word 7 syntax error

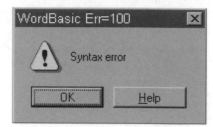

HOW TO FIND A BUG

Word has a nifty little trick for helping you find the bugs in your macros. Before you run a macro, place it in a macro-editing window. Then, open a new document window and run the macro there. If you get a syntax error, go back to the macro-editing window and Word will highlight the line with the error in red. You can fix the statement that is highlighted, and then return to the document window and run the macro again.

Let's put a bug in the Stationery macro and see what happens.

1. Click on **Tools**.
2. Click on **Macro...**
3. Click on **Stationery**.
4. Click on **Edit**. The Stationery macro appears in the macro-editing window.
5. Edit the Stationery macro by removing the comma in the FormatFont statement after the .Points argument.

```
FormatFont .Points = "36" .Underline = 0, .Color = 0,
.Strikethrough = 0, .Superscript = 0, .Subscript = 0, .Hidden
= 0, .SmallCaps = 0, .AllCaps = 0, .Spacing = "0 pt",
.Position = "0 pt", .Kerning = 0, .KerningMin = "", .Tab =
"0", .Font = "Algerian", .Bold = 1, .Italic = 0
```

6. Click on **Save** on the Standard toolbar.
7. Click on **Yes**.
8. Click on **Window**. If Global: Stationery is the only window listed, click on New to create a document window.
9. Click on **Document1**.
10. Click on the Stationery button on your toolbar.
    There's that syntax error message. Clicking on Help will bring you to the help screen on syntax errors. Clicking on OK will stop the macro from trying to run, and clear the screen. Let's get rid of the bug.
11. Click on **OK** to clear the syntax error message.
12. Click on **Window**.
13. Click on **Global: Stationery** to return to the macro-editing window.
    The FormatFont statement is highlighted and shaded on the screen.
14. Press → to remove the highlighting from the statement.

The FormatFont statement now appears in red letters in the macro-editing window.

15. Add a comma after the value "36" in the .Points argument.
    FormatFont .Points = "36", .Underline = 0, .Color = 0, .Strikethrough
16. Click on **Save** on the Standard toolbar.
17. Click on **Yes**.
18. Click on **Window**.
19. Click on **Document1**.
20. Click on the Stationery button on your toolbar to run the macro. The macro runs
    correctly and creates your stationery.
21. Click on **File, Close, No** to close the document window.
22. Click on **File, Close** to close the macro-editing window.

UNKNOWN COMMAND ERROR

The unknown command error message means that you misspelled a statement
name. Poor WordBasic doesn't know the meaning of the word you typed.

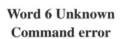

**Word 6 Unknown
Command error**

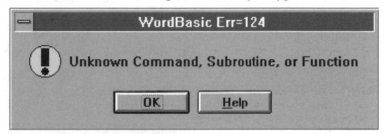

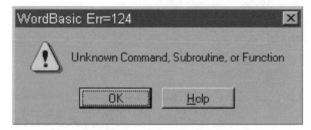

**Word 7 Unknown
Command error**

Let's create this error message by editing the Name macro.
1. Click on **New** on the Standard toolbar.
2. Click on **Tools**.
3. Click on **Macro...**
4. Click on **Name**.
5. Click on **Edit**. The Name macro appears in the macro-editing window.
6. Change *CenterPara* to **CenterPar**
7. Click on **Save** on the Standard toolbar.
8. Click on **Yes**.
9. Click on **Window**.
10. Click on **Document2**.
11. Press **Alt + N** to run the Name macro.
    The "Unknown Command" message appears. Word doesn't understand which
    instruction you want it to perform.
12. Click on **OK** to clear the error message from the screen.

13. Click on **Window**.
14. Click on **Global: Name** to return to the macro-editing window.
     The CenterPar statement is highlighted in red on the screen.
15. Change *CenterPar* to **CenterPara**
16. Click on **Save** on the Standard toolbar.
17. Click on **Yes**.
18. Click on **Window**.
19. Click on **Document2**.
20. Press **Alt + N** to run the Name macro.
     The macro runs correctly.
21. Click on **File, Close, No** to close the document window.
22. Click on **File, Close** to close the macro-editing window.

If you get an "Unknown Command" message and can't see anything wrong with your WordBasic statement, record a dummy little macro and see how Word *records* the statement. For example, you could record a macro called "Test" with the Center command as its only instruction. Then, click on Tools, Macro, Test, Edit to place the Test macro in the macro-editing window and check the spelling of the statement that Word created. It's always a good idea to record everything you can when you make a macro. Word always types the statements perfectly.

Getting Online Help

If you get an error message in a macro and can't see anything wrong with the highlighted statement, you can also use the Help features of Word to get more information about the syntax of the command. Word Help looks slightly different in version 6 and version 7.

TO GET HELP IN WORD 6

1. Click on **Help**.
2. Click on **Contents**.
3. Click on **Programming with Microsoft Word**.
    If you get an error message telling you that the requested topic in WRDBASIC.HLP is not installed, go to page 74 and follow the instructions labeled, "If Help is Not Available."
4. Click on **Index** for an alphabetical listing of all of the WordBasic statements and functions.

In Word 6, click on a command to see a detailed explanation

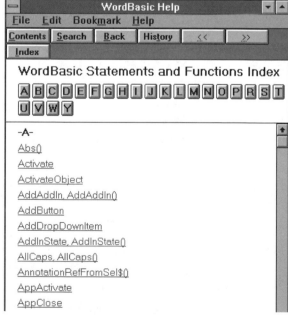

5. Click on **I** to see a list of commands that begin with the letter "I."
6. Click on **Insert** to see information about the Insert command.
   The Help screen for the Insert command appears.
7. Click on **Example** to see an example of the command.
   You can print the example for future reference by clicking on "Print."
8. Click on **Close** to close the example window.
9. Click on **Search** to find information on a particular WordBasic command.
10. Type: **macro error** to find information on macro errors.
11. Click on **Show Topics**.
    Word will place any related articles about your search string at the bottom of the screen.
12. Highlight the topic you want to read about at the bottom of the screen.
13. Click on **Go To**.
    The Help screen about error messages appears on the screen.
14. Click on **File, Exit** to get out of Help.

Help is a great way to learn more about WordBasic. Browse through the different topics and print pages that you can use as a reference later on.

To Get Help in Word 7

1. Click on **Help**.
2. Click on **Microsoft Word Help Topics**.
   If you get an error message telling you that the requested help topic is not installed, go to page 74 and follow the instructions labeled, "If Help is Not Available."
3. Click on **Index**.
4. Type: **Insert** to see a list of commands that begin with the word "Insert."
5. Click on **Insert statement** to see information about the Insert statement.
6. Click on **Display**.
   The Help screen for the Insert statement appears.
7. Click on **Example** to see an example of the command.
   You can print the example for future reference by clicking on "Print."
8. Click on **Close** to close the example window.

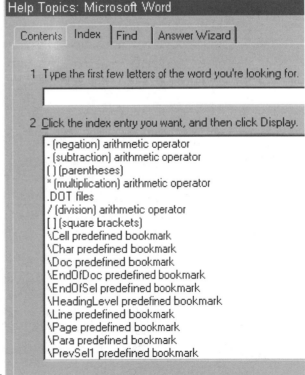

Word 7 Help Index

9.   Click on **Index** to find information on any WordBasic command.
10. Click on **C** to see a list of commands that begin with the letter "C."
11. Click on **CenterPara** to see information about the CenterPara command.
12. Click on **Search** to find information on a particular WordBasic command.

**Click on a command
to see a detailed
explanation**

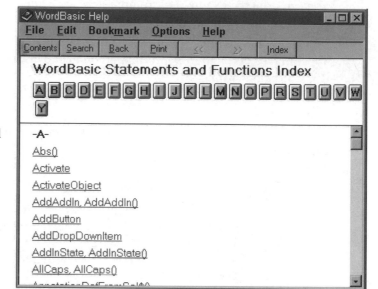

13. Type: **macro** to see a list of help topics that begin with the word "macro."
14. Click on **macro error messages**.
15. Click on **Display**. The Help screen about error messages appears on the screen.
16. Click on **File, Exit** to get out of Help.

IF HELP IS NOT AVAILABLE

If the help information about WordBasic does not appear and you get an obnoxious error message, it may be that the macro help files were not installed when the program was loaded onto your computer.

You can add the Help files to your computer by running the Microsoft Word installation program and installing just the WordBasic Help files. Make sure you have the original program disks handy before you start this process. If the WordBasic help files are already on your computer, skip this section.

To load WordBasic help files:

1.   Exit Word.
2.   In Word version 6, from the Windows Program Manager, click on **File**, **Run**.
     In Word version 7, click on **Start, Run...**
3.   Insert the Microsoft Word for Windows setup disk 1 into the disk drive.
4.   Type **a:\setup** and press Enter.
5.   Click on **Add/Remove...**
6.   In version 6, click on **Online Help, Examples, and Demos**
     In version 7, click on **Online Help**
7.   Click on **Change Option...**

Look at the option "WordBasic Help." If there isn't a check in the box in front of "WordBasic Help" it means that the help files are not loaded on your computer.

8.   Click on **WordBasic Help** to put a check in the check box.

9.   Click on **OK**.

10. Click on **Continue**.

11. Follow the instructions on your screen for loading the files onto your computer.

ANOTHER WAY TO GET HELP

If you have a macro in the macro-editing window and can't remember the syntax for a WordBasic command, you can use a really neat feature of Help to figure it out. Word allows you to point to the command you need help with, and it will bring up the help screen explaining the command you're pointing to. Here's how it works.

Put the DeleteLine macro in the macro-editing window.

1.   Click on **New** if you need to display the Word main menu.

2.   Click on **Tools, Macro...**

3.   Click on **DeleteLine**

4.   Click on **Edit**.

5.   Position the insertion point at the beginning of the *EndOfLine* statement.

6.   Press **F1**.
     The help screen appears with information about the EndOfLine command. The syntax of the command is shown at the top of the screen, followed by an explanation of how the statement or function works.

7.   In Word 6, click on **File, Print Topic...** to print the Help screen.
     In Word 7, click on **Options, Print Topic...** to print the Help screen.

8.   Click on **Example** to see an example of the command.

9.   In Word 6, click on **File, Exit** to get out of Help.   ⬛◻⬛ ◄—◄◄ **Close**
     In Word 7, click on **Close** to get out of Help.
     If you need help with a command but don't know how to spell the command name, position the insertion point on a blank line in the macro and press F1. The WordBasic Statements and Functions Index will appear. You can then click on the first letter of the command and look for the correct spelling in the alphabetical list of commands.

10. Click on **File, Close** to close the DeleteLine macro-editing window.

The Step Button

The Step button on the Macro toolbar is a great debugging tool. You can use it to run a macro one command at a time, or step by step. Each time you click on the Step button, Word highlights an instruction in the macro-editing window. When you click on Step again, Word runs the instruction and then highlights the next instruction. Let's check out the Step button on the HistoryReportFormat macro.

1.   Click on **Tools**.

2.   Click on **Macro...**

3.   Click on **HistoryReportFormat**.

4.   Click on **Edit**.

5. Click on **Window**.

    There should be two windows listed, the HistoryReportFormat macro-editing window and a document window. If you don't have a document window listed, click on New on the Standard toolbar to create one. If you have more than two windows listed, click on the extra window names, then click on File, Close to close them. In order to see the Step button clearly, we need two windows.

6. Click on **Arrange All**.

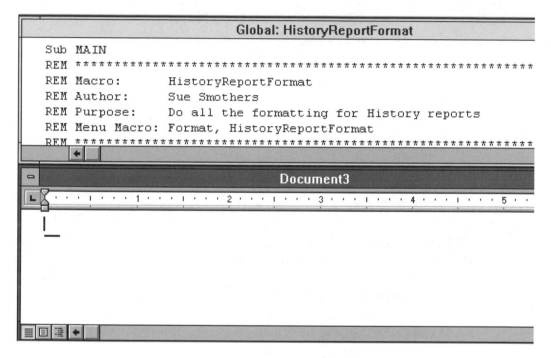

    You now have two windows showing on the screen at the same time. When you click anywhere in one of the windows, that window becomes active. Notice how the title bar changes color when you do this.

7. Click in the blank document window to make it the active window.

8. Click on the **Step** button on the Macro toolbar.

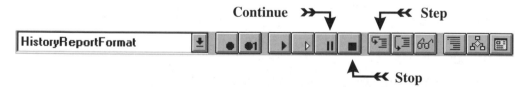

    The macro starts running and highlights the first command in the macro. Comments don't count as statements, so Word highlights the FilePageSetup statement.

9. Click on the **Step** button again.

    Word formats the page in the document window according to the arguments in the FilePageSetup command and highlights the FormatFont statement.

10. Click on the **Step** button again. Word executes the FormatFont statement and highlights the first Insert statement.

11. Continue clicking on **Step** to allow the macro to execute every command in the macro. When you get to the part of the macro that types information on the screen, notice how the information is typed in your document window. If you are stepping through a macro and find a bug, you can click on **Stop** to stop running the macro or **Continue** to run the remaining macro instructions without pausing.

Now, let's close the document window.

12. Click in the document window to select it.

13. Click on **File, Close, No** to close the document window.

14. Click on the maximize button on the right side of the HistoryReportFormat title bar to maximize the macro-editing window.

In version 6, click on ▲. In version 7, click on ☐

Debugging With Comments

Another useful technique for debugging a macro is to "comment out" part of the macro. What you're doing is telling the macro to ignore a group of instructions in the macro so that you can test another group of instructions. When the first part is working perfectly, you can remove the comments and test another part of the macro.

To turn macro instructions into comments, add REM or an apostrophe in front of the statement. Let's try it on the HistoryReportFormat macro.

1. Position the insertion point on the *StartOfDocument* statement (it's near the end of the macro).

2. Type: ' *(an apostrophe)* in front of the following three statements:

> **'StartOfDocument**
> **'LineDown 3**
> **'EndOfLine**

3. Click on **Save** on the Standard toolbar.

4. Click on **Yes**.

5. Click on **New**.

6. Click on **Format**.

7. Click on **HistoryReportFormat**.

The HistoryReportFormat macro runs without executing the three instructions that position the insertion point at the end of the Book Title line. Word ignored the statements because they are comments. Let's go back and remove the comments.

8. Click on **Window**.

9. Click on **Global: HistoryReportFormat**.

10. Remove the ' (apostrophes) from the StartOfDocument, LineDown and EndOfLine statements.

11. Click on **Save** on the Standard toolbar.

12. Click on **Yes**.

13. Click on **File**.

14. Click on **Close**.

15. Press **Alt + E** to erase the document window.
16. Click on **Format**.
17. Click on **HistoryReportFormat**.
    The entire macro runs now, because removing the apostrophes turned the comments into WordBasic instructions.

You can use the debugging tools you've learned in this chapter on any Word macro. As your macros become more and more complex, you'll use them a lot. In the next chapter we're going to look at how to create fill in the blanks macros. You'll see how a macro can ask questions on the screen, wait for your answer, and do something with it afterwards. It's beyond cool!

CHAPTER 5

Writing Macros

When you make a macro:

RECORD WHAT YOU CAN AND WRITE THE REST!!!!

Just about any macro you can think of will contain some commands that can be recorded with the macro recorder. Always, always, always, always record as much as you can. Word never makes a mistake when it records a command, so you'll never get an obnoxious syntax error. When you use the macro recorder, every WordBasic statement will be perfect.

After you have the recorded part of the macro done, add the WordBasic statements that go beyond the capabilities of the recorder. You can collect information, display messages on the screen, or make decisions about what happens next in the macro.

In this chapter, we look at the WordBasic statements that perform these incredible feats of magic. As we do, you'll turn into a computer programmer and dazzle non-macro-speaking mortals with the brilliance of your powerful, custom made programs.

Macros That Ask for Information

One of the most useful things a macro can do is let you enter information on the screen and then do something with what you entered inside the macro. In order to do this, a macro needs a place to put the information you enter. You can't have stuff flying around all over the place inside your computer. The macro would never be able to find anything. So in your macro, you'll create a storage bucket to hold the information. That storage bucket is called a variable.

Variables

A variable is a place in your computer's memory where information is stored. Each separate piece of information must have its own variable, so you could have a variable to hold the name of your report, a variable to hold your math grades or a variable to hold today's date.

There are two types of WordBasic variables: numeric variables and string variables.

Numeric variables are used to hold numbers. For example, you could have a numeric variable to hold your test scores.

String variables are used to hold a "string" or group of characters. They are used to hold text. You could have a string variable to hold the name of your report.

Each variable in a macro must have a name. You get to make up the name, so try to use names that tell how the variable is used inside the macro. You could use "x" as a variable name, but it would be difficult later on trying to figure what the "x" stands for. So, use names like "ReportName", or "MathGrades"—anything that makes sense to you. WordBasic has a few rules for naming variables.

◆ A variable name must begin with a letter.

◆ A variable name can contain only letters and numbers; punctuation marks and spaces are not allowed.

◆ A variable name cannot be longer that 40 characters (80 characters in Word 7).

◆ A variable name cannot be a WordBasic reserved word. A reserved word is a word that already has a meaning in WordBasic, such as statement names and arguments.

◆ A string variable name must end with a dollar sign ($). String variables end with dollar signs so that WordBasic knows immediately which variables contain numbers and which contain text.

Here are some examples of variable names:

String Variable Names	Numeric Variable Names
name$	total
report$	grade
answer$	count

Variables start out as empty containers, waiting to be filled when the macro runs. They stay empty until you put something in them.

The Input Statement

One of the ways to enter information into a macro is through an Input statement. When you run a macro with an Input statement, a question shows in the status bar at the bottom of the screen. The macro waits for you to type an answer, then continues running the rest of the macro. WordBasic holds the answer you entered in a variable until it needs it.

The syntax (or layout) of the Input statement is:

Input "*Question you want to appear in the status bar*", VariableName$

"Input" is the name of the statement. The question you want to see in the status bar is shown next, enclosed in quotation marks. Word will add a question mark when you run the macro, so you don't have to include a question mark in the Input statement. The variable name is shown after the message. This is where WordBasic will put the answer you type.

Including Input statements in your macros can make them easier to use. It sure would be nice if the Name macro contained an Input statement. The macro could start running, stop for a minute to let you type the title of your report, and then finish running.

Let's add an Input statement to the Name macro and see what happens. I think you'll agree that it makes the macro a lot more useful.

1.   Click on **Tools, Macro...**

2.   Click on **Name**.

3.   Click on **Edit**. The Name macro appears in the macro-editing window.

4. Position the insertion point on the statement: *Insert "by"*
5. Press **Enter** to create a blank line in the macro.

```
Sub MAIN
REM*****************************************************
REM Macro:      Name
REM Author:     Jeremy Jones
REM Purpose:    Type my name on a report, (Alt + N)
REM*****************************************************
FormatFont .Points = "14", .Underline = 0, .Color = 0,
.Strikethrough = 0, .Superscript = 0, .Subscript = 0, .Hidden
= 0, .SmallCaps = 0, .AllCaps = 0, .Spacing = "0 pt",
.Position = "0 pt", .Kerning = 0, .KerningMin = "", .Tab =
"0", .Font = "Arial", .Bold = 0, .Italic = 0
CenterPara
Insert "by"
```

←

Type the following WordBasic statements, starting at the blank line.

6. Type: **Input "What is the title of your report", title$**
   When the macro runs, "What is the title of your report?" will appear in the
   status bar at the bottom of your screen. After you type a title, it will be placed in
   the variable named title$.
7. Press **Enter** to position the insertion point on the next line.
8. Type: **Insert title$**
   The Insert statement types something on the screen. When it is used with a
   variable it types what is *in* the variable on the screen. It types the actual title, not
   the word "title."
9. Press **Enter** to position the insertion point on the next line.
10. Type: **InsertPara**
    After typing the title on the screen, the InsertPara statement will move the
    insertion point down to the next line. The Name macro should look like this.

```
Sub MAIN
REM*****************************************************
REM Macro:      Name
REM Author:     Jeremy Jones
REM Purpose:    Type my name on a report, (Alt + N)
REM*****************************************************
FormatFont .Points = "14", .Underline = 0, .Color = 0,
.Strikethrough = 0, .Superscript = 0, .Subscript = 0, .Hidden
= 0, .SmallCaps = 0, .AllCaps = 0, .Spacing = "0 pt",
.Position = "0 pt", .Kerning = 0, .KerningMin = "", .Tab =
"0", .Font = "Arial", .Bold = 0, .Italic = 0
CenterPara
Input "What is the title of your report", title$
Insert title$
InsertPara
Insert "by"
InsertPara
Insert "Jeremy Jones"
```

```
InsertPara
InsertPara
InsertPara
LeftPara
SpacePara2
End Sub
```

11. Click on **Save** on the Standard toolbar.
12. Click on **Yes**.
13. Click on **File**
14. Click on **Close** to close the macro-editing window.
15. Run the macro by pressing **Alt + N**

What is the title of your report?

When you run the Name macro, the question shows in the status bar.
As you type your answer, it will also appear in the status bar.

Look at the status bar at the bottom of the screen. The status bar shows "What is the title of your report?"

Word is waiting for you to enter the title of the report. Watch the status bar as you type a title (any old title is fine). As you type, the title appears on the status bar so you can check your typing and make corrections if necessary, before pressing Enter. Pressing Enter tells the macro you're done. Word types the report name on the screen and then finishes running the rest of the macro by typing the word "by" and your name. Pretty cool, isn't it?

The Big Bad Wolf
by
Jeremy Jones

The Input statement is a useful little fellow because it allows you to place a value in a variable. The variable can then be used inside the macro. In the Name macro, the contents of the variable are printed with the Insert statement, "Insert title$." This statement tells WordBasic to print whatever is in the variable title$. A lot of times you'll want to print what's in a variable and some text on the same line. No problem. WordBasic can handle it.

Combining Text and Variables in an Insert Statement

When you want WordBasic to type something on the screen, you use the Insert statement. When you want to type text on the screen, you enclose it in quotation marks, like:

Insert "by"

When you want to type what's in a variable, you type the variable name with no quotation marks.

Insert title$

A lot of times you'll want to type something on the screen that is part text and part variable. In that case, type the text in quotation marks, type the variable without quotations marks, and separate them with a plus sign (+). Like:

Insert "Name:" + Name$

> Types the word "Name:" then the value of the variable "Name$" right beside it.

Insert "Date:" + HomeworkDate$

> Types the word "Date:" then the value of the variable "HomeworkDate$" beside it.

INPUT STATEMENTS IN THE COMMENTS MACRO

The Comments macro allows you to add comments to your macros quickly and easily. If you add three Input statements to the Comments macro it will be even easier to get those comments into your macros.

1. Click on **Tools, Macro...**
2. Click on **Comments**.
3. Click on **Edit**. The Comments macro appears in the macro-editing window.
4. Position the insertion point on the following Insert statement.
    Insert "REM Macro:" + Chr$(9) + Chr$(9)
5. Press **Enter** to create a blank line in the macro.
6. Type: **Input "What is the name of the macro", Name$** in the blank line.
    This Input statement will display a message on the status bar at the bottom of the screen asking you to type the name of the macro. Your response will be stored in the variable "Name$."
    Modify the Insert statement that types the remark for the name of the macro.
7. Type: Insert "REM Macro:" + Chr$(9) + Chr$(9) **+ Name$**
    This Insert statement will type "REM Macro:" and the name of the macro that is stored in the variable "Name$."
8. Position the insertion point on the following Insert statement.
    Insert "REM Author:" + Chr$(9) + Chr$(9)
9. Press **Enter** to create a blank line in the macro.
10. Type: **Input "Who is the author", Author$** in the blank line.

This Input statement will display a message on the status bar asking you to type the name of the person who wrote the macro. Your response will be stored in the variable "Author$."

Modify the Insert statement that types the remark for the author.

11.   Type: Insert "REM Author:" + Chr$(9) + Chr$(9) **+ Author$**
12.   Position the insertion point on the following Insert statement.
Insert "REM Purpose:" + Chr$(9)
13.   Press **Enter** to create a blank line in the macro.
14.   Type: **Input "What is the purpose of this macro", Purpose$** in the blank line. This Input statement will display a message on the status bar asking you to type the purpose of the macro. Your response will be stored in the variable "Purpose$."

Modify the Insert statement that types the remark for the purpose of the macro.

15.   Type: Insert "REM Purpose:" + Chr$(9) **+ Purpose$**

The Comments macro should look like this:

```
Sub MAIN
LineDown 1
InsertPara
LineUp 1
Insert "REM ********************************************"
Insert "********"
InsertPara
Input "What is the name of the macro", Name$
Insert "REM Macro:" + Chr$(9) + Chr$(9) + Name$
InsertPara
Input "Who is the author", Author$
Insert "REM Author:" + Chr$(9) + Chr$(9) + Author$
InsertPara
Input "What is the purpose of this macro", Purpose$
Insert "REM Purpose:" + Chr$(9) + Purpose$
InsertPara
Insert "REM ********************************************"
Insert "********"
InsertPara
End Sub
```

16.   Click on **Save** on the Standard toolbar.
17.   Click on **Yes**.
18.   Click on **File**.
19.   Click on **Close**.

Run the Comments macro and add comments to the GiftCertificate macro.

1.   Click on **Tools, Macro...**
2.   Click on **GiftCertificate**
3.   Click on **Edit**.
4.   Press **Alt + C** to run the Comments macro.
Look at the status bar at the bottom of the screen. Word is waiting for you to type the name of the macro.

5. Type: **GiftCertificate**
6. Press **Enter**.
7. Type: *your name* as the author.
8. Press **Enter**.
9. Type: **Create a custom made gift certificate** as the purpose.
10. Press **Enter**.
11. Click on **Save** on the Standard toolbar.
12. Click on **Yes**.
13. Click on **File**.
14. Click on **Close**.

As helpful as Input statements are, there is one thing about them that some people don't like. Input statements are easy to miss because they're sort of hidden way down there on the status bar. While the macro is running, you can just sit there and sit there wondering what to do because you don't see the message at the bottom of the screen. Well I know we'd never do that, but some people would. Another way to get information into a macro is by using the InputBox$() function. When you use this command, a box will appear in the middle of the screen asking for information. You absolutely, positively can't miss it.

WordBasic Functions

We've seen that macros are made up of WordBasic statements and that statements are instructions that tell the macro what to do. Macros can also contain functions. The job of a function is to give information to the macro. A function can tell the macro things like what font is currently being used in the document or what is today's date. A function can also give the macro information that you type on the screen.

A function is easy to spot in a macro because it ends with parentheses ( ). Functions can give a macro numeric information or text information. Here are some functions that give a macro numeric information. They each have a function name, end with parentheses and will tell the macro something in the form of a number.

FontSize( )
    Tells the macro the font size in the document window.
Weekday( )
    Tells the macro the day of the week in the form of a number.
    1 is Sunday, 2 is Monday, 3 is Tuesday, 4 is Wednesday, 5 is Thursday,
    6 is Friday and 7 is Saturday.
Today( )
    Tells the macro today's date in the form of a number.

Some functions give macros text information. These functions always have a dollar sign ($) in the function name, right before the parentheses. They give information to a macro in the form of text or strings of information.

Font$( )
    Tells the macro which font is being used in the document window.

Date$( )

Tells the macro a date in the form of text (like January 1, 1997).

InputBox$( )

Tells the macro information you entered in an input box.

The important thing to remember about functions is that they give information to a macro that can be used inside the macro to do some job. Let's take a look at the InputBox$() function and see how we can use it to enter information into the Homework macro.

The Input Box$() Function

The InputBox$( ) function displays a box on the screen and lets you enter information into a macro by typing it in the box. The stuff you type will be stored in a variable as text information. The macro can then use whatever is in the variable to run the rest of the WordBasic statements.

You can make up a title for the box, a prompt that tells you what to enter, and a default response.

The title for the box shows in the title bar of the Input box when it is displayed on the screen. The prompt is shown inside the box and explains what you're suppose to do.

The default response is an answer that shows up automatically when the box appears on the screen. You'll use a default response if most of the time you type the same answer. The Input box can show that answer to save you from having to type it each time. Of course, you can change the answer if you want to.

The syntax of the InputBox$( ) function is:

VariableName$ = InputBox$(*"Prompt"* [, *"Title"*] [,*"Default"*])

"VariableName$" is the name of the variable that will hold whatever you type. Give the variable a name that reminds you of what it holds. The equal sign is used to tell Word to put what you type into the variable. It tells Word to make the variable *equal to* what you type in the Input box.

"InputBox$" is the name of the function. The InputBox$( ) function has three arguments; prompt, title and default. Prompt is the only argument that is required. In other words, you must have a prompt in all InputBox$( ) functions or WordBasic will give you one of its grouchy old error messages.

The title and default arguments are optional. You can put them into your InputBox$( ) functions if you want to, but the macro won't care a bit if you leave them out. Since title and default are optional arguments, they are shown with braces [ ] around them in the syntax example above. You don't put the braces in the actual command inside the macro, but they are always shown when you type the format of the command. It's one of those special programming rules to put stuff that's not absolutely necessary inside braces. That way, you can ignore any part of a command inside braces if you want to.

Let's take a look at the three arguments of the InputBox$( ) function.

Argument	*Explanation*
Prompt	This is the message that will appear in the box telling you what to type. Your answer cannot be longer than 255 characters (like that's a real problem). "Prompt" is a required argument. Word will give you an error message if you forget it.
Title	"Title" is what is shown in the title bar of the box on the screen. It is an optional argument. If you leave it out, WordBasic will use the title "Microsoft Word."
Default	This is the "answer" you want displayed automatically when the box appears on the screen. It is an optional argument. Lots of times you won't use a default because your answer will never be the same. You'll type something different each time you run the macro.

AN INPUTBOX$() FUNCTION IN THE HOMEWORK MACRO

Let's add an InputBox$() function to the Homework macro to let you enter the date at the top of the study planner. That way, you won't have to fill in the date after you print the study planner.

1. Click on **Tools, Macro...**
2. Click on **Homework**
3. Click on **Edit**. The Homework macro appears in the macro editing window.
4. Position the insertion point on the following Insert statement:
   Insert "Week of:"
5. Press **Enter** to insert a blank line into the macro.
6. Press ↑ to position the insertion point in the blank line.
7. Type: **WeekOf$ = InputBox$("What is the date?", "Homework Assignments")**

   This InputBox$() function will display a box on the screen asking you to type the date. The date you type will be stored in the variable "WeekOf$." Notice the prompt, "What is the date?" In an InputBox$() function, you always type the question exactly as you want it to appear inside the box. The Input statement adds a question mark to your prompt, but the InputBox$() function does not. You have to type it exactly as you want it to appear. The title of the Input box is "Homework Assignments."

   Modify the Insert statement that types the date.
8. Type: **Insert "Week of: " + WeekOf$**

   Press the spacebar two times after the word "of:" to add some space between the words "week of:" and the date that is stored in the variable "WeekOf$." This Insert statement will type the words "Week of: " and then the date that you entered in the Input box.
9. Delete the following three programming statements:
   Underline
   Insert Chr$(9) + Chr$(9) + Chr$(9) + Chr$(9) + Chr$(9)
   Underline

These statements were used to create a blank line on the study planner for writing in the date. Since the date will be typed on the study planner for you, you don't need the blank line. The section of macro statements you modified look like this:

```
Insert "Homework Assignments for Bobby Brown"
InsertPara
InsertPara
WeekOf$ = InputBox$("What is the date?", "Homework Assignments")
Insert "Week of: " + WeekOf$
InsertPara
InsertPara
```

10. Click on **Save** on the Standard toolbar.
11. Click on **Yes**.

Now, let's try it out. If you get an error message, return to the macro-editing window and fix the highlighted statement.

12. Click on **New** on the Standard toolbar.
13. Click on **Tools, Homework** to run the Homework macro.
     An Input box appears on the screen.
14. Type today's date and click on **OK**.
     Word types the date on the study planner, then finishes running the rest of the macro.
15. Click on **File, Close, No** to close the document window.
16. Click on **File, Close** to close the macro-editing window.

A couple of things to remember:

◆ Click on OK or press Tab to move to the OK button, and then press Enter to dismiss an Input box. Pressing Enter alone takes you down to the next line *inside* the Input box. It doesn't dismiss it.

◆ If you encounter an error while running a macro, use the debugging tools you learned in chapter four to correct the WordBasic statement. Most of the time the error is caused by missing quotation marks, missing commas or missing parentheses. Each left quotation mark must have a matching right quotation mark, each left parenthesis must have a matching right parenthesis. Those little "$" and "=" have to be there too.

An InputBox$() Function in the HistoryReportFormat Macro

Let's add some InputBox$( ) functions to the HistoryReportFormat macro.

Every time you run this macro, you need to type a name for the book you've read, its author and your rating of the book. If you enter this information in input boxes it'll make the macro easier to use.

1. Click on **Tools, Macro...**
2. Click on **HistoryReportFormat**.
3. Click on **Edit**. The HistoryReportFormat macro appears in the macro-editing window.

4. Position the insertion point after the last REM statement.
   Type an InputBox$( ) function that will let you enter the name of the book.

5. Type: **BookName$ = InputBox$("What is the title of your book?", "History Book Report")**
   When the macro runs, "What is the title of your book?" will appear on the screen inside an Input box to tell you what to type on the screen. "History Book Report" will appear as the title of the box. Since each book will have a different title, there is no default value. After you type a book title and click on OK, the title of your book will be placed in the variable named "BookName$."

6. Press **Enter** to position the insertion point on the next line.

7. Type: **Author$ = InputBox$("Who wrote the book?", "History Book Report")**
   When the macro runs, "Who wrote the book?" will appear on the screen inside an Input box to tell you what to type on the screen. "History Book Report" will appear as the title of the box. Since each book will have a different author, there is no default value. After you type the author's name and click on OK, the name will be placed in the variable named "Author$."

8. Press **Enter** to position the insertion point on the next line.

9. Type: **Rating$ = InputBox$("How would you rate this book?", "History Book Report", "C")**
   When the macro runs, "How would you rate this book?" will appear on the screen inside an Input box to tell you what to type. "History Book Report" will appear as the title of the box. Since you usually give the books you read a rating of "C" (you're tough on authors), the default value is already filled in as "C." After you type a rating and click on OK, your rating of the book will be placed in the variable named "Rating$."
   The name of the book you read is now safe and sound in the variable named BookName$. The author's name is sitting in the variable named Author$, and your rating of the book is relaxing in the variable named Rating$.
   All you've got to do now is get this information out of the variables and printed on your report. Use good old Insert statements once again.

10. Position the insertion point on the Insert statement that types the words "Book Title." Since you've already typed the title, and it's sitting in the variable named "BookName$," all you have to do is add the variable name to the Insert statement.

11. Type: Insert "Book Title:" **+ BookName$**
    This Insert statement types the words "Book Title:" and then the value of the variable "BookName$" beside it. Remember, enclose text that you want typed on the screen in quotation marks, and use a plus sign (+) to show the variable name beside it. WordBasic reads this statement as: type the stuff inside the quotation marks, then type whatever is in the variable named BookName$ right beside it.

12. Position the insertion point on the Insert statement that types the word "Author:" on the screen.

13. Type: Insert "Author:" **+ Author$**

The text information, "Author:" is typed on the screen first, then the name of the author that is in the variable Author$, beside it.

14. Position the insertion point on the Insert statement that types the word "Rating:" on the screen.

15. Type: Insert "Rating:" **+ Rating$**

    The text information, "Rating:" is typed on the screen first, then the actual rating you typed in the input box beside it.

16. Delete the following three WordBasic statements at the end of the macro.

    StartOfDocument

    LineDown 3

    EndOfLine

    These three WordBasic statements were used to position the insertion point in the original version of the HistoryReportFormat macro. The book report information will now be typed in the correct spot through the Input boxes, so these statements are unnecessary.

    The HistoryReportFormat macro should look like the example below. Check out those quotation marks, parentheses, and commas. Each left quotation mark should have a matching right quotation mark. Each left parenthesis should have a matching right parenthesis. There should be commas between all arguments. Make sure you've got punctuation where you need it and not where you don't.

```
Sub MAIN
REM **********************************************************
REM Macro:        HistoryReportFormat
REM Author:       Allison Brown
REM Purpose:      Do all the formatting for History reports
REM Menu Macro:   Format, HistoryReportFormat
REM **********************************************************
BookName$ = InputBox$("What is the title of your book?",
"History Book Report")
Author$ = InputBox$("Who wrote the book?", "History Book Report")
Rating$ = InputBox$("How would you rate this book?", "History
Book Report", "C")
FilePageSetup .Tab = "0", .PaperSize = "0", .TopMargin = "1.5" +
Chr$(34), .BottomMargin = "1.5" + Chr$(34), .LeftMargin = "1.25"
+ Chr$(34), .RightMargin = "1.25" + Chr$(34), .Gutter = "0" +
Chr$(34), .PageWidth = "8.5" + Chr$(34), .PageHeight = "11" +
Chr$(34), .Orientation = 0, .FirstPage = 0, .OtherPages = 0,
.VertAlign = 0, .ApplyPropsTo = 4, .FacingPages = 0,
.HeaderDistance = "0.5" + Chr$(34), .FooterDistance = "0.5" +
Chr$(34), .SectionStart = 2, .OddAndEvenPages = 0,
.DifferentFirstPage = 0, .Endnotes = 0, .LineNum = 0,
.StartingNum = "", .FromText = "", .CountBy = "0", .NumMode = - 1
 FormatFont .Points = "10", .Underline = 0, .Color = 0,
.Strikethrough = 0, .Superscript = 0, .Subscript = 0, .Hidden
= 0, .SmallCaps = 0, .AllCaps = 0, .Spacing = "0 pt",
.Position = "0 pt", .Kerning = 0, .KerningMin = "", .Tab =
"0", .Font = "Courier New", .Bold = 0, .Italic = 0
 Insert "Name: Sue Smothers" + Chr$(9) + Chr$(9) + Chr$(9) +
Chr$(9) + Chr$(9) + "Teacher: Mrs. Hanson"
```

```
InsertPara
Insert "Date: "
InsertDateTime .DateTimePic = "MMMM d, yyyy", .InsertAsField = 0
Insert Chr$(9) + Chr$(9) + Chr$(9) + Chr$(9) + Chr$(9) +
"Subject: History"
InsertPara
InsertPara
Insert "Book Title:" + BookName$
InsertPara
Insert "Author:" + Author$
InsertPara
Insert "Rating:" + Rating$
InsertPara
InsertPara
InsertPara
SpacePara2
End Sub
```

17. Click on **Save** on the Standard toolbar.

18. Click on **Yes**.

Check out the HistoryReportFormat macro with InputBox$( ) functions.

1. Click on **New** on the Standard toolbar.

2. Click on **Format, HistoryReportFormat**.

An Input box for entering the name of the book you read shows on the screen.

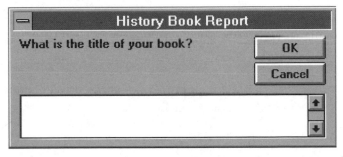

The title you entered in the title argument of the InputBox$( ) function "History
Book Report" appears in the title bar of the box. The prompt you entered in the
prompt argument of the InputBox$( ) function "What is the title of your book?"
appears inside the box, telling you what to do — type the name of the book.
You did not enter a default value in the InputBox$( ) function, so the area inside
the box where you type the name of the book is empty.

3. Type: **The Grinch From Next Door** as the title of the book.

4. Click on **OK**. To dismiss an Input box, you must click on OK or Cancel.
Pressing Enter will take you down to the second line inside the Input box. It
will *not* dismiss the Input box.

If you click on OK, the macro will keep running, performing each command in
order down the macro. If you click on Cancel, the macro will stop running and
the message "Command Failed" will appear on the screen. You can add
statements to the macro to check if the cancel button was pressed and if so,

display a nice message on the screen. But it's not really necessary. The macro will work just as well the way it is. So don't worry about the message. If you don't want to continue running a macro, it's no big deal to click on Cancel. It won't hurt anything inside your computer. The macro will just stop running.

The Input box for the author shows on the screen.

5.   Type: **Harry Hippo** as the author of the book.

6.   Click on **OK**. The rating Input box shows on the screen.

Check out the default value of "C" in the input box. Entering the "C" as the default value in the InputBox$( ) function caused the "C" to appear in the input box when you ran the macro. If you want to use the "C" click on OK. If you want to change the rating, Word makes it easy for you by highlighting the "C." All you have to do is type the new rating and Word will erase the old one.

7.   Click on **OK** to accept the rating of "C" and dismiss the input box.

The rest of the macro runs and types everything in the document window for you. The insertion point is at the bottom of the document window, waiting for you to type the report.

8.   Click on **File, Close, No** to close the document window.

Special Characters

I like this macro, I really do. Except one thing. Look at the way the title of the book, its author, and your rating are lined up on the page.

```
Book Title:The Grinch From Next Door
Author:Harry Hippo
Rating:C
```

It's hard to read. There needs to be some space in there between the headings and the stuff you typed. Wouldn't it look better like this?

```
Book Title:   The Grinch From Next Door
Author:       Harry Hippo
Rating:       C
```

If you press the tab key after the words "Book Title," "Author," and "Rating," the information will be a lot easier to read. To add a tab character to a macro you are recording, all you have to do is press the tab key on the keyboard. If you want to put a tab character in a WordBasic statement that cannot be recorded, then you need to write the *code* for the tab character.

Tab characters are one of the special characters that you can use in your macros to make the finished documents you're creating look good. The Chr$( ) function is used to put special characters into your macros.

THE CHR$( ) FUNCTION

The Chr$( ) function (which stands for "character") lets you add spaces, tabs and quotation marks to WordBasic statements.

Let's look at three special characters that can be used in macros. Each begins with the function name "Chr$" and ends with a number that tells WordBasic which special character you want.

Chr$(9)   Tab character (like pressing the tab key)

Chr$(32)   Space character (like pressing the spacebar)

Chr$(34)   Quotation mark
                 Since quotation marks are used in functions and statements to enclose strings, use the Chr$(34) function to include a quotation mark as part of the string. For example:

```
Insert "The book" + Chr$(32) + Chr$(34) +
BookName$ + Chr$(34) + Chr$(32) + "was
great!"
```

WordBasic types the words *The book*. It then types a space (the first Chr$(32) statement). The first Chr$(34) statement types a left quotation mark. The name of the book, in the variable "BookName$" is typed next, and the other Chr$(34) statement types the right quotation mark. The last Chr$(32) statement types another space. So, Word types:

The book "The Grinch From Next Door" was great!

CHR$() FUNCTIONS IN THE HISTORYREPORTFORMAt MACRO

Let's add tab characters to the HistoryReportFormat macro so the information will be lined up nicely.

1. If the HistoryReportFormat macro-editing window is not displayed on your screen, click on **Window, Global: HistoryReportFormat** to return to the macro-editing window.

2. Position the insertion point on the Insert statement that types the book title. Add a tab character to the Insert statement.

3. Type: Insert "Book Title:" **+ Chr$(9)** + BookName$
    This tells Word to type the words "Book Title:" press the tab key, and then type the name of the book.

4. Position the insertion point on the Insert statement that types the author. Add a tab character to the Insert statement.

5. Type: Insert "Author:" **+ Chr$(9)** + Author$

6. Position the insertion point on the Insert statement that types the rating of the book.
    Add a tab character to the Inset statement.

7. Type: Insert "Rating:" **+ Chr$(9)** + Rating$

8. Click on **Save** on the Standard toolbar.

9. Click on **Yes** to save the macro.

10. Click on **New** on the Standard toolbar.

11. Click on **Format, HistoryReportFormat** to run the macro.

12. Type the information in the Input boxes, and click on **OK**.

Looks a lot better doesn't it? If you need more than one tab or space character to make your document look good, add as many Chr$( ) functions as you need in the macro.

13. Click on **File, Close, No** to close the document window.
14. Click on **File, Close** to close the macro-editing window.

Macros That Display Messages

To have a conversation, both sides have to talk and listen. We've seen two ways that you can talk to a macro, the Input statement and the InputBox$( ) function. Macros can also talk to you and give you information. They can tell you something in the status bar at the bottom of the screen, or in a message box in the middle of the screen. We're going to look at three ways that macros talk to us: the Print statement, the MsgBox statement, and the MsgBox( ) function.

The Print Statement

The Print statement displays a message in the status bar at the bottom of the screen. It looks just like the message you saw in the Input statement, only it doesn't get any information from you. It is simply used to inform you of something, like what the macro is doing, or how far along it is in running.

The syntax of the Print statement is:

Print *"message you want printed in the status bar"*

One common use of the Print statement is to display the message "Working…" in the status bar when a macro takes a while to do something. You can look in the status bar and know that there really is something going on in there, even though you can't see it.

When you want the Print statement to type text information in the status bar, enclose the text in quotation marks. The print statement will also type numbers and variables in the status bar.

These are all valid Print statements:

Print "Hi gorgeous!"
    This Print statement will type the words "Hi gorgeous!" in the status bar.
Print ReportName$
    This Print statement will type whatever is in the string variable
    "ReportName$" in the status bar.
Print 587.12
    This Print statement will type the number 587.12 in the status bar.
Print Amount
    This Print statement will type whatever is in the numeric variable "Amount" in the status bar.

A PRINT STATEMENT IN THE NAME MACRO

Let's add a Print statement to the Name macro.

1. Click on **Tools, Macro…**
2. Click on **Name**.

3. Click on **Edit**. The Name macro appears in the macro-editing window.

4. Position the insertion point on the "End Sub" statement.

5. Press **Enter** to create a blank line in the macro.

6. Press ↑ to position the insertion point on the blank line.

7. Type: **Print "Type the report now, you amazing wonder–student."**

    When the macro runs, "Type the report now, you amazing wonder–student" will appear in the status bar at the bottom of the screen, after the program has typed your name. Just a gentle reminder to get started typing your report.

8. Click on **Save** on the Standard toolbar.

9. Click on **Yes**.

10. Click on **File, Close** to close the macro-editing window.

11. Press **Alt + E** to erase the screen if it is not blank.

12. Press **Alt + N** to run the Name macro.

13. Type the name of your report and press **Enter**.

    Now check out the status bar at the bottom of the screen. There's the message you created with the Print statement. As soon as you begin typing your report, the message will disappear. It was just there as a friendly reminder.

    In Word version 7, if your message flashes on the status bar for a minute, then another message appears in its place, check where your mouse pointer is pointing. If your mouse pointer happens to be pointing to a command on a toolbar, then the message explaining that Word feature will appear after your message. Just move the mouse pointer so that it's not pointing to a toolbar selection and run the macro again.

The MsgBox Statement

If you think a message in the status bar is too easy to miss, you can display a message in a message box in the middle of the screen. The MsgBox statement displays a message that you must tell Word you saw before the macro can continue running. You'll do this by clicking on the OK button that will be shown in the message box.

You can display any message you want to in the message box. You can also make up a title for the box, and choose which symbol appears in the box.

The syntax of the MsgBox statement is:

MsgBox "*message*" [, "*title*"] [, *type*]

"MsgBox" is the name of the WordBasic statement. The MsgBox statement has three arguments; message, title, and type. In the "message" argument, type the words that you want displayed on the screen. Since the point of a message box is to deliver a message, the message argument is required. Messages must be enclosed in quotation marks.

"Title" is an optional argument, so it is shown in braces [ ] in the syntax example. If you choose to give your message box a title, that title will appear in the title bar of the message box when it is displayed on the screen.

"Type" is also an optional argument. "Type" stands for the picture and buttons that appear in the box when the box is displayed on the screen.

Let's take a closer look at the three arguments of the MsgBox statement.

Argument	Explanation
Message	This is the message that will appear in the box. Your message cannot be longer than 255 characters. If it is, WordBasic will give you a message box of its own, an error message box. "Message" is a required argument.
Title	"Title" is what is shown in the title bar of the box on the screen. It is an optional argument. If you leave it out, WordBasic will use the title "Microsoft Word."
Type	"Type" is a numeric value that stands for the symbol and buttons displayed in the box. It is an optional argument. If you don't include a type argument, there will be an OK button in the message box and no symbol.

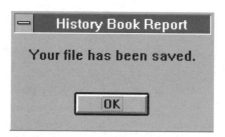
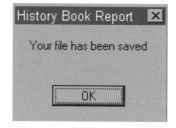

Word 6   **Word 7**

A message box with an OK button and no symbol

If you want to make your message box a little fancier, you can add a symbol to the box. There are four symbols to choose from: the stop symbol, the question mark, the attention symbol and the information symbol.

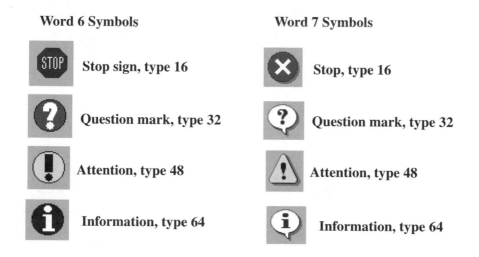

Word 6 Symbols   **Word 7 Symbols**

Stop sign, type 16   Stop, type 16

Question mark, type 32   Question mark, type 32

Attention, type 48   Attention, type 48

Information, type 64   Information, type 64

To place one of these symbols in a message box, type the number for the symbol as the type argument. This is a *numeric* argument, so it should NOT be placed in quotation marks. For example, a type argument of 16 in a MsgBox statement will produce a message box with a stop symbol.

Word 6	Word 7
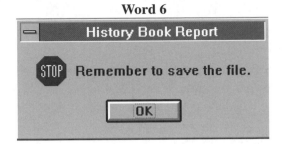	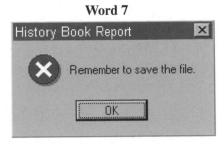

A Stop symbol will show in a message box with a type of 16

Let's add a MsgBox statement to the HistoryReportFormat macro. I hope you feel creative because you're going to pick the picture that appears in the box.

1. Click on **Tools, Macro...**
2. Click on **HistoryReportFormat**.
3. Click on **Edit**. The HistoryReportFormat macro appears in the macro-editing window.
4. Position the insertion point on the "End Sub" statement.
5. Press **Enter** to create a blank line.
6. Press ↑ to position the insertion point in the blank line.
7. Type: **MsgBox "Remember to use the spell checker.", "History Book Report", 48**

    Since this macro formats a report, the message should remind you of what your teacher focuses on when she grades reports. Use the message above if you want to, or create your own message. "History Book Report" will appear as the title of the message box. The attention symbol will be displayed in the box because of the third argument, 48. If you'd like a different symbol in your message box, choose 16 for a stop symbol, 32 for a question mark or 64 for the information symbol.
8. Click on **Save** on the Standard toolbar.
9. Click on **Yes**.
10. Click on **File, Close** to close the macro-editing window.
11. Press **Alt + E** to erase the screen if it is not empty.
12. Click on **Format, HistoryReportFormat** to run the macro and check it out.
    To remove the message box from the screen, you must tell Word that you saw it. Click on OK or press Enter to do this. Any time you want to change the message or the symbol, just edit the macro.

The MsgBox statement is helpful for telling you about things that are going on inside the macro, and reminding you of things you need to do when the macro is running. Another type of message box, the MsgBox() function, lets you ask a question in the message box, a question that can be answered with "yes" or "no." You might want to display the message "Are you sure you want to do that?" when your macro is about to delete something, or "Do you want to save the file?" when you're editing a document. The way you answer the question will determine what the macro does next. The macro will do one set of instructions when you answer "yes" and another set of instructions when you answer "no." This adds a lot of power to your macros.

The MsgBox( ) Function

The MsgBox( ) function displays a message box on the screen that contains a question. The question will be either a "yes/no" question or an "OK/Cancel" question. Your answer is placed in a variable and then used by the macro to figure out what to do next. If you answer "yes" the message box sends one value to the macro, and if you answer "no" the message box sends a different value to the macro.

The syntax of the MsgBox( ) function is:

Button = MsgBox(*"message"* [, *"title"*] [, *type*])

"Button" is the name of the variable that will hold your answer to the question in the message box. It is a numeric variable. It will hold a number.

The MsgBox( ) function has the same three arguments we looked at for the MsgBox statement, except that the arguments are placed in parentheses. In the "message" argument, you type the question you want displayed on the screen. Messages must be enclosed in quotation marks.

"Title" is an optional argument. If you choose to give your message box a title, it will appear in the title bar of the message box when it is displayed on the screen.

"Type" is also an optional argument. "Type" stands for the picture and buttons that appear in the box when the box is displayed on the screen. We already saw how the type argument will let you choose different pictures for the message box. It will also let you specify which buttons you want displayed in the box.

Let's take a closer look at the three arguments of the MsgBox( ) function.

Argument	*Explanation*
Message	This is the question that will appear in the box. Your question cannot be longer than 255 characters. "Message" is a required argument.
Title	"Title" is what is shown in the title bar of the box on the screen. It is an optional argument. If you leave it out, WordBasic will use the title "Microsoft Word."
Type	"Type" is a numeric value that stands for the symbol and buttons you want displayed in the box. WordBasic understands which buttons and symbols you want by the number you enter for "Type." "Type" is the sum of three values, one from each of the following groups:

Group	*Value*	*Meaning*
Button	0 (Zero)	OK button (default)
	1	OK and Cancel buttons
	2	Abort, Retry, and Ignore buttons
	3	Yes, No, and Cancel buttons
	4	Yes and No buttons

	5	Retry and Cancel buttons
Symbol	0 (Zero)	No symbol (default)
	16	Stop symbol
	32	Question mark symbol
	48	Attention symbol
	64	Information symbol
Action	0 (Zero)	First button is the default
	256	Second button is the default
	512	Third button is the default

"Action" is usually omitted from the "type" argument. If you leave it out, then the first button that appears in the box will always be the default button. This makes your life easier, because you can press Enter to select the first button in the box, the default button, instead of having to click on it.

So, to display "yes" and "no" buttons in a message box with the question mark symbol, the "type" argument would be 36 (32 for the question mark, plus 4 for the "yes" and "no" buttons).

$$32 + 4 = 36.$$

The default button is the "yes" button, because it's the first button in the box and we didn't include an action argument.

Here is an example of a MsgBox( ) function.

Button = MsgBox("Is it OK to delete this document?", "Delete Macro", 36)

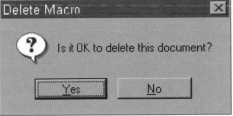

Word 6   **Word 7**

In this example, "Button" is the name of the variable that will hold your answer to the question "Is it OK to delete this document?" "Delete Macro" is the title of the box. The type argument of 36 represents the symbol and buttons that will appear in the box (32 for the question mark symbol, 4 for "yes" and "no" buttons). So, the type argument is 36.

After you answer the question in the message box, WordBasic puts your answer into a numeric variable. The value of that variable indicates which button you selected. The following values are what WordBasic can put into a variable. They each have a special meaning to WordBasic.

Value	Button Choice	Button Name
–1	First (leftmost) button	OK, Yes or Abort
0 (Zero)	Second button	Cancel, No or Retry
1	Third button	Cancel, Ignore

When you run the macro that contains the MsgBox() function:

Button = MsgBox("Is it OK to delete this document?", "Delete Macro", 36)

the variable "Button" will hold -1 if you clicked on "Yes," or pressed Enter. "Yes" is the default button, the first button in the box, the button on the left. "Button" will hold 0 if you clicked on "No," the second button in the box.

Choices, Choices — So Many Choices!

In message boxes that contain choices, your macro needs to know what you want it to do when you answer the question "yes" and what you want it to do when you answer the question "no." You tell it by putting a conditional statement in the macro. A conditional statement reads the variable that contains your answer and then tells the macro what you want it to do next. The macro will do different things depending on the value that is passed to it from the message box. A conditional statement tells the macro, "Do this if I answer yes, and do that if I answer no."

Conditional Statements

In the world of macros, a condition is a sentence that is either true or false.

The sentence "Today is Saturday." is either true or false. If today is Saturday, then it's a true condition. If today is not Saturday, then it's a false condition. It has to be one or the other.

A condition is always the first part of a conditional statement. The second part of the statement tells what happens when the condition is true. In a conditional statement, something always happens as a result of the condition. So, the first part of a conditional statement is the *If* and the second part of a conditional statement is the *Then*. Let's look at an example of a conditional statement.

If today is Saturday, **Then** I'll go to my baseball game.

The first part of the conditional statement is the condition, "If today is Saturday." It will either be true or false. The second part of the conditional statement tells what happens if the condition is true. It is *only* done if the condition is true. I'll go to my baseball game, *only* if it's Saturday. If it's not Saturday, (a false condition) there won't be a game, so I'll do something else.

To put a conditional statement in a macro, all you have to do is tell WordBasic:

If this is true, *Then* follow these instructions.

The "If" Conditional Statement

The most common WordBasic conditional statement is the "If" conditional.

The first part of the statement is the "**If**" part. What are you checking for? What has to happen before the macro follows the instructions after the word "then?"

If you press the OK button…

If today is Monday…

The second part of the statement is the "**Then**" part. This part of the statement will only be done if the condition is true.

If you press the OK button, **Then WordBasic will delete the line.**
If today is Monday, **Then WordBasic will display a message on the screen.**

The "Then" part of the statement will only be done if the condition is true. When WordBasic sees a condition that is false, it skips the whole statement and goes to the next instruction in the macro after the "If" statement. WordBasic says "That's not true, so forget about it."

There are several ways to write an "If" conditional statement, depending on how complex your question is. The simplest form of the If conditional statement is:

If *condition* Then *instruction*

This conditional statement says that if one sentence (condition) is true, then perform one macro instruction. This form of the "If" statement is used for a single instruction. The condition and the instruction must be on the same line. To check if something is true, use the equal sign (=). For example:

If Underline( ) = 1 Then Underline 0

This statement checks to see if underlining is turned on, Underline( ) = 1. If it is, WordBasic will turn it off, Underline 0.

If Button = –1 Then FileSave

This statement checks to see if the OK button in a message box was pressed. If it was, the value of –1 will be in the variable "Button." If WordBasic finds the variable –1, it will save the file with the FileSave statement. If the variable "Button" contains anything other than –1, then the macro will keep on going and will not save the file.

AN "IF" STATEMENT IN THE HISTORYREPORTFORMAT MACRO

Let's put all this stuff together and see how it works. Suppose you have trouble remembering to save your files. It's gotten you in trouble before when the power has gone out or you're rushing to get to the dinner table and forget to save. Let's modify the HistoryReportFormat macro to add a message box that asks if you want to save the file. You'll need a MsgBox( ) function and an "If" conditional statement.

1. Click on **Tools, Macro…**
2. Click on **HistoryReportFormat**.
3. Click on **Edit**. The first thing you need to do is add a MsgBox( ) function that asks if you'd like to save the file.
4. Position the insertion point on the MsgBox statement that displays the message "*Remember to use the Spell Checker*" (or whatever your message is). Type the following MsgBox() function in place of the old MsgBox statement.
5. Type: **Button = MsgBox ("Would you like to save the file now?", "History Book Report", 36)**
    This MsgBox() function will display a message box on the screen asking the question "Would you like to save the file now?" The message box will have the

title "History Book Report" and contain a question mark (32 for the type argument) and "yes" and "no" buttons (4 for the type argument).

6.   Press **Enter** to position the insertion point on the next line.

Now you need an "If" conditional statement to check which button you chose.

7.   Type: **If Button = -1 Then FileSave**

This statement checks the value of the variable "Button." If "Button" contains -1 (meaning that you clicked on "yes"), then the macro will save the file. If "Button" does not contain -1 (meaning that you clicked on "no"), then the macro will not save the file.

8.   Click on **Save** on the Standard toolbar.

9.   Click on **Yes**.

10.   Click on **Window, Document1** (or whatever document window is listed).

      If the HistoryReportFormat macro-editing window is the only window listed when you click on Window, click on **New** on the Standard toolbar to create a blank document window.

11.   Click on **Format, HistoryReportFormat** to test the macro.

      Run the macro a few times. Answer "yes" and "no" to make sure your macro works every time — no matter how you answer the question.

12.   Click on **File, Close, No** to close the document window.

13.   Click on **File, Close** to close the macro-editing window.

If...EndIf

What if you want a macro to do more than one thing if a condition is true? No problem.

The "If...EndIf" conditional statement tells Word to do all of the instructions between the word "If" and the word "EndIf" if the condition is true.

The syntax of the "If...EndIf" conditional statement is:

> **If** *condition* **Then**
> > ***More than one instruction***
> **EndIf**

The instructions to be performed are indented to make them easier to read, and the statement always ends with the word "EndIf."

For example,

> **If** Underline( ) = 1 **Then**
> > Underline 0
> > Italic 1
> > Bold 1
> **EndIf**

This statement says that if underlining is turned on, Underline( ) = 1, then WordBasic will turn it off and then turn on italic and bold type.

THE PRINTSAVE MACRO

Let's write a macro that will print and save any document. We'll assign it to a keyboard shortcut key so it will be fast to run and have it display a message box on the screen asking if we want to save and print. The macro will need an "If...EndIf" conditional statement.

1. Click on **New** on the Standard toolbar.
2. Click on **Tools, Macro...**
3. Type **PrintSave** as the name of the macro.
4. Type **Print a document and save a file** as the description.
5. Click on **Create**.

    When you're writing a macro from scratch, click on Create to make a blank macro-editing window. Assign the macro to a toolbar, menu or shortcut key after the macro is finished.

    A macro-editing window shows on the screen with a Sub MAIN statement and an End Sub statement. Type your macro statements between those two statements.

6. Press **Alt + C** to add comments to your macro. Answer the questions in the Status bar at the bottom of your screen and press Enter.

    REM***

    REM Macro: PrintSave (Alt + P)
    REM Author: Jimmy James George Groverton (you can put your name)
    REM Purpose: Show a message box asking if I want to print and save
    REM***

7. Press **Enter** to move the insertion point down to the next line in the macro.
8. Type: **Button = MsgBox("Do you want to save and print?" , "Save and Print Helper", 36)**

    "Button" is the name of the variable that will hold your answer. The message box will display the message "Do you want to save and print?" The title of the message box is "Save and Print Helper." The number 36 means that a question mark and "yes" and "no" buttons will appear on the screen.

9. Type: **If Button = -1 Then**
    > **FileSave**
    > **FilePrint**
    > **EndIf**

    When the macro runs, Word will look in the variable "Button." If it finds the value - 1, then it will follow the instructions to save and print. If it does not find the value - 1 in the variable "Button" then it will skip the whole thing and the macro will end. Your macro should look like this:

```
Sub MAIN
REM*************************************************************
REM Macro:      PrintSave (Alt + P)
REM Author:     Jimmy James George Groverton
REM Purpose:    Show a message box asking if I want to print
and save
REM*************************************************************
```

```
Button = MsgBox ("Do you want to save and print?", "Save and
Print Helper", 36)

If Button = -1 Then
   FileSave
   FilePrint
EndIf

End Sub
```

10.   Click on **Save** on the Standard toolbar.
11.   Click on **Yes**.

Let's run the PrintSave macro and see how it works.
1.   Click on **New** on the Standard toolbar.
2.   Type: **Now is the time for all good kids to come to the aid of their parents.**
3.   Click on **Tools**.
4.   Click on **Macro…**
5.   Click on **PrintSave**.
6.   Click on **Run**.
7.   Click on **Yes** to save and print the file. This brings up the Save As dialog box.
8.   Type a file name and click on **OK** (Word 6) or **Save** (Word 7) to save the file. The file is saved and printed. Now, test the macro by answering "no" to the question in the message box.
9.   Click on **Tools**.
10.   Click on **Macro…**
11.   Click on **PrintSave**.
12.   Click on **Run**.
13.   Click on **No**.
      The macro ends without saving or printing your document. Always test your macros by answering the question in the message box every way it can be answered. That way, you'll know your macros will work *all* of the time.
14.   Click on **File, Close** to close the document window.
15.   Click on **File, Close** to close the macro-editing window.

Assigning an Existing Macro

When you write a macro from scratch, you'll have to assign it to a menu, toolbar or keyboard shortcut key after you finish writing the macro. You can use this method any time you want to add an assignment to a new macro or change the assignment of an old macro.
1.   Click on **New** on the Standard toolbar.
2.   Click on **Tools**.
3.   Click on **Customize…**
4.   Click on the **Keyboard** file folder.
5.   Click on **Macros** under Categories (use ↓ to find Macros).
6.   Click on **PrintSave** under Macros
7.   Click in the box titled "Press New Shortcut Key"
8.   Press **Alt + P** as the shortcut key.

Look at the area of the Customize dialog box labeled "Currently Assigned To."
It's below the "Press New Shortcut Key" text box. It should contain the word
"unassigned." If this shortcut key is already assigned to some other function on
your computer, choose a different shortcut key.

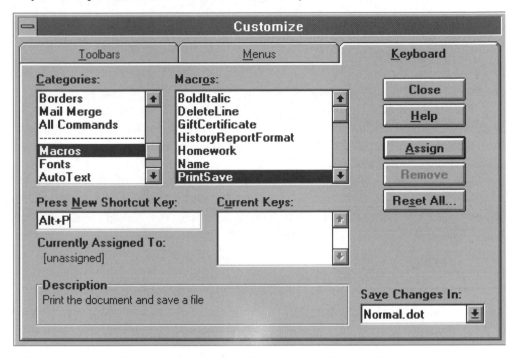

The Customize dialog box lets you assign macros after they have been written

9. Click on **Assign**.
10. Click on **Close**.

Let's try out the PrintSave shortcut key. You can run the PrintSave macro any
time you're working on a document. Try it out on the Homework Study Planner.

1. Click on **Tools**.
2. Click on **Homework**.
3. Type today's date.
4. Click on **OK**.
5. Press **Alt + P** to run the PrintSave macro.
6. Click on **Yes** to save and print the file.
7. Type a name in the File Name text box that will remind you that this file is a
    homework planner.
8. Click on **OK** (Word 6) or **Save** (Word 7) to save the file.
9. Click on **File, Close** to close the Homework file.

Let's do another.

10. Click on **New** on the Standard toolbar.
11. Press **Alt + N** to run the Name macro.
12. Type a report name and press **Enter**.

13.   Press **Alt + P** to run the PrintSave macro.
14.   Click on **No**.
15.   Click on **File, Close, No** to close the report file.

Remember, test your macros every which way. Answer the question in the message box every way it can be answered and test it each time.

Now you've got a macro that will let you save and print automatically any time you are working on a document.

If...Then...Else...EndIf

The final and fanciest structure for the "If" conditional statement is the "If...Then...Else...EndIf" statement. This statement contains the "If" conditional and instructions for WordBasic to follow if the condition is true, and *also* instructions to follow if the condition is false.

The "If ...Then...Else...EndIf" statement tells WordBasic to do the set of instructions that are found after the word "Then" when the condition is true, and to do the set of instructions that are found after the word "Else" when the condition is false. The syntax of this statement is:

If *condition* **Then**
   One or more instructions (will be done if the condition is true)
Else
   One or more instructions (will be done if the conditoin is false)
EndIf

Let's modify the PrintSave macro to see how this works.

"IF...THEN...ELSE...ENDIF" IN THE PRINTSAVE MACRO

When the PrintSave macro runs and you answer "yes," Word automatically prints the document in the document window, and saves the file. We always want to save the file, but we don't always want to print it. Let's add an "If...Then...Else...EndIf" conditional statement that will let us choose whether to print or not.
1.   Click on **Tools, Macro...**
2.   Click on **PrintSave**.
3.   Click on **Edit**.
4.   Position the insertion point on the MsgBox() function.
      The first thing you need to do is change the message in the message box. It needs to ask if you want to print and save or just save.
5.   Type: Button = MsgBox("**Do you want to print after saving the file?**", "Print and Save Helper", 36)
6.   Position the insertion point on the If statement. Modify the If statement.
7.   Type: **If Button = -1 Then**
            FileSave
            FilePrint
      Else
            FileSave
      EndIf

This statement checks to see if the "yes" button was pressed in the message box (If Button = -1). If the "yes" button was pressed, then Word will save the file and then print the document in the document window. If the "no" button was chosen, then Word will just save the file. The PrintSave macro should look like this:

```
Sub MAIN
REM ********************************************************
REM Macro:     PrintSave (Alt + P)
REM Author:    Jimmy James George Groverton
REM Purpose:   Show a message box asking if I want to print
and save
REM ********************************************************

Button = MsgBox("Do you want to print after saving the file?",
"Print and Save Helper", 36)

If Button = -1 Then
   FileSave
   FilePrint
Else
   FileSave
EndIf
End Sub
```

8. Click on **Save** on the Standard toolbar.
9. Click on **Yes**.
10. Click on **File, Close** to close the macro-editing window.
11. Test the macro by placing a document in the document window or typing something on the screen.
12. Press **Alt + P** to test the macro. Make sure you test your macros every which way. Answer "yes" and "no."

"IF...THEN...ELSE...ENDIF" IN THE DELETELINE MACRO

The DeleteLine macro deletes a line of typing from the insertion point to the end of the line. Let's add a message box to the macro asking if you are sure you want to delete the line. If you answer "yes" the line will be deleted. If you answer "no" Word will remove the highlighting from the screen.

1. Click on **Tools, Macro...**
2. Click on **DeleteLine**.
3. Click on **Edit**.

There are two statements in the DeleteLine macro.

   "EndOfLine 1" highlights the text from the insertion point to the end of the line
   "EditClear" deletes the line

The first thing you need to do is add a message box that asks if you're sure about deleting the line.

4. Delete the EditClear statement.

5.   Type: **Button = MsgBox("Are you sure you want to delete this line?",** **"Delete Line", 36)**

6.   Press **Enter** to position the insertion point on the next line.

7.   Type: **If Button = –1 Then**
           EditClear
           Print "The line has been deleted."
       Else
           CharLeft 1
       EndIf

This statement checks to see if the "yes" button was pressed in the message box (If Button = –1). If "yes" was pressed, then Word will delete a line of typing and display a message in the status bar telling you it has been deleted. If you decided not to delete the line, and pressed the "no" button, then Word will follow the instruction for the "Else" part of the statement and remove the highlighting from the screen with the CharLeft 1 statement.

The DeleteLine macro should look like this:

```
Sub MAIN
REM ********************************************************
REM Macro:     DeleteLine
REM Author:    Betty Jones
REM Purpose:   Delete a line of typing (Alt + D)
REM ********************************************************

EndOfLine 1
Button = MsgBox("Are you sure you want to delete this
line?","Delete Line", 36)
If Button = -1 Then
   EditClear
   Print "The line has been deleted."
Else
   CharLeft 1
EndIf
End Sub
```

8.   Click on **Save** on the Standard toolbar.

9.   Click on **Yes**.

10.   Click on **Window, Document1** to return to a document window.

Test the macro by placing a document in the document window, or typing something on the screen. Position the insertion point on the first character of the text you want to delete. The insertion point can be at the beginning of the line or in the middle of the line. Press **Alt + D** to delete the line. Look at the status bar at the bottom of the screen. A message appears informing you that the line has been deleted. Test the macro for "yes" and test the macro for "no."

If you encounter an error running the macro, use the debugging techniques from chapter four to find the bug. Click on **Window, Global: DeleteLine**. Then check for syntax errors. Is MsgBox spelled correctly (one word)? Do the left parenthesis have matching right parenthesis? Do the left quotation marks have matching right quotation marks? Are there commas between the arguments? Does the If statement have a matching EndIf statement? Bugs are easy to find, if you know where to look.

11. Click on **File, Close, No** to close the document window.
12. Click on **File, Close** to close the macro-editing window.

Chapter Review — Absolutely, Positively the Most Important Stuff

1. Record what you can and write the rest!
2. A variable is a storage container for holding information used by a macro.
3. There are two ways to talk to a macro:

   ◆ **Input** *"Question you want to appear in the status bar"*, VariableName$

   ◆ VariableName$ = **InputBox$**("Prompt" [, "Title"] [, "Default"])

4.   There arc three ways to get a macro to talk to you.

   ◆ **Print** *"message you want printed in the status bar"*

   ◆ **MsgBox** "message" [, "title"] [, type]

   ◆ Button = **MsgBox**("message" [, "title"] [, type])

5.   The **Chr$( )** function is used to put spaces, tabs and quotation marks into your macros.

6.   There are three formats to the "If" conditional statement.

   ◆ **If** *condition* **Then** *instruction*

   ◆ **If** *condition* **Then**
           More than one instruction
     EndIf

   ◆ **If** *condition* **Then**
           One or more instructions
     Else
           One or more instructions
     EndIf

7.   Test your macros thoroughly. Answer every possible way when you run them.

Projects for Practice

Party Invitation Macro

1.   Make a macro that will create custom made party invitations. The changeable stuff in the invitation will be filled in with Input boxes, and the macro will

It's Party Time!

For Michael Simon

When: Saturday, March 16, 1997

at 3:00 p.m.

Meet at The Fun Factory

3425 Cedar Landing

Shhhhhh! It's a surprise!

contain an "If" statement so that you can tell your friends if the party is a surprise or not. A lot of this macro can be recorded, so do that part first. Assign the macro to your toolbar.

◆ Click on **View, Toolbars...**

◆ Check four toolbars: **standard, formatting, drawing** and **your toolbar**

◆ Click on **OK**.

◆ Double-click on **REC** on the Status Bar to turn on the macro recorder

◆ Type "**Party**" for the macro name

◆ Type "**Fill in the blanks party invitation**" for the description

◆ Click on **Toolbars** to assign the macro to your toolbar

◆ Assign the macro to your personal macro toolbar by dragging the word "party" to the toolbar. Make sure you overlap the new empty box with the gift certificate box (the happy face box) a little.

◆ In the Custom Button dialog box, click on the picture that looks like an empty comics bubble (second row, fifth picture). You can modify this picture to create a button face that will remind you of a party announcement.

◆ Click on **Edit...** The Button Editor dialog box appears.

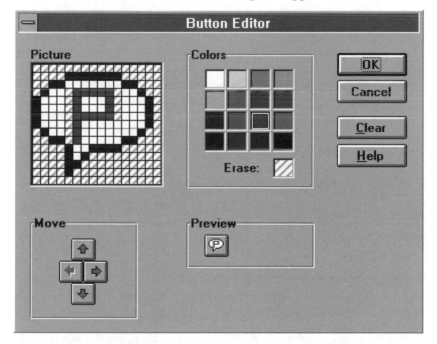

◆ Add the letter "P" (for party) to the bubble. Click on the color you want to use in the Colors section of the dialog box. Then, click in the Picture section to draw the letter. Click once to fill in a square, click again to erase it.

When you've got the picture just like you want it,

◆ Click on **OK**.

You are taken back to the Customize dialog box. The button face you created appears on your toolbar. If you don't like the way the button face looks, you can

remove it and try again. You can do this any time the Customize dialog box is
displayed on your screen.

◆ To remove a button from a toolbar:

Position the insertion point on the button you want to remove.

Click the mouse button and drag the button down into the document
window.

Release the mouse button.

Follow the steps to add a button to the toolbar and design a new button
face.

◆ Click on **Close** to close the Customize dialog box.
The button face you created appears on your toolbar and the macro record
toolbar is displayed reminding you that the macro recorder is running.

◆ Click on **View, Page Layout**

◆ Click on **Whole Page**

◆ Click on **Insert, Frame**

◆ Click on **Format, Frame...**

◆ Set the size of the frame as:
Width = **Exactly 3**, Height = **Exactly 3**
Horizontal Position = **Center**, Relative to **Page**
Vertical Position = **Top**, Relative to **Margin**

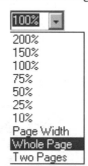

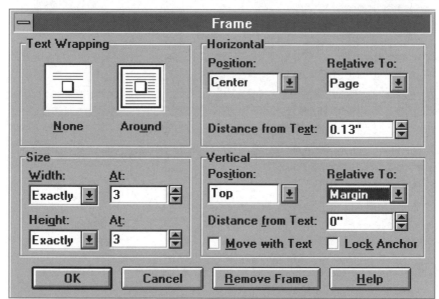

◆ Click on **OK**.

◆ Click on **Insert, Picture...**

◆ Click on **party.wmf** as the picture name. If you don't have this figure, choose
another one that you like that reminds you of a party.

◆ Click on **OK**.

◆ Press **Enter**

◆ Click on **Text Box** (6th button from the left) on the drawing toolbar (toolbar at the bottom of the screen)

◆ Click on **Format, Drawing Object...**

◆ Click on **Line**

◆ Click on **None**

◆ Click on **Size and Position**

◆ Set the size of the text box as:
Horizontal Position = **1.2"** From **Page**
Vertical Position = **3.8"** From **Margin**
Height = **5.8"**
Width = **6"**

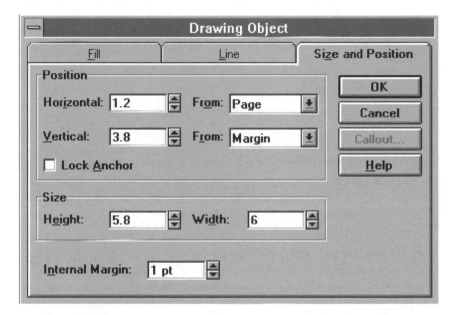

◆ Click on **OK**.

◆ Click on **Format, Font...**

◆ Select Font = **CaslonOpenface BT**, Font Style = **Regular**, Size = **32**
If your computer doesn't show this font listed in the Font dialog box, choose

one that looks kind of fancy like this: Caslon Openface is fancy.

◆ Click on **OK**.

◆ Press **Ctrl + E** to turn on centering.

◆ Type "**It's Party Time!**"

◆ Press **Enter** two times.

◆ Click on **Format, Font...**

◆ Select Font = **Arial**, Font Style = **Regular**, Size = **24**

If your computer doesn't show this font listed in the Font dialog box, choose one that looks plain and neat, like printing: Arial is plain and neat.

◆ Click on **OK**.

◆ Type "**For**"

◆ Press **Enter** two times.

◆ Type "**When:**"

◆ Press **Enter** two times.

◆ Type "**at**"

◆ Press **Enter** two times.

◆ Type "**Meet at**"

◆ Press **Enter** two times.

◆ Click on **Format, Font…**

◆ Select Font = **Brush Script MT**, Font Style = **Italic**, Size = **14**
If your computer doesn't show this font listed in the Font dialog box, choose one that looks like handwriting. *Brush Script MT looks like handwriting.*

◆ Click on **OK**.

◆ Click on **Stop** on the Macro Record Toolbar to turn off the macro recorder.

Now let's add the statements that can't be recorded.

◆ Click on **Tools, Macro, Party, Edit**

◆ Type the WordBasic statements that cannot be recorded. The macro needs remarks to explain the macro. Input boxes to allow you to type the changeable information, a message box asking if the party is a surprise or not, and an "If" statement to read the answer.

◆ Press **Alt + C** to add comments to the macro. Look at the Status bar at the bottom of the screen as you type the following comments.
REM**

REM Macro: **Party**

REM Author: **Ashley Burlington**

REM Purpose: **Create fill in the blanks party invitations**
REM**

◆ Type the InputBox functions next. Each piece of information about the party will be typed in an Input box and stored in its own variable until the macro uses it later in the program. The variable names make it easy to recognize what each one stands for. After the remark statements, type:

Who$ = InputBox$("Who is the party for?", "Party Time")

PartyDate$ = InputBox$("When is the party?", "Party Time")

PartyTime$ = InputBox$("What time?", "Party Time")

Where$ = InputBox$("Where is the party?", "Party Time")

◆ Type a MsgBox( ) function asking if the party is a surprise or not. Type:
Button = MsgBox("Is the party a surprise?", "Party Time", 36)

◆ If you're using **Word 7**, modify the InsertPicture statement to include the exact location of the picture file. If you're using **Word 6**, you can skip this step.

InsertPicture .Name = "**C:\MSOffice\Winword\Clipart\Party.wmf**"

◆ Now, modify the Insert statements that type information on the invitation. Find the Insert statement that types the word *For.* Add the variable name *Who$* to the Insert statement.

Insert "For" + Chr$(32) + Who$

◆ Modify the Insert statement that tells the date of the party.

Insert "When:" + Chr$(32) + Chr$(32) + PartyDate$

◆ Modify the Insert statement that tells the time of the party.

Insert "at" + Chr$(32) + PartyTime$

◆ Modify the Insert statement that tells where the party is going to be held.

Insert "Meet at" + Chr$(32) + Where$

◆ One last thing — an "If" statement to ask if the part is a surprise or not. Make a blank line just before the End Sub statement. Type the "If" statement in the blank line.

     If Button = -1 Then

         Insert "Shhhhhh! It's a surprise!"

     EndIf

The Party macro should look like this.

```
Sub MAIN
REM ******************************************************
REM Macro:      Party
REM Author:     Ashley Burlington
REM Purpose:    Create fill in the blanks party invitations
REM ******************************************************

Who$ = InputBox$("Who is the party for?", "Party Time")
PartyDate$ = InputBox$("When is the party?", "Party Time")
PartyTime$ = InputBox$("What time?", "Party Time")
Where$ = InputBox$("Where is the party?", "Party Time")
Button = MsgBox("Is the party a surprise?", "Party Time", 36)

ViewPage
ViewZoom .FullPage
InsertFrame
FormatFrame .Wrap = 1, .WidthRule = 1, .FixedWidth = "3" +
Chr$(34), .HeightRule = 2, .FixedHeight = "3" + Chr$(34),
.PositionHorz = "Center", .PositionHorzRel = 1, .DistFromText
= "0.13" + Chr$(34), .PositionVert = "Top", .PositionVertRel =
0, .DistVertFromText = "0" + Chr$(34), .MoveWithText = 0,
.LockAnchor = 0
InsertPicture .Name = "C:\WINWORD\CLIPART\PARTY.WMF",
.LinkToFile = "0"
InsertPara

DrawTextbox
```

```
FormatDrawingObject .Tab = "2", .FillColor = "1", .LineColor =
"", .FillPatternColor = "8", .FillPattern = "0", .LineType =
0, .LineStyle = - 1, .LineWeight = "", .ArrowStyle = - 1,
.ArrowWidth = - 1, .ArrowLength = - 1, .Shadow = 0,
.RoundCorners = 0, .HorizontalPos = "1.2" + Chr$(34),
.HorizontalFrom = 1, .VerticalPos = "3.8" + Chr$(34),
.VerticalFrom = 0, .LockAnchor = 0, .Height = "5.8" +
 Chr$(34), .Width = "6" + Chr$(34), .InternalMargin = "1 pt"
FormatFont .Points = "32", .Underline = 0, .Color = 0,
.Strikethrough = 0, .Superscript = 0, .Subscript = 0, .Hidden
= 0, .SmallCaps = 0, .AllCaps = 0, .Spacing = "0 pt",
.Position = "0 pt", .Kerning = 0, .KerningMin = "", .Tab =
"0", .Font = "Braggadocio", .Bold = 0, .Italic = 0
CenterPara
Insert "It's Party Time!"
InsertPara
InsertPara
FormatFont .Points = "24", .Underline = 0, .Color = 0,
.Strikethrough = 0, .Superscript = 0, .Subscript = 0, .Hidden
= 0, .SmallCaps = 0, .AllCaps = 0, .Spacing = "0 pt",
.Position = "0 pt", .Kerning = 0, .KerningMin = "", .Tab =
"0", .Font = "Arial", .Bold = 0, .Italic = 0
Insert "For" + Chr$(32) + Who$
InsertPara
InsertPara
Insert "When:" + Chr$(32) + Chr$(32) + PartyDate$
InsertPara
InsertPara
Insert "at" + Chr$(32) + PartyTime$
InsertPara
InsertPara
Insert "Meet at" + Chr$(32) + Where$
InsertPara
InsertPara
FormatFont .Points = "14", .Underline = 0, .Color = 0,
.Strikethrough = 0, .Superscript = 0, .Subscript = 0, .Hidden
= 0, .SmallCaps = 0, .AllCaps = 0, .Spacing = "0 pt",
.Position = "0 pt", .Kerning = 0, .KerningMin = "", .Tab =
"0", .Font = "Brush Script MT", .Bold = 0, .Italic = 0
If Button = - 1 Then
    Insert "Shhhhhhh! It's a surprise!"
EndIf
End Sub
```

◆ Click on **Save** on the Standard toolbar.

◆ Click on **Yes**.

◆ Click on **New** on the Standard toolbar to open a new document window.

◆ Try out the macro by clicking on the cool looking button you created on your personal toolbar.

If you encounter a syntax error, click on Window, Global: Party to return to the macro-editing window. Look for the highlighted statement, fix the error, and re-save the macro. Then click on Window, Document1 to return to the document window and run the macro again.

◆ Fill in the information in the Input boxes and click on OK. In the Input box for the location of the party, you can type two lines for the address.

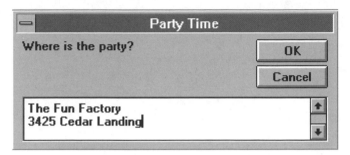

You can type two lines in an Input box

Now you can have parties any time you want—for birthdays, real holidays, made up holidays, Fridays, days off — any excuse will do!

◆ Click on **Window, Global: Party** to return to the macro-editing window.

◆ Click on **File, Close** to close the macro-editing window.

Daily Reminder Macro

2. Write a macro that will display a message box on the screen displaying a different message each day of the week. With your busy schedule, you need help keeping track of everything! In order to make this macro, you'll have to use two new WordBasic functions, *Weekday* and *Today*. Assign the macro to the keyboard shortcut key Alt + R (for reminders). You can use this macro to remind yourself of things that you have to do each day.

◆ Click on **Tools, Macro...**

◆ Type **Reminders** as the macro name.

◆ Type **Message Boxes for each day of the week** as the description.

◆ Click on **Create**.

◆ Press **Alt + C** to run the Comments macro. Look in the Status bar at the bottom of the screen as you type the following comments.

REM ***

REM Macro: **Reminders (Alt + R)**

REM Author: **Jonathan Walsh**

REM Purpose: **Display messages based on the day of the week**

REM ***

◆ Type: **title$ = "Reminders"**

"Reminders" is the title of the message boxes that will be displayed on the screen. Use the variable "title$" to make the message box statements easier to type.

◆ Create numeric variables for each day of the week. These variables correspond to the way the computer holds the day of the week, as a number. Type:

Sunday = 1

Monday = 2

Tuesday = 3

Wednesday = 4

Thursday = 5

Friday = 6

Saturday = 7

◆ Your computer knows what day of the week it is on any given date. You tell it the date and it can tell you what day it is. In WordBasic, the day of the week is found in the function "Weekday( )." "Weekday( )" holds a numeric value. The days of the week are stored as numbers (1 for Sunday, 2 for Monday, and so on). Your computer also knows today's date. In WordBasic, today's date is found in the function "Today( )." We can combine these two functions in a macro so that WordBasic can figure out what day of the week it is every day we run the macro.

◆ Type: **MyDay = Weekday(Today( ))**

The variable "MyDay" will hold the day number, 1 through 7 for today's date.

◆ Type "If" conditional statements to check for each day of the week.

If MyDay = Monday Then MsgBox "Piano lessons tonight.", title$, 64

If MyDay = Tuesday Then MsgBox "Basketball practice at 4:30.", title$, 64

If MyDay = Wednesday Then MsgBox "Book report due on Thursday.", title$, 64

If MyDay = Thursday Then MsgBox "Better study spelling list.", title$, 64

If MyDay = Friday Then MsgBox "You made it! Party down!", title$, 64

If MyDay = Saturday Or MyDay = Sunday Then

    MsgBox "Relax and recharge!", title$, 64

EndIf

Here's how it works. The variable "MyDay" contains a number between one and seven which stands for what day of the week it is today, as determined by the date inside your computer. In the list of variables at the beginning of the macro, you assigned numeric variables to each day using the name of the day as the variable name. Since your variables are numeric, the "If" statements compares the value in the variable "MyDay" (from the computer date) with the day of the week in your numeric variable. It's a pretty slick trick.

For Saturday and Sunday, a compound conditional If statement is used. When you have two statements joined by the word "Or," Word will execute the instruction after the word "Then," if *either* statement is true.

The Reminders macro should look like this:

```
Sub MAIN
REM *********************************************************
REM Macro:      Reminders (Alt + R)
REM Author:     Jonathan Walsh
REM Purpose:    Display messages based on the day of the week
REM *********************************************************

title$ = "Reminders"
Sunday = 1
Monday = 2
Tuesday = 3
Wednesday = 4
Thursday = 5
Friday = 6
Saturday = 7

MyDay = Weekday(Today())

If MyDay = Monday Then MsgBox "Piano lessons tonight.",
title$, 64
If MyDay = Tuesday Then MsgBox "Basketball practice at 4:30.",
title$, 64
If MyDay = Wednesday Then MsgBox "Book report due on
Thursday.", title$, 64
If MyDay = Thursday Then MsgBox "Better study spelling list.",
title$, 64
If MyDay = Friday Then MsgBox "You made it! Party down!",
title$, 64
If MyDay = Saturday Or MyDay = Sunday Then
   MsgBox "Relax and recharge!", title$, 64
Endif
End Sub
```

- ◆ Click on **Save** on the Standard toolbar.
- ◆ Click on **Yes**.
- ◆ Click on **Window**.
- ◆ Click on **Document1** or whatever document window is listed.
- ◆ Assign the macro to the keyboard shortcut key Alt + R. We usually do this at the beginning of a macro recording session, but since we didn't record any of this macro, we can assign it now.
- ◆ Click on **Tools, Customize…**
- ◆ Click on **Keyboard**
- ◆ Under Categories, Click on **Macros**
- ◆ Under Macros, Click on **Reminders**
- ◆ Click in the box **Press new shortcut key**
- ◆ Press **Alt + R**
  Look below the Alt + R, in the section of the screen labeled, "Press new shortcut key." The word "unassigned" should be displayed, letting you know

that this shortcut key has not been assigned to any other function and is available to use for this macro. If Alt + R is already assigned to another function, pick a different shortcut key.

◆ Click on **Assign**

◆ Click on **Close**

Run the macro by pressing Alt + R. Run it every day this week and check for the new message. If you encounter a syntax error, click on **Window, Global: Reminders** to return to the macro-editing window. Look for the highlighted statement, fix the error, and re-save the macro. Then click on Window, Document1 to return to the document window and run the macro again.

◆ Click on **Window**.

◆ Click on **Global: Reminders**.

◆ Click on **File, Close** to close the macro-editing window.

You've seen how to record and write powerful custom made programs using Word's programming language, WordBasic. The next chapter shows you how to design and use your own dialog boxes in macros. You will actually write programs as slick looking as Word itself! It's totally awesome!

CHAPTER 6

Dialog Boxes in Macros

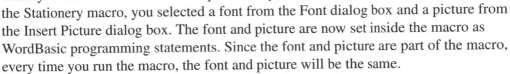

Dialog boxes are used to select options in Word. The selected options tell Word how you want it to work. For example, you select the file you want to open, the font you want to use, and the margins you want to set in dialog boxes.

When you record a macro, the selections you make in dialog boxes are written into the macro as WordBasic programming statements. The statements don't change when you run the macro. For example, when you recorded the Stationery macro, you selected a font from the Font dialog box and a picture from the Insert Picture dialog box. The font and picture are now set inside the macro as WordBasic programming statements. Since the font and picture are part of the macro, every time you run the macro, the font and picture will be the same.

Wouldn't it be great if you could display a dialog box while a macro is running and make selections on-the-fly? It would make the macro much more useful and powerful. In the Stationery macro, it would mean you could create a different type of stationery every time you ran the macro. Well, guess what? Macros can display Word dialog boxes. They can even display dialog boxes that you design yourself (which is totally cool). In this chapter you're going to add Word dialog boxes and homemade dialog boxes to your macros.

Word Dialog Boxes

Let's modify the Stationery macro to display the Font dialog box and the Insert Picture dialog box. Then, when the macro runs, you'll be able to choose which font and picture you want to use. You'll be able to create different stationery to suit your mood at the time—funny one time, serious another.

In order to display a dialog box in a macro, the macro must contain a dialog record to hold the dialog box information and a Dialog () function to display the dialog box.

The Dialog Record

A dialog record is a special variable that holds the settings of a dialog box. Any time you want to use a piece of information in a macro, it must be stored in a variable. The dialog record variable lets you use the information from a dialog box in a macro.

Use a Dim statement to define a dialog record to a macro. The syntax of the Dim statement is:

Dim *DialogRecord* As *DialogBoxName*

"Dim" is the name of the macro statement. It defines a dialog record to a macro. "DialogRecord" is the name of the variable that holds the dialog box information. Dialog record names can be any name you choose that isn't a reserved word. If you're not sure if a word is a reserved word, check the Statements and Functions Index section in the Help screens. Or, use names that you know don't sound official enough to be reserved words. The dialog record name is the name you will refer to in the macro any time you need to access information from the dialog box.

"DialogBoxName" is the name of any Word dialog box. Dialog box names correspond to the menu selections that access the dialog box. For example, to open a file you click on File, Open. The name of the dialog box for opening a file is FileOpen.

Here are some examples of valid Dim statements:

Dim FontRecord As FormatFont
> Creates a dialog record called FontRecord that holds the FormatFont dialog box information.

Dim PictureRecord As InsertPicture
> Creates a dialog record called PictureRecord that holds the InsertPicture dialog box information.

Dim OpenRecord As FileOpen
> Creates a dialog record called OpenRecord that holds the FileOpen dialog box information.

Displaying a Dialog Box

Once you've defined the dialog record, use the Dialog () function to display the dialog box. The syntax of the Dialog () function is:

ButtonChoice = Dialog (*DialogRecord*)

"ButtonChoice" is the name of the variable that will tell the macro how you closed the dialog box. It will hold,

-1	If you clicked on OK to close the dialog box
0 (zero)	If you clicked on Cancel to close the dialog box

"Dialog" is the name of the function. It commands the macro to display the dialog box named in *DialogRecord*. The name in DialogRecord must be the same name you used in the Dim statement when you defined the dialog record. For example,

> Dim **FontRecord** As FormatFont
>> Defines a dialog record called FontRecord
> ButtonChoice = Dialog (**FontRecord**)
>> Displays the dialog box FontRecord

In this example, the Font dialog box will be displayed on the screen. The selections you make on the dialog box will be stored in the FontRecord dialog record. You can then access the information on the FontRecord inside the macro.

The variable ButtonChoice will hold - 1 if you clicked on OK and 0 if you clicked on Cancel to close the dialog box. Your macro will use an If statement to read the variable ButtonChoice and decide what to do next. If you clicked on OK, then the macro will continue and create the stationery. If you clicked on Cancel, a GoTo statement will direct the macro to the end of the macro, where it will end.

The GoTo Statement

In all of the macros you've seen so far, Word starts at the top of the macro on the Sub MAIN statement and executes each of the instructions one-by-one down the macro until it reaches the End Sub statement. Sometimes it is necessary to control the flow of a macro — the order in which Word performs the instructions.

For example, in the Stationery macro if you click on Cancel to close the Font and Insert Picture dialog boxes, it means that you don't want to create any stationery right now. You want the macro to end so you can do something else. A GoTo statement in the macro will tell the macro to skip all of the instructions that create the stationery, go to the end of the macro, and quit.

To use a GoTo statement in a macro, the macro must include two key elements, a Label statement, and a conditional statement. A Label statement is a name that identifies where you want the macro to go. A conditional statement tells the macro to go to the label only if a certain condition is true. Here's how it works.

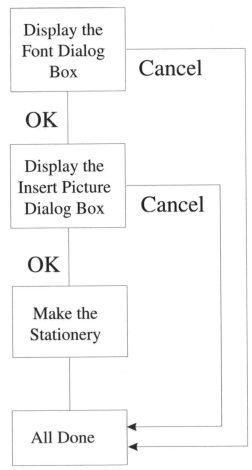

Macro instructions to display the Font and Insert Picture dialog boxes

If ButtonChoice = 0 Then   *Conditional statement*
         GoTo Quit:
EndIf

Macro instructions to create stationery

     Quit: *Label statement*

In this example, the macro displays the Font and Insert Picture dialog boxes. If you click on OK to close the dialog boxes, then the macro will continue by dropping down to the next instruction and formatting the stationery. If you click on Cancel, the macro will go to the label "Quit" and stop.

DIALOG BOXES IN THE STATIONERY MACRO

Let's put all this stuff together in the Stationery macro. We're going to edit the macro so that it displays the Font dialog box and the Insert Picture dialog box. We'll use Dim statements and Dialog () functions to accomplish this mission.

1. Click on **Tools**.
2. Click on **Macro...**
3. Click on **Stationery**.
4. Click on **Edit**. The Stationery macro appears in the macro-editing window.
5. Position the insertion point after the last REM statement.
6. Type: **Dim FontRecord As FormatFont**
   This statement defines the dialog record, FontRecord, for the Font dialog box.
7. Press the **Tab** key two times to add a comment.
8. Type: **'Define a dialog record FontRecord**
   If the comment wraps to the next line, take out one of the Tab statements. If you still need to shorten the comment, abbreviate it in some way, maybe by typing rec for record.
9. Press **Enter** to move the insertion point down to the next line.
10. Type: **ButtonChoice = Dialog(FontRecord)**
    This function displays the Font dialog box. "ButtonChoice" is the name of the variable that will hold the answer to the question, "How did you close the dialog box?"
11. Press the **Tab** key to add a comment.
12. Type: **'Display the Font dialog box**
    The comment is used to clarify the macro. It doesn't affect the execution of the program, but may help you understand the macro later.
13. Press **Enter** to move the insertion point down to the next line.
14. Type: **If ButtonChoice = 0 Then**   **'Check if Cancel button chosen**
             GoTo Quit:
    EndIf

This If statement checks to see how you closed the dialog box by reading the variable "ButtonChoice." If you clicked on Cancel, the value 0 (zero) will be in "ButtonChoice." If you canceled the dialog box, then a GoTo statement will direct the macro to the label Quit and the program will end. If the OK button was clicked, then the macro will continue by moving down to the next line and executing the macro instruction it finds there.

15. Press **Enter** to move the insertion point down to the next line.

16. Type: **Dim PictureRecord As InsertPicture**

    This statement defines the dialog record, PictureRecord, for the Insert Picture dialog box.

17. Press the **Tab** key to add a comment.

18. Type: **'Define a dialog record**

    This comment explains the Dim macro statement.

19. Press **Enter** to move the insertion point down to the next line.

20. Type: **PictureChoice = Dialog(PictureRecord)**

    This function displays the Insert Picture dialog box. PictureChoice is the name of the variable that will hold the answer to the question, "How did you close the dialog box?"

21. Press the **Tab** key.

22. Type: **'Display Picture dialog box** as the comment for the Dialog () function.

23. Press **Enter** to move the insertion point down to the next line.

24. Type: **If PictureChoice = 0 Then   'Check if Cancel button chosen**
    GoTo Quit:
    EndIf

    This If statement checks to see how you closed the dialog box by reading the variable "PictureChoice." If you clicked on Cancel, then the macro will go to the label "Quit" and end. If you clicked on OK, then the macro will continue by moving down to the next line and executing the macro instruction it finds there.

25. Position the insertion point on the first line of the FormatFont statement for the Algerian font (or the font you used instead of Algerian).

26. Press **Shift + ↓** to highlight the entire statement. Make sure you highlight the whole statement by pressing ↓. It's a long one.

```
FormatFont .Points = "36", .Underline = 0, .Color = 0,
.Strikethrough = 0, .Superscript = 0, .Subscript = 0,
.Hidden = 0, .SmallCaps = 0, .AllCaps = 0, .Spacing = "0
pt", .Position = "0 pt", .Kerning = 0, .KerningMin = "",
.Tab = "0", .Font = "Algerian", .Bold = 1, .Italic = 0
```

27. Press the **Delete** key to delete the FormatFont statement.

28. Press **Enter** to insert a blank line into the macro.

29. Type: **FormatFont FontRecord** in the blank line.

    The FormatFont statement sets the font in a document. This statement tells the macro to select the font it finds in the dialog record FontRecord. The font you selected when the dialog box was displayed will be the value in FontRecord.

30. Press the **Tab** key four times to add a comment. Line up the comments as much as you can in a macro, so press the Tab key as many times as necessary to do this.

31. Type: **'Sets font in document** as the comment.

32. Position the insertion point on the InsertPicture statement.

33. Press **Shift +** ↓ to highlight the statement.

34. Press the **Delete** key to delete the InsertPicture statement.

35. Press **Enter** to insert a blank line into the macro.

36. Type: **InsertPicture PictureRecord** in the blank line.
    The InsertPicture statement inserts a picture into the current document. This statement tells the macro to use the picture you selected when the Insert Picture dialog box was displayed. The picture you selected is in the dialog record PictureRecord.

37. Press the **Tab** key three times to add a comment. Line up this comment with the one you typed for the "FormatFont" statement. Press the Tab key as many times as necessary to do this.

38. Type: **'Places picture in document** as the comment.

39. Position the insertion point on the End Sub statement.

40. Press **Enter** to create a blank line in the macro.

41. Type: **Quit:** in the blank line. This label statement tells the macro where to go when you cancel the dialog boxes.

The Stationery macro should look like this:

```
Sub MAIN
REM *********************************************************
REM Macro:      Stationery
REM Author:     John Gulliver
REM Purpose:    Create custom made stationery
REM Toolbar:    Located on personal toolbar
REM *********************************************************

Dim FontRecord As FormatFont    'Define a dialog record FontRecord
ButtonChoice = Dialog(FontRecord) 'Display the Font dialog box
If ButtonChoice = 0 Then         'Check if Cancel button chosen
   GoTo Quit:
EndIf

Dim PictureRecord As InsertPicture 'Define a dialog record
PictureChoice = Dialog(PictureRecord) 'Display Picture dialog box
If PictureChoice = 0 Then        'Check if Cancel button chosen
   GoTo Quit:
EndIf

FormatFont FontRecord                'Sets font in document
CenterPara
InsertPicture PictureRecord          'Places picture in document
InsertPara
Insert "John Gulliver"
InsertPara
InsertPara
```

```
LeftPara
FormatFont .Points = "10", .Underline = 0, .Color = 0,
.Strikethrough = 0, .Superscript = 0, .Subscript = 0, .Hidden
= 0, .SmallCaps = 0, .AllCaps = 0, .Spacing = "0 pt",
.Position = "0 pt", .Kerning = 0, .KerningMin = "", .Tab =
"0", .Font = "Courier New", .Bold = 0, .Italic = 0
Quit:
End Sub
```

42. Click on **Save** on the Standard toolbar.

43. Click on **Yes**.

Let's run the new and improved Stationery macro.

1. Click on **New** on the Standard toolbar.

2. Click on the **Stationery** button on your toolbar to run the macro. If your toolbar
    is not displayed, click the right mouse button on a blank portion of the
    Standard toolbar, then click on your toolbar name to display it.
    The Font dialog box appears.

3. Click on Font = **Teletype**, Font Style = **Bold**, Size = **36**
    Click on any font that looks good to you. If your computer doesn't have the
    Teletype font, pick another font instead. The font you choose should be bold,
    and about 36 points.

4. Click on **OK** to close the Font dialog box. The Insert Picture dialog box
    appears.

5. Click on **Computer.wmf** as the picture name. If you don't have the picture
    Computer.wmf, choose another picture that looks good to you.

6. Click on **OK**.

Isn't that cool!

7. Click on **Print** on the Standard toolbar to print a copy of your stationery.

8. Click on **File, Close, No** to close the document window.

9. Click on **File, Close** to close the macro-editing window.

Run the macro a few more times, experimenting with different fonts and pictures.
If you want to see what a font looks like, click on the font name and look at the
preview section of the screen for an example. If you want to see what a picture looks
like, click on the file name, click on "Preview Picture" and look at the preview
section of the screen for an example.

Custom Dialog Boxes

You can use Word's dialog boxes in a macro, or create a dialog box of your own,
called a custom dialog box.

A custom dialog box is a dialog box that you design for use inside a macro. A
custom dialog box can contain all of the features that can be found in a Word dialog
box. Custom dialog boxes are used to give information to a macro. They allow you to
enter any type of information in any order on a screen that you design. For example,
in the HistoryReportFormat macro, there are three different Input boxes for giving
information to the macro: an Input box for the book title, an Input box for the author

and an Input box for the rating of the book. You can create a dialog box that will allow you to enter all of that information on one screen.

Creating a Dialog Box — A Five-Step Process

When you create a dialog box for use inside a macro, you'll follow a five step process. Here are the steps in the order they should be performed.

1. Design the dialog box with the Dialog Editor.
    Use the Dialog Editor to design the dialog box. This is the fun part. You get to choose how the dialog box looks—how big it is, what information is displayed in the dialog box and the order the information is displayed. When you design a dialog box with the Dialog Editor, Word creates statements for the macro called dialog box definition statements. These statements tell the macro everything it needs to know about the dialog box. It's similar to what happens when you record a macro. When you record a macro, Word creates WordBasic statements that tell the macro what to do. When you design a dialog box, the Dialog Editor creates dialog box definition statements that tell the macro all about the dialog box.

2. Copy the dialog box definition into the macro.
    When you design a dialog box, the Dialog Editor writes the macro statements for you. To use the statements, copy them into your macro.

3. Create a dialog record.
    Use the Dim statement to create a dialog record for the dialog box you designed. The Dim statement for custom dialog boxes works the same way it does for Word dialog boxes.

4. Display the dialog box.
    Use the Dialog() function to display the dialog box. The Dialog() function for custom dialog boxes works the same way it does for Word dialog boxes.

5. Use the data from the dialog box inside the macro. Each piece of information in the dialog box will be stored in a variable. You can use those variables inside the macro to perform the task you're asking the macro to accomplish.

Creating a Dialog Box in the History Report Format Macro

Let's follow the five step process to add a dialog box to the HistoryReportFormat macro. We'll use the Dialog Editor to create the dialog box. Before you start the Dialog Editor, have the macro that will display the dialog box open in a macro-editing window.

1. Click on **Tools**.
2. Click on **Macro...**
3. Click on **HistoryReportFormat**.
4. Click on **Edit**. The HistoryReportFormat macro appears in the macro-editing window.
5. Click on the **Dialog Editor** button on the Macro toolbar.

Dialog Editor ≫

The Dialog Editor screen appears with an empty dialog box displayed.

The Dialog Editor is a separate application included in the Word package. It should already be installed on your computer. If it's not, then you'll see an error message telling you that Word can't run the Dialog Editor program.

If you see this error message, run the Word installation program to install the Dialog Editor files. If the Dialog Editor is already installed, skip this section and go to page 130, Step 1.

INSTALLING THE DIALOG EDITOR

1. Click on **OK** to close the message box.

2. Click on **File, Exit** to exit Word.

3. In Word version 6, from the Windows Program Manager, click on **File, Run...**

    In Word version 7, click on **Start, Run...**

4. Insert the Microsoft Word for Windows **Disk 1 Setup** disk into the disk drive.

5. Type: **a:\setup** and press **Enter**.

6. Click on **Add/Remove...**

7. In version 6, click on **Tools**.

    In version 7, click on **Word Tools**.

8. Click on **Change Option...**

    The option "Dialog Editor" should be checked. If it is not checked, that means that the Dialog Editor files are not loaded on your computer.

9. Click on **Dialog Editor** to put a check in the box.

10. Click on **OK**.

11. Click on **Continue**.

12. Follow the instructions on your screen for loading the files onto your computer.

    When the installation is complete, start Word and reload the HistoryReportFormat macro into the macro-editing window. Then you can run the Dialog Editor.

13. In Word 6: Double-click on the program group **Word for Windows**.

    Double-click on the program item **Word for Windows**.

    In Word 7: Click on **Start**.

    Click on **Programs**.

    Click on **Microsoft Word.**

14. Click on **Tools**.

15. Click on **Macro...**

16. Click on **HistoryReportFormat**.

17. Click on **Edit**. The HistoryReportFormat macro appears in the macro-editing window.

18. Click on the **Dialog Editor** button on the Macro toolbar. The Dialog Editor appears with an empty dialog box displayed.

STEP 1: DESIGN THE HISTORYREPORT DIALOG BOX
USING THE DIALOG EDITOR

The first thing you'll want to do when you design a dialog box is to give the dialog box a title. The Dialog Editor automatically displays "Microsoft Word" as the title of the dialog box, which is kind of boring. Let's change the name.

1.   Click on **Edit**.
2.   Click on **Info...**
     The Dialog Information screen appears. The Dialog Information screen contains all the technical information about the dialog box. The name of the dialog box is shown in the text box labeled "Text$." To change the name of the dialog box, change what's in this box.
3.   Click in the text box to the right of the word "Text$" to position the insertion point.
4.   Delete "**Microsoft Word**"
5.   Type: **History Book Report** as the title of the dialog box.
6.   Click on **OK**. "History Book Report" now appears as the title of the empty dialog box on the screen.

Dialog Box Items

A custom dialog box contains the same features as a Word dialog box. A custom dialog box can contain OK and Cancel buttons, push buttons, option buttons, check boxes, text boxes, list boxes and group boxes. These features are called items and can be arranged in any order in the dialog box.

Dialog Box Design Tips

Designing a custom dialog box means choosing which items you want to include in the dialog box and how you want those items arranged. Here are a few tips for designing a custom dialog box.

1. Plan the arrangement
    Before you begin placing items in a dialog box, think about how you want the information in the dialog box arranged. Think about how you want to enter the data. The order of the items in a dialog box determines the focus of the dialog box when the macro is running. Place items in the dialog box in the same order you want to enter the information when the macro is running.

2. Top to bottom, left to right
    Build a dialog box from top to bottom and from left to right. The Dialog Editor always starts placing items in the upper-left corner of a dialog box and works down to the lower-right corner. This is called the top to bottom, left to right design method. In the Dialog Editor everything is relative to the upper-left corner of the dialog box.

3. Selecting items
    When an item is placed in a dialog box, the item is shown with dotted lines around it. The dotted lines mean that the item is selected—it has the Dialog Editor's attention at the moment. When you are adding items to a dialog box, the Dialog Editor will place each item directly below the selected item. So, to make items line up and look good in a dialog box, click on an item to select it, then add another item below the selected item. The Dialog Editor will place the second item directly below the first.

4. Command buttons
    Always include command buttons (OK and Cancel buttons) in every dialog box so that there's a way out of the dialog box.

5. Add a group box first, then add the option buttons and check boxes inside it.
    A group box is a box that encloses several options. It is used to separate an area of the dialog box and keep related choices together. If you create the group box first, then it's easy to add the option buttons and check boxes inside it.

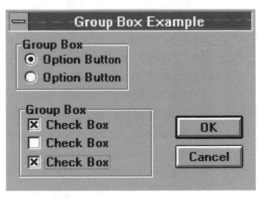

6. Deleting Items
    If you don't like the way an item looks in your dialog box, you can delete it and try again. Click on the item first to select it, then press the Delete key.

    Let's create a custom dialog box for the HistoryReportFormat macro that will allow you to enter the book title, the author and your rating of the book. This dialog box will contain text items, text boxes and command buttons.

Text Items and Text Boxes

The most common items in a custom dialog box are text items and text box items. A text box is a box in which you can enter information while the dialog box is displayed. Each text box is like one Input box. Using text boxes in a dialog box instead of Input boxes gives you the ability to enter all of your information on one screen instead of on several screens. A text item is a label, or text explaining what information to type in the text box.

Command Buttons

Every dialog box must contain at least one command button—an OK button, a Cancel button, or a Push button. These buttons provide a way out of the dialog box, so you can see that they are really important. As much as you might like your beautiful homemade dialog box, you don't want it displayed forever!

Let's add text items, text boxes and command buttons to the History Book Report dialog box.

1. Click on **Item**.

    The Item menu appears showing the available dialog box controls, or items that are available in designing dialog boxes.

2. Click on **Text**.

    The Dialog Editor places a text item in the dialog box containing the word "Text." Notice how the Dialog Editor places the text item in the upper left corner of the dialog box. It always starts at the upper left corner and works its

Dialog Box Items

way down the dialog box. The purpose of a text item is to explain what to enter in the text box that follows, so you'll always need to change the word "text" to something more descriptive.

3. Type: **Book Title**

    The Dialog Editor changes the text item to the words "Book Title." The size of the text item expands to fit the words you type. When you run the HistoryReportFormat macro, you'll know to enter the book title in the text box that follows. The dotted lines around "Book Title" mean that this item is selected and the Dialog Editor will place the next item directly below this one.

4. Click on **Item**.

5. Click on **Text Box**.

    A text box appears in the dialog box, directly below the text item "Book Title." This is where you will type the title of your book when the macro is running and the dialog box is displayed on the screen.

6. Click on **Item**.

7. Click on **Text**.

    The Dialog Editor places a text item in the dialog box below the text box for entering the book title, containing the word "text."

8. Type: **Author**

The Dialog Editor changes the text item to the word "Author." When you use the dialog box in the HistoryReportFormat macro, you'll know to enter the author's name in the text box that follows.

9. Click on **Item**.

10. Click on **Text Box**.
    A text box appears in the dialog box, directly below the text item "Author."

11. Click on **Item**.

12. Click on **Text**.
    The Dialog Editor places a text item in the dialog box directly below the Author text box.

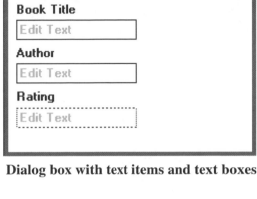

13. Type: **Rating**
    The Dialog Editor changes the text item to the word "Rating."

14. Click on **Item**.

15. Click on **Text Box**.
    When the macro runs, you'll be able to enter all the information for the book report on this one screen.

Dialog box with text items and text boxes

The dialog box needs command buttons so that you'll have a way of closing the dialog box.

16. Click on **Item**.

17. Click on **Button...**
    The New Button dialog box appears showing the different types of buttons you can place in a custom dialog box.
    When you display the New Button dialog box for the first time, the OK button type is selected.

18. Press **Enter** or click on **OK** (the OK at the bottom of the New Button dialog box) to place an OK button in your dialog box.
    The Dialog Editor places an OK button below the text box for "Rating."

The dialog box looks a little crowded, don't you think? It would look better if you moved the OK button over to the right side of the dialog box.

℗ositioning ℐtems in a 𝒟ialog ℬox

You can move dialog box items around to make your dialog box look as good as one of Microsoft Word's.

Use the mouse pointer to position an item in a dialog box. When the mouse pointer is positioned over an item, the pointer turns into a funny-looking four-headed arrow. Click the mouse button and drag the item where you want to position it in the dialog box.

1. Move the mouse pointer to the OK button.

The mouse pointer looks like a four-headed arrow. The OK button has dotted lines around it. That means that the OK button is selected. An item must be selected before it can be moved and positioned.

2. Click the mouse button, and drag the OK button to the right side of the dialog box, to the right of the text box for entering the rating. Leave enough room for a Cancel button below the OK button.

3. Release the mouse button when you have the OK button positioned where you want it.

    Now, finish the History Book Report dialog box by placing a Cancel button in the dialog box.

4. Press **Enter**.

    The Dialog Editor places a Cancel button below the OK button. The Dialog Editor knows that you already have an OK button in your dialog box, so it makes it easy for you to place a Cancel button in the box too. All you have to do is press

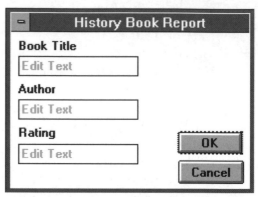

Position items in a dialog box by moving them with the mouse

Enter. The Dialog Editor placed the Cancel button below the OK button because the OK button was selected (it had dotted lines around it).

You can also click on **Item, Button, Cancel, OK** to add a Cancel button to your dialog box.

Sizing a Dialog Box

You can size a dialog box by dragging its border with the mouse. A border is the outer edge of the dialog box. When the mouse pointer is positioned over a border, the pointer turns into a two-headed arrow. Click and drag the two-headed arrow to make the dialog box larger or smaller.

1. Move the mouse pointer to the lower right corner of the dialog box.
    The mouse pointer turns into a two-headed arrow.

2. Click the mouse button to select the dialog box.
    Dotted lines appear around the dialog box. That means the dialog box is selected. An item must be selected before it can be sized.

3. Click and drag the two-headed arrow down, and to the right to enlarge the dialog box.

4. Release the mouse button when the dialog box is the size you want.

5. Click and drag the lower-right corner of the dialog box up and to the left to make the dialog box smaller. Play with that until you like the size of the dialog box.

Sizing Items in a Dialog Box

You can size an item in a dialog box by dragging its border with the mouse. A border is the outer edge of an item. When the mouse pointer is positioned over a border, the pointer turns into a two-headed arrow. Click and drag the two-headed arrow to make an item larger or smaller.

The text boxes in your dialog box are all the same size. When the Dialog Editor places a text box in a custom dialog box, it is set to a default size. The Book Title and Author text boxes need to be large enough to hold long names. The Rating text box can be smaller. The simplest way to change the size of a text box is to drag the side of the box.

1. Click on the Book Title text box, on the words "Edit Text" to select the box.
2. Position the mouse pointer on the right edge of the text box. The mouse pointer looks like a two-headed arrow.
3. Click the mouse button and drag the right side of the box to the right to expand the size of the text box.
4. Release the mouse button to set the size of the text box.
   Now you can enter long names, like Jonathan Christopher Hadjigeorghiou.
5. Click on the Author text box, on the words "Edit Text" to select the box.
6. Position the mouse pointer on the right edge of the box.
7. Click the mouse button and drag the right side of the box to the right to expand the size of the text box.

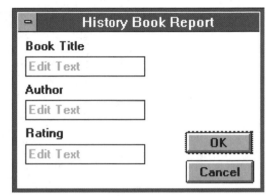

Click and drag the edge of a text box to make the text box larger or smaller

8. Release the mouse button to set the size of the text box.
9. Click on the Rating text box, on the words "Edit Text."
10. Position the mouse pointer on the right edge of the box.
11. Click the mouse button and drag the right side of the box to the left to shorten the size of the text box.
12. Release the mouse button to set the size of the text box.
    Ratings will not need as much room as names, so this text box can be smaller than the other two.

Records and Fields

You will enter three pieces of information in the History Book Report dialog box: the book title, the author and the rating. All of that information will be stored in a dialog record. Within the dialog record are fields for holding each piece of information you enter in the dialog box.

Any field you refer to inside the macro must be given a unique field name in the dialog record. When you want to refer to a particular piece of information in your macro, you identify the name of the dialog record and the name of the field within that record. Name fields in a dialog record just like you would name any other variable in a macro. Choose names that describe what the field holds. Choose names you can remember.

Variable Names in a Dialog Box

In the HistoryReportFormat macro, there are three fields that need to have field names: the book title field, the author field, and the rating field. Use the Text Box Information screen to name those fields.

1.   Double-click on the text box for book title (the first box that contains "Edit Text"). The Text Box Information screen appears. You can also click on Edit, Info to display the Text Box Information screen. The top portion of the screen shows the position and size of the text box. "X" is the horizontal position of the text box and "Y" is the vertical position of the text box.

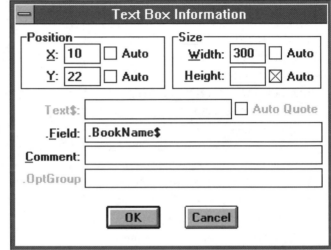

Type the variable name in the Field text box

2.   Click in the text box for .Field to position the insertion point.
3.   Delete **.TextBox1**
     Each piece of data that will be used inside the macro must have a unique name. The Dialog Editor labels each item with the name of the item, and consecutive numbers, TextBox1, TextBox2, CheckBox1, CheckBox2, etc. It's hard to remember what TextBox1 and TextBox2 represent inside a macro, so change the field names to something meaningful to make your macros clear.
4.   Type: **.BookName$**
     Don't forget the period. Field names begin with a period.
5.   Press **Enter** or click on **OK** to close the Text Box Information dialog box.
6.   Double-click on the text box for author. The Text Box Information screen appears.
7.   Click in the text box for .Field to position the insertion point.
8.   Delete **.TextBox2**
9.   Type: **.Author$**
10.   Press **Enter** or click on **OK**.
11.   Double-click on the text box for rating.
12.   In the .Field text box, delete .TextBox3 and type **.Rating$**
13.   Press **Enter** or click on **OK**.

STEP 2: COPY THE DIALOG BOX DEFINITION INTO THE HISTORY MACRO

You've got a great looking dialog box! The next step is to copy the dialog box definition into your macro. When you design a dialog box, the Dialog Editor writes dialog box statements for you. To use the statements, all you have to do is copy them into your macro. Select the dialog box first, then copy it into the macro.

1. Click on the title bar of the dialog box to select it.
    The dialog box has dotted lines around it, showing that it has been selected. You can also click on **Edit, Select Dialog** to select a dialog box.
2. Click on **Edit**.
3. Click on **Copy**.
    This command places a copy of the dialog box definition on the clipboard.
4. Click on **File**.
5. Click on **Exit** to exit the Dialog Editor and return to the macro-editing window.
    The dialog box definition is now sitting on the clipboard. Use the paste command to paste it into your macro.
6. Position the insertion point on the line after the last REM statement.
7. Press **Enter** to insert a blank line into the macro, then _ to position the insertion point on the blank line.
8. Press **Ctrl + V** to paste the dialog box definition from the clipboard into the macro. You can also click on **Edit, Paste** to paste the dialog box definition into the macro.

    Voilà! A dialog box definition, written by the Dialog Editor, appears with all the technical information the macro needs to display and use the dialog box.

The Dialog Box Definition

The dialog box definition appears as a series of instructions that begin with **Begin Dialog** and end with **End Dialog**. All dialog box definitions begin and end with those two statements, just like Sub MAIN and End Sub begin and end all macros.

The dialog box definition you just created looks like this.

```
Begin Dialog UserDialog 324, 150, "History Book Report"
    Text 10, 6, 79, 13, "Book Title", .Text1
    TextBox 10, 22, 300, 18, .BookName$
    Text 10, 46, 51, 13, "Author", .Text2
    TextBox 10, 62, 300, 18, .Author$
    Text 10, 86, 51, 13, "Rating", .Text3
    TextBox 10, 102, 80, 18, .Rating$
    OKButton 218, 90, 88, 21
    CancelButton 218, 114, 88, 21
End Dialog
```

Let's take a look at what the statements mean.

Begin Dialog UserDialog 324, 150, "History Book Report"

The first statement in a dialog box definition is always a "Begin Dialog" statement. After the words "Begin Dialog" you'll find "UserDialog." The Dialog

Editor places the UserDialog argument in the statement so that the macro will know immediately that this is a custom dialog box. It is a *user* dialog box, because it was created by a user (a person using Word). The numbers following UserDialog specify the size and dimensions of the dialog box. If the numbers in your dialog box definition are different than those shown above, don't worry about it. It means that your dialog box ended up a different size when you clicked and dragged to size the box. "History Book Report" is the title of the dialog box.

The indented statements between Begin Dialog and End Dialog are the statements the Dialog Editor created for each item in the dialog box. They are in the order you created them, which is the order the insertion point will follow when the macro runs.

Text 10, 6, 79, 13, **"Book Title"**, **.Text1**	Text item for the book title
TextBox 10, 22, 300, 18, **.BookName$**	Text box for entering the book title
Text 10, 46, 51, 13, **"Author"**, **.Text2**	Text item for the author
TextBox 10, 62, 300, 18, **.Author$**	Text box for entering the author
Text 10, 86, 51, 13, **"Rating"**, **.Text3**	Text item for the rating of the book
TextBox 10, 102, 80, 18, **.Rating$**	Text box for entering the rating
OKButton 218, 90, 88, 21	OK button
CancelButton 218, 114, 88, 21	Cancel button

The last statement in a dialog box definition is always an "End Dialog" statement. It is just like the End Sub statement at the end of every macro—a stop sign that tells the macro the dialog box definition is done.

The HistoryReportFormat macro now contains a dialog box definition. When the macro runs, the dialog box will be displayed on the screen and all of the information about the book report will be entered on that one screen. Originally, you entered the book report information in Input boxes. Now that you have a spiffy new dialog box, you don't need the Input boxes any more, so delete the InputBox() functions in the macro.

1. Position the insertion point on the first InputBox() function for entering the book name. You'll find it right after the End Dialog statement.

2. Press **Shift +** ↓ to highlight all three InputBox() functions.

```
BookName$ = InputBox$("What is the title of your book?",
"History Book Report")
Author$ = InputBox$("Who wrote the book?", "History Book
Report")
Rating$ = InputBox$("How would you rate this book?", "History
Book Report", "C")
```

3. Press the **Delete** key to delete the three InputBox () functions for BookName$, Author$ and Rating$.

STEP 3: CREATE A DIALOG RECORD FOR THE HISTORYREPORTFORMAT MACRO

Every macro that uses a dialog box, either a custom dialog box or a Word dialog box, must contain a Dim statement that defines the dialog record. You saw the syntax of the Dim statement when you used it to create dialog records for the Word "Font" dialog box and the Word "Insert Picture" dialog box. Dim statements work the same way for custom dialog boxes.

Dim *DialogRecord* As *UserDialog*

"Dim" is the name of the macro statement. It defines a dialog record to the macro. "DialogRecord" is the name of the variable that holds the dialog box information. It can be any name you choose. A Dim statement for a custom dialog box always ends with *UserDialog* as the name of the dialog box. This argument tells the macro that the dialog box is a custom box created by a person using Word.

Let's add a Dim statement to the HistoryReportFormat macro.

1. Position the insertion point on the line after the **End Dialog** Statement.
2. Type: **Dim HistoryRecord As UserDialog**
    "HistoryRecord" is the name of the dialog record. "UserDialog" is required by Word to tell the macro that this is a dialog record for a custom dialog box, not a dialog record for a Word dialog box.
3. Press the **Tab** key three times to add a comment to the statement.
4. Type: **'Define the dialog record** as the comment

STEP 4: DISPLAYING A CUSTOM DIALOG BOX

Your macro has a dialog box definition. Your macro has a dialog record. Now you need to display the dialog box. Use the Dialog() function to display a custom dialog box just like you did when you displayed a Word Dialog box.

ButtonChoice = Dialog (*DialogRecord*)

"ButtonChoice" is the name of the variable that will tell the macro how you closed the dialog box. It will hold,

> -1   If you clicked on OK to close the dialog box
> 0 (zero)   If you clicked on Cancel to close the dialog box

"Dialog" is the name of the function. It commands the macro to display the dialog box named in *DialogRecord*. The name in DialogRecord must be the same name you used in the Dim statement when you defined the dialog record. For example, your Dim statement is:

Dim HistoryRecord As UserDialog

The name of the dialog record in the Dialog () function must match the name of the dialog record in the Dim statement.

ButtonChoice = Dialog(HistoryRecord)

Add a Dialog () function to the HistoryReportFormat macro.

1. Position the insertion point on the next line after the Dim statement.
2. Type: **ButtonChoice = Dialog(HistoryRecord)**
    "ButtonChoice" is the name of the variable that will tell the macro how you closed the dialog box. If you clicked on OK, then - 1 will be the value in ButtonChoice. If you clicked on Cancel, then 0 will be the value in ButtonChoice.

"HistoryRecord" is the name of the dialog record that was defined in the Dim statement.

3. Press the **Tab** key to add a comment to the statement. Line this comment up with the comment you wrote for the Dim statement.

4. Type: **'Display the dialog box** as the comment.

STEP 5: USE THE DIALOG BOX IN THE HISTORY MACRO

You're on the last step in using a custom dialog box in a macro—using the information from the dialog box in your macro. Whenever you want to use a piece of information from a custom dialog box in a macro, you must tell the macro the name of the dialog record and the name of the field within that record. The name of the dialog record is typed first, then the name of the field within the dialog record. The syntax for accessing a field from a custom dialog box is:

DialogRecordName.FieldName

For example,

HistoryRecord.BookName$

> Reads the book title that you entered in the History Book Report dialog box. "HistoryRecord" is the name of the dialog record, and ".BookName$" is the name of the field within that record.

HistoryRecord.Author$

> Reads the author's name that you entered in the History Book Report dialog box. "HistoryRecord" is the name of the dialog record, and ".Author$" is the name of the field within that record.

Let's finish the HistoryReportFormat macro by using the book title field, the author field and the rating field from your custom dialog box. The macro needs to extract the information from the dialog box and print it on the screen. You'll modify the Insert statements that are already in the macro to accomplish this.

1. Position the insertion point on the line after the Dialog() function.

2. Type: **If ButtonChoice = 0 Then   'Check if Cancel button chosen**
        GoTo Quit:
        EndIf

> This If statement checks how you closed the dialog box. If you clicked on OK, then the macro will continue and execute the next instruction it finds, which begins formatting the book report. If you clicked on Cancel, then the macro will go to the label "Quit" and end.

3. Position the insertion point on the Insert statement that types the book title. Add the dialog record name to the Insert statement.

4. Type: Insert "Book Title:" + Chr$(9) + **HistoryRecord.BookName$**

5. Position the insertion point on the Insert statement that types the author. Add the dialog record name to the Insert statement.

6. Type: Insert "Author:" + Chr$(9) + **HistoryRecord.Author$**

7. Position the insertion point on the Insert statement that types the rating of the book.

8. Type: Insert "Rating:" + Chr$(9) + **HistoryRecord.Rating$**

The Insert statements now contain the name of the dialog record as well as the variable name for the three fields.

9. Position the insertion point on the End Sub statement.

10. Press **Enter** to insert a blank line into the macro.

11. Type: **Quit:** in the blank line.

    This label statement is necessary to tell the macro where to go when you click on Cancel to close the dialog box.

The HistoryReportFormat macro statements should look like this:

```
Sub MAIN
REM ***************************************************
REM Macro:        HistoryReportFormat
REM Author:       Sue Smothers
REM Purpose:      Do all the formatting for History reports
REM Menu Macro:   Format, HistoryReportFormat
REM ***************************************************

Begin Dialog UserDialog 324, 150, "History Book Report"
    Text 10, 6, 79, 13, "Book Title", .Text1
    TextBox 10, 22, 300, 18, .BookName$
    Text 10, 46, 51, 13, "Author", .Text2
    TextBox 10, 62, 300, 18, .Author$
    Text 10, 86, 51, 13, "Rating", .Text3
    TextBox 10, 102, 80, 18, .Rating$
    OKButton 218, 90, 88, 21
    CancelButton 218, 114, 88, 21
End Dialog

Dim HistoryRecord As UserDialog     'Define the dialog record
ButtonChoice = Dialog(HistoryRecord)   'Display the dialog box

If ButtonChoice = 0 Then        'Check if Cancel button chosen
    GoTo Quit:
EndIf

FilePageSetup .Tab = "0", .PaperSize = "0", .TopMargin = "1.5" +
Chr$(34), .BottomMargin = "1.5" + Chr$(34), .LeftMargin = "1.25"
+ Chr$(34), .RightMargin = "1.25" + Chr$(34), .Gutter = "0" +
Chr$(34), .PageWidth = "8.5" + Chr$(34), .PageHeight = "11" +
Chr$(34), .Orientation = 0, .FirstPage = 0, .OtherPages = 0,
.VertAlign = 0, .ApplyPropsTo = 4, .FacingPages = 0,
.HeaderDistance = "0.5" + Chr$(34), .FooterDistance = "0.5" +
Chr$(34), .SectionStart = 2, .OddAndEvenPages = 0,
.DifferentFirstPage = 0, .Endnotes = 0, .LineNum = 0,
.StartingNum = "", .FromText = "", .CountBy = "0", .NumMode = - 1
FormatFont .Points = "10", .Underline = 0, .Color = 0,
.Strikethrough = 0, .Superscript = 0, .Subscript = 0, .Hidden
= 0, .SmallCaps = 0, .AllCaps = 0, .Spacing = "0 pt",
.Position = "0 pt", .Kerning = 0, .KerningMin = "", .Tab =
"0", .Font = "Courier New", .Bold = 0, .Italic = 0
Insert "Name: Sue Smothers" + Chr$(9) + Chr$(9) + Chr$(9) +
Chr$(9) + Chr$(9) + "Teacher: Mrs. Hanson"
InsertPara
```

```
Insert "Date: "
InsertDateTime .DateTimePic = "MMMM d, yyyy", .InsertAsField = 0
Insert Chr$(9) + Chr$(9) + Chr$(9) + Chr$(9) + "Subject: History"
InsertPara
InsertPara
Insert "Book Title:" + Chr$(9) + HistoryRecord.BookName$
InsertPara
Insert "Author:" + Chr$(9) + HistoryRecord.Author$
InsertPara
Insert "Rating:" + Chr$(9) + HistoryRecord.Rating$
InsertPara
InsertPara
InsertPara
SpacePara2
Button = MsgBox("Would you like to save the file now?",
"History Book Report", 36)
If Button = - 1 Then FileSave

Quit:
End Sub
```

12. Click on **Save** on the Standard toolbar.
13. Click on **Yes**.

Check out the new and improved HistoryReportFormat macro.

1. Click on **New** on the Standard toolbar.
2. Click on **Format**.
3. Click on **HistoryReportFormat**. Your very own extremely radical dialog box appears on the screen. The insertion point is in the Book Title field, waiting for you to type the title of the book.
4. Type: **Dazzling Dialog Boxes** as the book title.
5. Press the **Tab** key to move the insertion point to the Author field.
6. Type: *your name* as the author.
7. Press the **Tab** key to move the insertion point to the Rating field.
8. Type: **A** as the rating for the book you wrote.
9. Press **Enter** or click on **OK** to close the dialog box. The macro types the book report information on the screen.
10. Click on **No** when the message box asks if you want to save the file. Is that cool — or what?

Now, check out what happens when you click on Cancel to close the dialog box.

1. Press **Alt + E** to erase the screen.
2. Click on **Format**.
3. Click on **HistoryReportFormat**. The History Book Report dialog box appears on the screen.
4. Click on **Cancel** to close the dialog box. The macro quietly ends. It doesn't give you an obnoxious error message or anything.

Filling a Dialog Box With Default Values

A text box is usually empty when a dialog box is displayed on the screen. You can place a default value in a text box if the data entered in the text box is often the same. When the dialog box is displayed on the screen, the value that is usually entered in the text box will already be typed in the box. It's the same idea as placing default values in Input boxes.

Place a default value in a text box by assigning it to the field identifier that corresponds to the text box. This statement must be placed before the Dialog () function in the macro. You have to assign the value you want to appear in the dialog box before you display the box. The syntax for assigning default values to a text box is:

DialogRecordName.FieldName = *Default Value*

For example,

HistoryRecord.Rating$ = "C"

places the default value "C" in the rating field of the HistoryRecord dialog record.

Let's add this statement to the HistoryReportFormat macro. Since you're usually brutal to writers (giving them a boring old "C" on their books), placing a default value in the rating field will save you from having to type the "C" each time.

1. Click on **Window.**
2. Click on **Global: HistoryReportFormat**.
3. Position the insertion point on the statement *ButtonChoice = Dialog(HistoryRecord)*
4. Press **Enter** to place a blank line into the macro.
   The statement to assign a value to a field in a dialog record must appear before the Dialog() function. That's so when you display the dialog box with the Dialog() function, the value of the field will already be filled in.
5. Type: **HistoryRecord.Rating$ = "C"** in the blank line.
   This statement places the value "C" in the variable "HistoryRecord.Rating$." Add a comment to the statement to clarify what you're doing.
6. Press the **Tab** key three or four times. Line the insertion point up with the comment for the Dim statement above.
7. Type: **'Assign a value to .Rating$** as the comment.
8. Click on **Save** on the Standard toolbar.
9. Click on **Yes**.

Now, run the HistoryReportFormat macro.

1. Click on **Window**.
2. Click on **Document1**.
3. Click on **Format**.
4. Click on **HistoryReportFormat**.
   The History Book Report dialog box appears on the screen with the Rating field filled in with the value of "C."

5. Type a book title, real or fake.
6. Press **Tab** to move to the author field.
7. Type the name of an author, real or fake.
8. Press **Enter** or click on **OK** to close the dialog box.
9. Click on **No** when asked about saving the file.
    The macro types the book title, the author, and the rating "C."
10. Press **Alt + E** to erase the screen.

Modifying a Dialog Box

Sometimes after you work with a custom dialog box for a while, you discover that you'd like to modify it in some way—maybe add a field, or take out a field. But you sure don't want to start all over again and build the dialog box from scratch. You just want to add a few finishing touches. The Dialog Editor makes it easy for you to modify a dialog box. All you have to do is copy the dialog box definition from the macro, back into the Dialog Editor.

Let's modify the HistoryReportFormat dialog box and see how this works. Suppose your teacher wants you to write a short paragraph rating the book in your book report instead of giving it a letter grade. Let's change the rating field to a multiple-line text box (a box that holds more than one line of typing) and enter the rating paragraph in the History Book Report dialog box. The HistoryReportFormat macro is still in the macro-editing window.

1. Click on **Window**.
2. Click on **Global: HistoryReportFormat**
3. Position the insertion point on the **Begin Dialog** statement.
4. Press **Shift +** ↓ to highlight the entire dialog box definition.
    Make sure you include the "End Dialog" statement in the highlighting.
5. Press **Ctrl + X**
    This places the dialog box definition on the clipboard and removes it from the macro. When you're done modifying the dialog box, you'll paste it back into the macro in its new and improved form.
6. Click on the **Dialog Editor** button on the macro toolbar. The Dialog Editor appears with an empty dialog box displayed.
7. Press **Ctrl + V** to paste the dialog box definition from the clipboard into the Dialog Editor.
8. Click in a blank area of the dialog box to remove the highlighting from the screen.
    Now you can modify the dialog box without having to start all over again. This is how the modified dialog box will look.

Create a multiple line text box by changing the height of the box

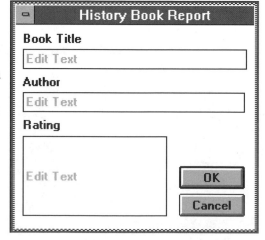

9. Click and drag the bottom edge of the dialog box down to make the dialog box a little taller.

10. Double-click on the Rating edit box (the third "Edit Text" box).
The Text Box Information screen appears. Let's change the height of the text box to accommodate multiple lines. Text boxes are automatically set to single line boxes. "Height" is set to "Auto" which means that the Dialog Editor set the height to hold one line of data. To change a text box to a multiple line box, change the height of the box.

11. If the "Auto" check box to the right of the word "Height" is checked, click on Auto to remove the check mark. This tells the Dialog Editor that you don't want the height automatically set any more.

12. Type: **75** as the height of the text box.

13. Press **Enter** or click on **OK** to close the Text Box Information dialog box.

14. Click and drag the right edge of the Rating text box to the right to expand the width of the box.

15. Click and drag the OK and Cancel buttons to the lower right corner of the dialog box.
That should just about do it.

Now, copy the new dialog box definition back into the HistoryReportFormat macro.

1. Click on the title bar of the dialog box to select it.

2. Click on **Edit**.

3. Click on **Copy**.

4. Click on **File**.

5. Click on **Exit**.
The HistoryReportFormat macro-editing window appears with the insertion point on the Dim statement. This is the correct spot for pasting a dialog box definition into a macro because the dialog box definition statements will be pasted *before* the Dim statement.

6. Press **Ctrl + V** to paste the dialog box definition from the clipboard into the macro.

7. Delete the following statement: **HistoryRecord.Rating$ = "C"**
You don't want the value "C" to appear in the Rating field.

8. Click on **Save** on the Standard toolbar.

9. Click on **Yes**.

10. Click on **File**.

11. Click on **Close**.

Run the new and improved HistoryReportFormat macro.

1. Click on **Format**.

2. Click on **HistoryReportFormat**.

3. Type a book title.

4. Press **Tab** to move to the Author field.

5. Type an author.

6. Press **Tab** to move to the Rating field.

7.   Type: **This was an excellent book. It was interesting and gave a lot of information. I would recommend this book to anyone who has to do a book report.**
8.   Click on **OK** to close the dialog box.
9.   Click on **No** when asked about saving the file.
10.   Click on **File, Close, No** to close the document window.

Basketball Card Collection Macro

One of the things a computer does well is keep track of things. We're going to write a macro that will help you keep track of your basketball card collection. This macro will allow you to keep track of what basketball cards you have, what you paid for each card, and the current price of the card. You will create a dialog box to enter the information about each card and a macro to add that information to a master list. Part of the macro will be recorded, part of it will be designed with the Dialog Editor and part of it will be written in the macro-editing window.

CREATE THE BASKETBALL CARD FILE

The first thing you need to do is create a file to hold the basketball card information. Then, you'll write a macro that will open that file and add information to it that you will enter in a custom dialog box.

1.   Click on **New** on the Standard toolbar.
2.   Click on **File**.
3.   Click on **Page Setup...**
4.   Click on **Margins**.
5.   Set the following margins:
      Top: **1"**
      Bottom: **1"**
      Left: **1"**
      Right: **1"**
6.   Click on **OK**.
7.   Click on **Format**.
8.   Click on **Font...**
9.   Click on Font = **Courier New**, Font Style = **Bold**, Size = **20**
      If you don't have a Courier New font, choose another 20-point bold font that looks good to you.
10.   Click on **OK**.
11.   Press **Ctrl + E** to turn on centering.
12.   Type: **Basketball Card Collection**
13.   Press **Enter**.
14.   Press **Ctrl + L** to turn on left justification.
15.   Click on **Format**.
16.   Click on **Font...**

17. Click on Font = **Courier New**, Font Style = **Regular**, Size = **12**
    If you don't have a Courier New font, choose another 12-point font.
18. Click on **OK**.
19. Press **Enter** two times.
20. Click on **Format**.
21. Click on **Tabs...**
22. Click on **Clear All**.
23. Set the following tab stops:
    Tab Stop Position = **2.5**, Alignment = **Left**
    Click on **Set**.
    Tab Stop Position = **3.8**, Alignment = **Left**
    Click on **Set**.
    Tab Stop Position = **5.2**, Alignment = **Right**
    Click on **Set**.
    Tab Stop Position = **6.3**, Alignment = **Right**
    Click on **Set**.
24. Click on **OK**.
25. Type: **Player**
26. Press the **Tab** key.
27. Type: **Card Type**
28. Press the **Tab** key.
29. Type: **Year**
30. Press the **Tab** key.
31. Type: **Purchase**
32. Press the **Tab** key.
33. Type: **Current**
34. Press **Enter**.
35. Press the **Tab** key three times.
36. Type: **Price**
37. Press the **Tab** key.
38. Type: **Price**
39. Press **Enter** two times.
40. Press the **Delete** key.
    Every time we add new information to this file, we want the font to be the same.
    The end-of-document paragraph marker sets the font back to the default font for
    your computer. So, we're deleting it.
41. Press the **Enter** key.

The Basketball Card file should look like this:

Basketball Card Collection

Player	Card Type	Year	Purchase Price	Current Price

42. Click on **Save** on the Standard toolbar.

43. Type: **bball** as the file name.

44. Click on **OK** (Word 6) or **Save** (Word 7) to save the file.

45. Click on **File**.

46. Click on **Close**.

RECORD THE BASKETBALLCARDS MACRO

Record a macro that will open the basketball card file and position the insertion point at the bottom of the document. When the macro runs, the insertion point will be in the correct spot for adding new cards to the list. Assign this macro to your toolbar, so it will be easy to run. If your toolbar is displayed on the screen, skip to step three. If your toolbar is not displayed, display it now.

1. Click the right mouse button on a blank spot on the Standard toolbar. The list of available toolbars appears on the screen.

2. Click on your toolbar name to display it.

3. Double-click on **REC** on the Status Bar to turn on the macro recorder.

4. Type: **BasketballCards** for the macro name

5. Click in the **Description** box at the bottom of the screen to position the insertion point.

6. Type: **Add cards to a basketball card collection file** for the description.

7. Click on **Toolbars** to assign the macro to your toolbar.

8. Drag the name **BasketballCards** to your toolbar.
   The Custom Button dialog box appears. Create your own design for the button face.

9. Click on **Edit...** The Button Editor dialog box appears.

Create a button face design and click on OK

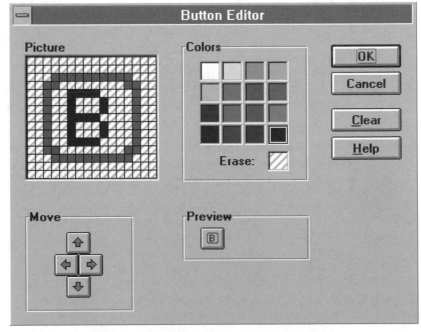

10. Use this example, or create your own design for the button face.

Click on the colors you want to use in the Colors section of the dialog box. Then, click in the Picture section to draw a picture. Click once to fill in a square and click again to erase it. When you've got the picture just like you want it,

11. Click on **OK**.

12. Click on **Close**.

The button you created appears on your toolbar and the macro record toolbar is displayed reminding you that the macro recorder is running.

13. Click on **Open** on the Standard toolbar (button that looks like an open folder).

14. Click on **bball.doc** (Word 6) or **bball** (Word 7) as the document to open.

15. Click on **OK** (Word 6) or **Open** (Word 7).

16. Press **Ctrl + End** to position the insertion point at the bottom of the document.

17. Click on **Stop** on the Macro Record toolbar.

Check out the BasketballCards macro to make sure it works.

1. Click on **File**.

2. Click on **Close**.

3. Click on the BasketballCards button on your toolbar to run the macro.

The Basketball cards file appears on the screen, with the insertion point at the bottom of the document. The recorded part of the macro is finished.

DESIGN THE BASKETBALL CARDS DIALOG BOX

Create a dialog box for entering the basketball card information. Put the basketball card file away and place the BasketballCards macro in the macro-editing window before you start designing the dialog box.

1. Click on **File**.

2. Click on **Close**.

3. Click on **Tools**.

4. Click on **Macro. . .**

5. Click on **BasketballCards** as the macro name.

6. Click on **Edit**.

7. Press **Alt + C** to add comments to the macro. Look at the Status bar at the bottom of the screen as you type the following comments.

REM ***

REM Macro: BasketballCards

REM Author: Harold Bishop

REM Purpose: Add cards to a basketball card collection file

REM ***

8. If you're using Word 7, modify the FileOpen statement to include the exact location of the Basketball Cards file. If you're using Word 6, you can skip this step.

Type: FileOpen **.Name = "C:\My Documents\bball.doc"**,

9. Click on the **Dialog Editor** button on the macro toolbar. A blank dialog box appears in the Dialog Editor. Change the title of the dialog box.

10. Click on **Edit**.

11. Click on **Info...** The Dialog Information screen appears.

12. Click in the text box to the right of the word "Text$" to position the insertion point.

13. Delete "**Microsoft Word**"

14. Type: **Basketball Card Collection** as the title of the dialog box. "Basketball Card Collection" is a long title. When you type it in the text box, a few of the letters roll off the left side of the box as you type. Don't worry, the entire title will appear on the title bar of the Basketball Card Collection dialog box.

15. Click on **OK**. "Basketball Card Collection" now appears as the title of the empty dialog box on the screen.

Adding Items to the Dialog Box

The Basketball Card Collection dialog box

This is how the finished dialog box will look. It contains text items, text boxes, command buttons, option buttons and a group box. Option buttons are used to allow you to choose one option from a group of options. A Group box is used to surround the list of options and keep them together as related items in the dialog box. In the Basketball Card Collection dialog box, there are option buttons for each type of basketball card you collect. When the macro runs, you can click on the option button for the card type instead of having to type it each time. The group box is the box that surrounds the names of the different types of cards.

Whenever you use group boxes and option buttons in a dialog box, make the group box first, then add the option buttons.

This dialog box holds a lot of information, so begin by expanding the size of the dialog box.

1. Move the mouse pointer to the lower right corner of the dialog box. The mouse pointer turns into a double-headed arrow.

2. Click and drag the double-headed arrow down and to the right to expand the size of the dialog box.

3. Release the mouse button when the dialog box is the size you want.
   Now that you've got plenty of space to work with, add the items to the dialog box.
4. Click on **Item**.
5. Click on **Text**.
6. Type: **Player**
   The first field in basketball card file is the name of the basketball player. So, that should be the first field you enter in the dialog box when the macro runs.
7. Click on **Item**.
8. Click on **Text Box**.
   A text box for entering the name of the basketball player appears below the text item.
9. Click on the right edge of the text box and drag it to the right with the double-headed arrow to expand the size of the box.
   Lots of basketball players have long names, so make your text box large enough to accommodate them. Leave some space to the right of the text box for another field.
10. Double-click on the basketball player text box. The Text Box information screen appears.
11. Click in the text box for **.Field** to position the insertion point.
12. Delete **.TextBox1**
13. Type: **.Player**
    "Player" is the name of the field that will be used inside the macro when you're referring to the name of the basketball player.
14. Click on **OK**.
    Add a group box and option buttons for the different types of cards.
15. Click on **Item**.
16. Click on **Group Box**.
    An empty group box appears in the dialog box.
17. Type: **Card Type**
    The title of the group box is now "Card Type."
18. Press **Enter**.
    An option button is inserted into the group box. When a group box is selected, all you have to do to place an option button inside the group is press Enter.
19. Type: **Fleer**
    The option button has dotted lines around it. That means it's selected. To change the title of a selected option button, just type the new name.
    You have lots of "Fleer" cards in your collection, so that will be the first option button you can choose from when the macro runs. There will be five option buttons for different types of cards.

The macro will need to figure out which option button you selected when the macro runs, so you need to create an option group identifier that the macro can use to make this decision. Within the group, only one option button can be selected at a time. The Option Group identifier returns a value corresponding to the selected option button.

20.   Double-click on **Fleer**. The Option Button Information screen appears.

```
┌──────────────────────────────────────────────────────────┐
│  ▬        Option Button Information                        │
├──────────────────────────────────────────────────────────┤
│  ┌─Position──────────────┐  ┌─Size──────────────────┐     │
│     X: [20]   □ Auto         Width: [67]   □ Auto         │
│     Y: [18]   □ Auto         Height: [16]  □ Auto         │
│  └───────────────────────┘  └───────────────────────┘     │
│                                                            │
│        Text$: [Fleer              ]    ⊠ Auto Quote        │
│        .Field: [                  ]                        │
│       Comment: [                  ]                        │
│      .OptGroup [.CardType         ]                        │
│                                                            │
│              [   OK   ]      [  Cancel  ]                  │
└──────────────────────────────────────────────────────────┘
```

**Change the OptGroup
variable name**

21.   Click in the text box for **.OptGroup** to position the insertion point.

22.   Delete **.OptionGroup1**

23.   Type: **.CardType**
      "CardType" is the name of the variable that will be used inside the macro when you are looking at which option button was selected.

24.   Click on **OK**.

25.   Press **Enter** to place the second option button in the group box.
      Each time you press Enter, another option button will be inserted into the group box.

26.   Type: **SkyBox**

27.   Press **Enter** to place the third option button into the group box.

28.   Type: **Topps**

29.   Press **Enter** to place the fourth option button in the group box.

30.   Type: **Ultra**

31.   Press **Enter** to place the fifth option button in the group box.

32.   Type: **Upper Deck**
      The five different types of cards you collect are now listed in the group box. When the macro runs, you will click on one of the option buttons to specify the type of card.

33.   Click on **Item**.

34.   Click on **Text**.

35.   Type: **Year**

36.   With the four-headed arrow, click and drag the text item "Year" below the group box.

37.   Click on **Item**.

38.   Click on **Text Box**.

39.   With the two-headed arrow, click and drag the right side of the text box to the left to shorten the size of the box.

It doesn't take a lot of space to type a year, so the text box for entering the year can be shorter than the other text boxes in the dialog box.

40. Double-click on the "Year" text box.

41. In the .Field text box, delete .TextBox2 and type **.Year**
    "Year" is the name of the variable that will be used inside the macro when you're referring to the year of the basketball card.

42. Click on **OK**.

43. Click on **Item**.

44. Click on **Text**.

45. Type: **Purchase Price**

46. Click and drag the text item "Purchase Price" to the right side of the dialog box to the right of the text item "Player."

47. Click on **Item**.

48. Click on **Text Box**.
    A text box is inserted into the dialog box below the text item "Purchase Price." If your dialog box is getting a little crowded, or if the Purchase Price text box doesn't all fit in the dialog box, click on the right side of the dialog box and drag the two-headed arrow to the right to expand the size of the box. If the box is too large, drag the two-headed arrow to the left.

49. Double-click on the text box for entering the purchase price.

50. In the .Field text box, delete .TextBox3 and type **.Purchase**
    "Purchase" is the name of the variable that will be used inside the macro when referring to the price you paid for the basketball card.

51. Click on **OK**.

52. Click on **Item**.

53. Click on **Text**.

54. Type: **Current Price**

55. Click on **Item**.

56. Click on **Text Box**.
    A text box is inserted in the dialog box below the text item "Current Price."

57. Double-click on the text box for entering the current price.

58. In the .Field text box, delete .TextBox4 and type **.Current**
    "Current" is the name of the variable that will be used inside the macro when referring to the current price of the basketball card.

59. Click on **OK**.
    The final ingredients in a custom dialog box are command buttons.

60. Click on **Item.**

61. Click on **Button...**

62. Press **Enter** to place an OK button in the dialog box.

63. Click and drag the OK button down to the lower right corner of the dialog box. Leave enough room for a Cancel button below it.

64. Press **Enter** to place a Cancel button in the dialog box.

Now that the Basketball Card Collection dialog box has all the pieces, click and drag the items around inside the box if you need to fine-tune its appearance.

Your dialog box looks great! Copy it onto the clipboard, then into the BasketballCards macro.

COPY THE DIALOG BOX DEFINITION INTO THE MACRO

1.   Click on the title bar of the dialog box to select it.
2.   Click on **Edit**.
3.   Click on **Copy**.
      The dialog box definition is now on the clipboard.
4.   Click on **File**.
5.   Click on **Exit** to exit the Dialog Editor and return to the macro-editing window.
6.   Position the insertion point on the End Sub statement at the end of the macro.
7.   Press **Enter** to insert a blank line into the macro.
8.   Press **Ctrl + V** to paste the dialog box definition from the clipboard into the macro.

The dialog box definition should look like this:

```
Begin Dialog UserDialog 470, 218, "Basketball Card Collection"
    Text 10, 6, 48, 13, "Player", .Text1
    TextBox 10, 22, 261, 18, .Player
    GroupBox 10, 46, 204, 108, "Card Type"
    OptionGroup .CardType
    OptionButton 20, 58, 67, 16, "Fleer", .OptionButton1
    OptionButton 20, 75, 85, 16, "SkyBox", .OptionButton2
    OptionButton 20, 92, 76, 16, "Topps", .OptionButton3
    OptionButton 20, 109, 65, 16, "Ultra", .OptionButton4
    OptionButton 20, 126, 120, 16, "Upper Deck", .OptionButton5
    Text 13, 170, 36, 13, "Year", .Text2
    TextBox 13, 186, 83, 18, .Year
    Text 299, 6, 116, 13, "Purchase Price", .Text3
    TextBox 299, 22, 160, 18, .Purchase
    Text 299, 46, 100, 13, "Current Price", .Text4
    TextBox 299, 62, 160, 18, .Current
    OKButton 338, 160, 88, 21
    CancelButton 338, 184, 88, 21
End Dialog
```

There are five fields that receive information in the Basketball Card Collection dialog box. The order of the dialog box definition statements determines the order the insertion point will travel to those five fields when the macro runs. The text box for entering the player's name appears first in the dialog box definition, so the "Player" field will be the field that has the initial focus when the dialog box is displayed on the screen. The insertion point starts out in the player text box, when the dialog box is displayed. This is the order the insertion point will follow when the macro runs.

TextBox 10, 22, 261, 18, **.Player**	First
OptionGroup **.CardType**	Second
TextBox 13, 186, 83, 18, **.Year**	Third
TextBox 299, 22, 160, 18, **.Purchase**	Fourth
TextBox 299, 62, 160, 18, **.Current**	Fifth

The OptionGroup statement was created by the Dialog Editor when you placed the first option button in the group box. Notice the name of the option group, "CardType." When the macro runs, it will look at the value in "CardType" to see which option button you selected. The values in "CardType" correspond to the order of the option buttons in the group box. If you select the first option button, "Fleer," then 0 (zero) will be the value in "CardType." If you select the second option button, "SkyBox," then 1 will be the value in "CardType," and so on. These are the possible values in the variable "CardType."

OptionGroup **.CardType**

OptionButton 20, 58, 67, 16, "**Fleer**", .OptionButton1	0
OptionButton 20, 75, 85, 16, "**SkyBox**", .OptionButton2	1
OptionButton 20, 92, 76, 16, "**Topps**", .OptionButton3	2
OptionButton 20, 109, 65, 16, "**Ultra**", .OptionButton4	3
OptionButton 20, 126, 120, 16, "**Upper Deck**", .OptionButton5	4

DEFINE THE DIALOG RECORD

To use the Basketball Card Collection dialog box in the BasketballCards macro, you need to define the dialog record and display the dialog box.

1. Position the insertion point on the **End Sub** statement.
2. Press **Enter** to insert a blank line into the macro.
3. Type: **Dim BBallRecord As UserDialog**   **'Define the dialog record**
   "BBallRecord" is the name of the dialog record. Any time you refer to a field in the macro, you'll type the record name, "BBallRecord" and then the field name.

DISPLAY THE DIALOG BOX

Use the Dialog() function to display the Basketball Card Collection dialog box.

1. Position the insertion point on the next line after the **Dim** statement.
2. Type: **ButtonChoice = Dialog(BBallRecord) 'Display the dialog box**
   "ButtonChoice" is the name of the variable that will tell the macro how you closed the dialog box. "BBallRecord" is the name of the dialog record for the Basketball Card Collection dialog box.

USE THE DIALOG BOX INFORMATION IN THE MACRO

The last step in completing this masterpiece of a macro is to use the information from the dialog box in the macro. Think about the logic of the macro for a minute. What do you want the macro to do?

The Basketball Card Collection Flowchart, shown on the next page, illustrates the logic of the BasketballCards macro. Actions the macro performs are shown in boxes and decisions it has to make are shown in diamonds. The flow of the BasketballCards macro is:

1. Open the basketball card master file.
2. Position the insertion point at the end of the file.
3. Display the Basketball Card Collection dialog box.
4. Check how you closed the dialog box.

The Basketball Card Collection Flowchart

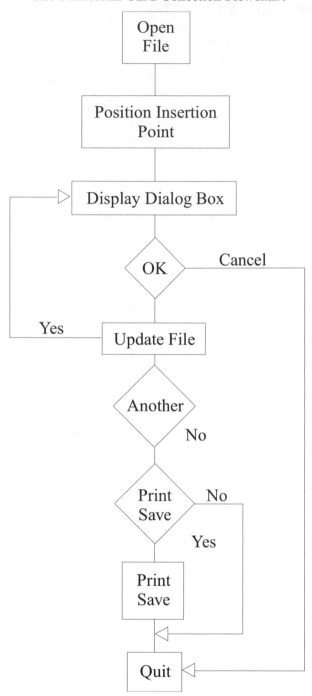

5. If you clicked on OK to close the dialog box, update the basketball card file by writing the information you entered in the dialog box to the master file.

6. If you clicked on Cancel to close the dialog box, go to "Quit" and end the macro.

7. Ask if you'd like to enter the information for another card.

The macro wouldn't be very useful if you had to run it for each card you wanted to enter. So, the macro needs a loop to go back and display the dialog box again and let you enter the information for another card.

8. Check how you answered the question "Do you want to enter another card?"
9. If you clicked on "Yes" to enter another card, loop back up and display the dialog box again.
10. If you clicked on "No" to enter another card, continue running the macro by executing the next instruction.
11. Ask if you'd like to print and save the file.
12. Check how you answered the question "Do you want to save and print the file?"
13. If you clicked on "Yes" to save and print the file, execute the save and print commands in the macro.
14. If you clicked on "No" to save and print the file, end the macro.

The BasketballCards macro already includes WordBasic statements for the first three steps. The FileOpen statement opens the basketball card file. The EndOfDocument statement positions the insertion point at the end of the document. The Dialog box definition statements, the Dim statement and the Dialog() function display the dialog box.

Let's write the WordBasic statements for the rest of the macro.

The BasketballCards macro will contain a loop to allow you to enter more than one basketball card at a time. Type a label statement to tell the macro where to go when it loops.

1. Position the insertion point on the **Begin Dialog** statement.
2. Press **Enter** to place a blank line into the macro.
3. Type: **Continue:** in the blank line.
4. Position the insertion point on the End Sub statement.
5. Press **Enter** to place a blank line into the macro.
6. Type the following statements, beginning at the blank line.
7. Type: **If ButtonChoice = 0 Then   'Check if Cancel button chosen**
   GoTo Quit:
   EndIf

   If you clicked on Cancel the macro will end. If you clicked on OK, the macro will continue and execute the next instruction in the macro.
8. Type: **Insert BBallRecord.Player**

   This Insert statement types the basketball player's name in the document window.
9. Type: **Insert Chr$(9)** to press the Tab key in the document window.
10. Type:
    If BBallRecord.CardType = 0 Then   'Check which card chosen
        Insert "Fleer"
    EndIf

    If the "Fleer" option button was selected, then 0 will be the value in the variable "BBallRecord.CardType."

11. Type: **If BBallRecord.CardType = 1 Then**
    Insert "SkyBox"
    EndIf

12. Type: **If BBallRecord.CardType = 2 Then**
    Insert "Topps"
    EndIf

13. Type: **If BBallRecord.CardType = 3 Then**
    Insert "Ultra"
    EndIf

14. Type: **If BBallRecord.CardType = 4 Then**
    Insert "Upper Deck"
    EndIf

15. Type: **Insert Chr$(9)** to press the Tab key in the document window.

16. Type: **Insert BBallRecord.Year**
    This Insert statement types the year of the basketball card in the document window.

17. Type: **Insert Chr$(9)** to press the Tab key in the document window.

18. Type: **Insert BBallRecord.Purchase**
    This Insert statement types the purchase price of the basketball card in the document window.

19. Type: **Insert Chr$(9)** to press the Tab key in the document window.

20. Type: **Insert BBallRecord.Current**
    This Insert statement types the current price of the basketball card in the document window.

21. Type: **InsertPara**
    The InsertPara statement moves the insertion point down to the next line in the document window.

22. Type: **Again = MsgBox("Do you want to enter another card?", "Basketball Card Collection", 36)**
    This message box will allow you to choose whether you want to enter the information for another basketball card. You'll click on "Yes" if you want to enter another card, and "No" if you don't want to enter another card.

23. Type:
    If Again = -1 Then   **'Check if you want to enter another card**
    GoTo Continue:
    EndIf
    If you want to enter the information for another card, the macro will loop to the label "Continue." If you don't want to enter another card, the macro will drop down and execute the next instruction in the macro.

24. Type: **PrintSave = MsgBox("Do you want to print and save the file?", "Basketball Card Collection", 36)**
    This message box will allow you to choose whether you want to print and save the basketball card file.

25. Type:

   If PrintSave = -1 Then   'Check if you want to print and save
   FileSave
   FilePrint
   EndIf

   This If statement checks the value in the variable "PrintSave" to see if you want to print and save the file. If you do, then the macro will execute the FileSave and FilePrint commands. If you don't, the macro will drop down to the next line and end.

26. Type: **Quit:**

   This label statement is necessary to tell the macro where to go when you Click on Cancel to close the dialog box.

The BasketballCards macro statements should look like this:

```
Sub MAIN
REM ***********************************************************
REM Macro:      BasketballCards
REM Author:     Harold Bishop
REM Purpose:    Add cards to a basketball card collection file
REM ***********************************************************
FileOpen .Name = "C:\My Documents\BBALL.DOC",
.ConfirmConversions = 0, .ReadOnly = 0, .AddToMru = 0,
.PasswordDoc = "", .PasswordDot = "", .Revert = 0,
.WritePasswordDoc = "", .WritePasswordDot = ""
EndOfDocument
Continue:
Begin Dialog UserDialog 434, 220, "Basketball Card Collection"
   Text 10, 6, 48, 13, "Player", .Text1
   TextBox 10, 22, 227, 18, .Player
   GroupBox 10, 46, 204, 108, "Card Type"
   OptionGroup .CardType
      OptionButton 20, 58, 67, 16, "Fleer", .OptionButton1
      OptionButton 20, 75, 85, 16, "SkyBox", .OptionButton2
      OptionButton 20, 92, 76, 16, "Topps", .OptionButton3
      OptionButton 20, 109, 65, 16, "Ultra", .OptionButton4
      OptionButton 20, 126, 120, 16, "Upper Deck", .OptionButton5
   Text 16, 170, 36, 13, "Year", .Text2
   TextBox 16, 186, 69, 18, .Year
   Text 268, 6, 116, 13, "Purchase Price", .Text3
   TextBox 268, 22, 160, 18, .Purchase
   Text 268, 46, 100, 13, "Current Price", .Text4
   TextBox 268, 62, 160, 18, .Current
   OKButton 322, 166, 88, 21
   CancelButton 322, 190, 88, 21
End Dialog
Dim BBallRecord As UserDialog      'Define the dialog record
ButtonChoice = Dialog(BBallRecord)      'Display the dialog box
```

```
If ButtonChoice = 0 Then        'Check if Cancel button chosen
    Goto Quit:
EndIf
Insert BBallRecord.Player
Insert Chr$(9)
If BBallRecord.CardType = 0 Then     'Check which card chosen
    Insert "Fleer"
EndIf
If BBallRecord.CardType = 1 Then
    Insert "SkyBox"
EndIf
If BBallRecord.CardType = 2 Then
    Insert "Topps"
EndIf
If BBallRecord.CardType = 3 Then
    Insert "Ultra"
EndIf
If BBallRecord.CardType = 4 Then
    Insert "Upper Deck"
EndIf
Insert Chr$(9)
Insert BBallRecord.Year
Insert Chr$(9)
Insert BBallRecord.Purchase
Insert Chr$(9)
Insert BBallRecord.Current
InsertPara
Again = MsgBox("Do you want to enter another card?",
"Basketball Card Collection", 36)
If Again = - 1 Then        'Check if you want to enter another card
    Goto Continue:
EndIf
PrintSave = MsgBox("Do you want to print and save the file?",
"Basketball Card Collection", 36)
If PrintSave = - 1 Then      'Check if you want to print and save
    FileSave
    FilePrint
EndIf
Quit:
End Sub
```

27. Click on **Save** on the Standard toolbar.

28. Click on **Yes**.

Let's try it out. If you get an error the first time you run the macro, click on Window, Global: BasketballCards and fix the highlighted statement in the macro.

1.   Click on **New** on the Standard toolbar.

2.   Click on the **Basketball Card** button on your toolbar.
      The Basketball Card Collection dialog box appears on the screen. The insertion point is in the Player field, waiting for you to enter the name of a player.

3.   Type: **Michael Jordan**

4. Click on the **SkyBox** option button.
5. Press the **Tab** key to move to the year field.
6. Type: **1996**
7. Press the **Tab** key to move to the Purchase Price field.
8. Type: **10.00**
9. Press the **Tab** key to move to the Current Price field.
10. Type: **12.50**
11. Press **Enter** or click on **OK** to close the dialog box.
12. Click on **Yes** when a message box appears asking if you'd like to enter another card.
13. Type: **Shaquille O'Neal**
14. Click on the **Ultra** option button.
15. Press the **Tab** key to move to the year field.
16. Type: **1995**
17. Press the **Tab** key to move to the Purchase Price field.
18. Type: **5.00**
19. Press the **Tab** key to move to the Current Price field.
20. Type: **6.50**
21. Press **Enter** or click on **OK** to close the dialog box.
22. Click on **No** when a message box appears asking if you'd like to enter another card.
23. Click on **Yes** when a message box appears asking if you'd like to print and save the file.

   Pretty cool, dude!

24. Click on **File**.
25. Click on **Close**.
   When you're done running the BasketballCards macro, make sure you close the file so that it will be safe and sound on disk until you need it again.
26. Run the BasketballCards macro again and enter some of your favorite basketball players.
27. Click on **Window**.
28. Click on **Global: BasketballCards**.
29. Click on **File, Close** to close the macro-editing window.

Chapter Review — Absolutely, Positively the Most Important Stuff

1. Every macro that uses a dialog box must contain a Dim statement to define the dialog record. The syntax of the Dim statement is:

Dim *DialogRecord* As *DialogBoxName*   For Word dialog boxes
Dim *DialogRecord* As *UserDialog*   For custom dialog boxes

2. Every macro that uses a dialog box must contain a Dialog() function to display the dialog box. The syntax of the Dialog() function is:

ButtonChoice = Dialog(*DialogRecord*)

3. Follow a five step process to use a custom dialog box in a macro.

    ◆ Design the dialog box with the Dialog Editor.

    ◆ Copy the dialog box definition into the macro.

    ◆ Create the dialog record.

    ◆ Display the dialog box.

    ◆ Use the data from the dialog box inside the macro.

4. Keep these tips in mind when you're designing a custom dialog box.

    ◆ Plan the arrangement of the dialog box in advance. Place items in the dialog box in the same order you want to enter the information when the macro is running.

    ◆ Build the dialog box from top to bottom, left to right.

    ◆ Click on an item to select it, then add another item below the selected item.

    ◆ Always include command buttons (OK and Cancel buttons) in every dialog box.

    ◆ Add a group box first, then add the option buttons and check boxes inside it.

    ◆ To delete items in a dialog box, click on the item first to select it, then press the Delete key.

5. To use a field from a custom dialog box in a macro, type the record name first, then the field name, like: *RecordName.FieldName*

Projects for Practice

The Party Macro

Let's add a dialog box to the Party macro. With a dialog box, you'll be able to enter all of the information about the party on one screen instead of having to go through five Input boxes. Follow the famous 5-step process to use a dialog box in the Party macro.

Design the Dialog Box

When we are done, the Party Time dialog box will look like the illustration on the next page. Pretty cool, isn't it?

1. Click on **Tools**.
2. Click on **Macro...**
3. Click on **Party**.
4. Click on **Edit**. The Party macro appears in the macro-editing window.

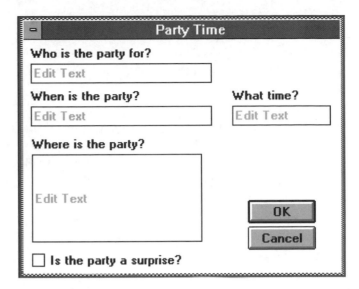

The Party Time
dialog box

5. Click on **Dialog Editor** on the Macro toolbar. A blank dialog box appears in the Dialog Editor. Change the title of the dialog box.

6. Click on **Edit**.

7. Click on **Info...**

8. Click in the text box to the right of the word "Text$" to position the insertion point.

9. Delete "**Microsoft Word**"

10. Type: **Party Time**

11. Click on **OK**.

This dialog box holds a lot of information, so make the dialog box larger so everything will fit.

12. Position the mouse pointer on the lower right corner of the dialog box.

13. Click and drag the two-headed arrow down and to the right to expand the size of the dialog box.

Add items to the dialog box.

14. Click on **Item**.

15. Click on **Text**.

16. Type: **Who is the party for?**

17. Click on **Item**.

18. Click on **Text Box**.

19. Click and drag the right edge of the text box to the right to expand the size of the text box.

20. Double-click on the text box, on the words "Edit Text."

The Text Box Information screen appears.

21. Click in the text box for **.Field** to position the insertion point.

22. Delete **.TextBox1**

23. Type: **.Who$**

"Who$" is the name of the field that will be used inside the macro when you're referring to the person you're having the party for.

24. Click on **OK**.

25. Click on **Item**.

26. Click on **Text**.

27. Type: **When is the party?**

28. Click on **Item**.

29. Click on **Text Box**.

30. Click and drag the right edge of the text box to the right to expand the size of the text box. Make this text box the same size as the text box for entering the name of the person you're having the party for above.

31. Double-click on the text box for enter the date of the party.
   The Text Box Information screen appears.

32. In the .Field text box, delete .TextBox2 and type **.PartyDate$**
   "PartyDate$" is the name of the field that will be used inside the macro when referring to the date of the party.

33. Click on **OK**.

34. Click on **Item**.

35. Click on **Text**.

36. Type: **What time?**

37. Click and drag the text item "What time?" to the right side of the dialog box, across from the text item "When is the Party?"

38. Click on **Item**.

39. Click on **Text Box**.
   A text box appears on the screen directly below the text item "What time?"

40. Click and drag the right edge of the text box to the left to make the text box smaller.

41. Double-click on the text box for entering the time of the party.

42. In the .Field text box, delete .TextBox3 and type **.PartyTime$**
   "PartyTime$" is the name of the field that will be used inside the macro when referring to the time of the party.

43. Click on **OK**.

44. Click on **Item**.

45. Click on **Text**.

46. Type: **Where is the party?**
   The text item is positioned below the text box for entering the time of the party. Move it over to the left side of the dialog box.

47. Click and drag the text item "Where is the party?" to the left side of the dialog box, below the text box for entering the party date.

48. Click on **Item**.

49. Click on **Text Box**.

50. Click and drag the right edge of the text box to the right to expand the size of the text box. Make this text box the same size as the text box for entering the date of the party above.

51. Double-click on the text box for entering the location of the party.

52. In the .Field text box, delete .TextBox4 and type **.Where$**

"Where$" is the name of the field that will be used inside the macro when referring to the location of the party.

Now, change the size of the text box to accommodate multiple line addresses.

53. Click on the "Auto" check box to the right of the word "Height" to remove the check mark designating this as a single line text box.

54. Type: **80** as the height of the text box.

55. Click on **OK**.

Add a check box to indicate whether the party is a surprise or not.

56. Click on **Item**.

57. Click on **Button...**

58. Click on **Check Box**.

59. Click on **OK**.

60. Type: **Is the party a surprise?**

61. Click and drag the check box "Is the party a surprise?" down a little bit so that your dialog box doesn't look crowded.

62. Double-click on the check box, "Is the party a surprise?"

63. Click in the text box for **.Field** to position the insertion point.

64. Delete **.CheckBox1**

65. Type: **.Surprise**

66. Click on **OK**.

The final items needed in the dialog box are the command buttons.

67. Click on **Item**.

68. Click on **Button...**

69. Press **Enter** to place an OK button in the dialog box.

70. Click and drag the OK button to the right side of the dialog box. It will fit nicely in the blank area to the right of the text box for entering the location of the party.

71. Press **Enter** to place a Cancel button in the dialog box.

72. If your dialog box is too small or too large, click and drag any edge of the dialog box to make it look good. Rearrange the items as necessary to tidy up the dialog box.

Copy the Dialog Box Definition Into the Macro

The second step in creating a custom dialog box macro is to copy the dialog box definition into the macro.

1. Click on the title bar of the dialog box to select it.

2. Click on **Edit**.

3. Click on **Copy**. The dialog box definition is now on the clipboard.

4. Click on **File**.

5. Click on **Exit** to exit the Dialog Editor and return to the macro-editing window.

6. Position the insertion point at the beginning of the macro after the last REM statement.

7. Press **Enter** to insert a blank line into the macro.

8. Press **Ctrl + V** to paste the dialog box definition from the clipboard into the macro.

Create the Dialog Record Using the Dim Statement

1. Position the insertion point on the line after the **End Dialog** Statement.
2. Press **Enter** then ↑ to position the insertion point on a blank line.
3. Type: **Dim PartyRecord As UserDialog   'Create the dialog record**
    "PartyRecord" is the name of the dialog record. "UserDialog" is required by Word to show that this is a custom dialog box.

Display the Dialog Box With the Dialog() Function

1. Press **Enter** to position the insertion point on the next line.
2. Type: **ButtonChoice = Dialog(PartyRecord)   'Display the dialog box**
    "ButtonChoice" is the name of the variable that will tell the macro how you closed the dialog box. "PartyRecord" is the name of the dialog record for the Party Time dialog box.

Use the Dialog Box Information in Your Macro

In the original version of the Party macro, you typed the information for the party in Input boxes. Now that the macro uses a dialog box to get its information, you'll need to delete the InputBox$() functions in the macro. You'll also add some statements to read the data that was entered in the dialog box and check how the dialog box was closed.

1. Position the insertion point on the "Who$" InputBox$() function. It should be on the next line after the Dialog() function.
2. Press **Shift +** ↓ to highlight the four InputBox$() functions and the MsgBox() function.
    Who$ = InputBox$("Who is the party for?")
    PartyDate$ = InputBox$("When is the party?")
    PartyTime$ = InputBox$("What time?")
    Where$ = InputBox$("Where is the party?")
    Button = MsgBox("Is the party a surprise?", "Party Time", 36)
3. Press the **Delete** key to delete the statements.
4. Press **Enter** to create a blank line.
    Type an If statement that will check how you closed the dialog box, starting at the blank line.
5. Type: **If ButtonChoice = 0 Then   'Check if Cancel button chosen**
                    GoTo Quit:
             EndIf
6. Modify the statement that types the name of the person you're having the party for to include the dialog record name as well as the field name.
    Type: Insert "For" + Chr$(32) + **PartyRecord.**Who$
7. Modify the statement that types the date of the party.
    Type: Insert "When:" + Chr$(32) + Chr$(32) + **PartyRecord.**PartyDate$
8. Modify the statement that types the time of the party.

Type: Insert "at" + Chr$(32) + **PartyRecord.**PartyTime$

9. Modify the statement that types the location of the party.

Type: Insert "Meet at" + Chr$(32) + **PartyRecord.**Where$

10. With the insertion point at the beginning of the Insert statement for the location of the party, press **Enter** to insert a blank line into the macro.

11. Type: **SpacePara2** in the blank line. When the macro runs, you will enter the address of the party in a multiple line text box. The "SpacePara2" statement doublespaces that address on the invitation.

12. Position the insertion point on the InsertPara statement after the "Where$" Insert statement.

```
Insert "at" + Chr$(32) + PartyRecord.PartyTime$
InsertPara
InsertPara
SpacePara2
Insert "Meet at" + Chr$(32) + PartyRecord.Where$
InsertPara
InsertPara
```

13. Delete the InsertPara statement.

The SpacePara2 statement turned on double spacing, so you only need one InsertPara statement to get two blank lines printed on the invitation.

14. Modify the If statement that tells the macro if you want the party to be a surprise or not. In place of the old If statement (If Button = –1 Then),

Type: **If PartyRecord.Surprise = 1 Then**

In the Party Time dialog box you indicate if the party is a surprise or not by clicking on the check box. If the party is a surprise, then the value of the variable "Surprise" will be 1. If the party is not a surprise, then the check box will not be checked and the value of the variable will be 0.

15. Position the insertion point on the End Sub statement at the end of the macro.

16. Press **Enter** to insert a blank line.

17. Type: **Quit:** in the blank line.

This label tells the macro where to go when you click on the Cancel button to close the Party Time dialog box.

The Party macro should look like this:

```
Sub MAIN
REM **********************************************************
REM Macro:     Party
REM Author:    Ashley Burlington
REM Purpose:   Create fill in the blanks party invitations
REM **********************************************************

Begin Dialog UserDialog 420, 216, "Party Time"
   Text 10, 6, 160, 13, "Who is the party for?", .Text1
   TextBox 10, 22, 240, 18, .Who$
   Text 10, 46, 144, 13, "When is the party?", .Text2
   TextBox 10, 62, 240, 18, .PartyDate$
   Text 278, 46, 87, 13, "What time?", .Text3
   TextBox 279, 62, 128, 18, .PartyTime$
```

```
    Text 12, 90, 149, 13, "Where is the party?", .Text4
    TextBox 12, 106, 225, 80, .Where$, 1
    CheckBox 12, 195, 203, 16, "Is the party a surprise?", .Surprise
    OKButton 298, 149, 88, 21
    CancelButton 298, 173, 88, 21
End Dialog

Dim PartyRecord As UserDialog    'Create the dialog record
ButtonChoice = Dialog(PartyRecord)  'Display the dialog box

If ButtonChoice = 0 Then        'Check if Cancel button chosen
    Goto Quit:
EndIf
ViewPage
View Zoom$ .FullPage
InsertFrame
FormatFrame .Wrap = 1, .WidthRule = 1, .FixedWidth = "3" +
Chr$(34), .HeightRule = 2, .FixedHeight = "3" + Chr$(34),
.PositionHorz = "Center", .PositionHorzRel = 1, .DistFromText
= "0.13" + Chr$(34), .PositionVert = "Top", .PositionVertRel =
0, .DistVertFromText = "0" + Chr$(34), .MoveWithText = 0,
.LockAnchor = 0
InsertPicture .Name = "C:\WINWORD\CLIPART\PARTY.WMF",
.LinkToFile = "0"
InsertPara
DrawTextbox
FormatDrawingObject .Tab = "2", .FillColor = "1", .LineColor =
"", .FillPatternColor = "8", .FillPattern = "0", .LineType =
0, .LineStyle = - 1, .LineWeight = "", .ArrowStyle = - 1,
.ArrowWidth = - 1, .ArrowLength = - 1, .Shadow = 0,
.RoundCorners = 0, .HorizontalPos = "1.2" + Chr$(34),
.HorizontalFrom = 1, .VerticalPos = "3.8" + Chr$(34),
.VerticalFrom = 0, .LockAnchor = 0, .Height = "5.8" +
Chr$(34), .Width = "6" + Chr$(34), .InternalMargin = "1 pt"
FormatFont .Points = "32", .Underline = 0, .Color = 0,
.Strikethrough = 0, .Superscript = 0, .Subscript = 0, .Hidden
= 0, .SmallCaps = 0, .AllCaps = 0, .Spacing = "0 pt",
.Position = "0 pt", .Kerning = 0, .KerningMin = "", .Tab =
"0", .Font = "Caslon Openface", .Bold = 0, .Italic = 0
CenterPara
Insert "It's Party Time!"
InsertPara
InsertPara
FormatFont .Points = "24", .Underline = 0, .Color = 0,
.Strikethrough = 0, .Superscript = 0, .Subscript = 0, .Hidden
= 0, .SmallCaps = 0, .AllCaps = 0, .Spacing = "0 pt",
.Position = "0 pt", .Kerning = 0, .KerningMin = "", .Tab =
"0", .Font = "Arial", .Bold = 0, .Italic = 0

Insert "For" + Chr$(32) + PartyRecord.Who$
InsertPara
InsertPara
Insert "When:" + Chr$(32) + Chr$(32) + PartyRecord.PartyDate$
InsertPara
```

```
InsertPara
Insert "at" + Chr$(32) + PartyRecord.PartyTime$
InsertPara
InsertPara
SpacePara2
Insert "Meet at" + Chr$(32) + PartyRecord.Where$
InsertPara

FormatFont .Points = "14", .Underline = 0, .Color = 0,
.Strikethrough = 0, .Superscript = 0, .Subscript = 0, .Hidden
= 0, .SmallCaps = 0, .AllCaps = 0, .Spacing = "0 pt",
.Position = "0 pt", .Kerning = 0, .KerningMin = "", .Tab =
"0", .Font = "Brush Script MT", .Bold = 0, .Italic = 0
If PartyRecord.Surprise = 1 Then
    Insert "Shhhhhhh! It's a surprise!"
EndIf
Quit:
End Sub
```

18. Click on **Save** on the Standard toolbar.

19. Click on **Yes**.

Let's have a party!

1. Click on **New** on the Standard toolbar.

2. Click on the **Party** button on your toolbar.
   The Party Time dialog box appears on the screen with the insertion point in the first text box, waiting for you to type who the party is for.

3. Type: **Gail Booker**

4. Press the **Tab** key to move the insertion point to the next text box, the "When" text box.

5. Type: **Saturday, December 12, 1997**

6. Press the **Tab** key to move the insertion point to the next text box, the "Time" text box.

7. Type: **1:00 p.m.**

8. Press the **Tab** key to move the insertion point to the next text box, the "Address" text box.

9. Type   **Mary Smith's House** *(press Enter)*
            1987 Laurel Hill

10. Click on the check box to tell the macro that this is a surprise party.

11. Press **Enter** or click on **OK** to close the dialog box.

12. Click on **Print** on the Standard toolbar to print a copy of your beautiful party invitation.

Great! Now, make a party invitation of your own.

13. Click on **File, Close, No** to close the document window.

14. Click on **Window**.

15. Click on **Global: Party**

16. Click on **File, Close** to close the macro-editing window.

The Baseball Games Tracker

Let's write a macro that will help you keep track of your baseball game stats. You'll create a master file that contains all the stuff you want to keep track of: your "at bats," hits, walks, RBI's, home runs and runs scored for each game you played. You will create a dialog box to enter all of that information and a macro to add the information to the master list. Part of the macro will be recorded, part of it will be designed with the Dialog Editor and part of it will be written in the macro-editing window.

Create the Baseball Games File

The first thing you need to do is create a file to hold the baseball game information. Then, you'll write a macro that will open the file and add new information to it that you will enter in a custom dialog box.

1. Click on **New** on the Standard toolbar.
2. Click on **File**.
3. Click on **Page Setup...**
4. Click on **Margins**.
5. Set the following margins:
    Top: **1"**   Left: **1"**
    Bottom: **1"**   Right: **1"**
6. Click on **OK**.
7. Click on **Format**.
8. Click on **Font...**
9. Click on Font = **Courier New**, Font Style = **Bold**, Size = **20**
10. Click on **OK**.
11. Press **Ctrl + E** to turn on centering.
12. Type: **Maggie's Baseball Stats** (*Use your name*)
13. Press **Enter**.
14. Press **Ctrl + L** to turn on left justification.
15. Click on **Format**.
16. Click on **Font...**
17. Click on Font = **Courier New**, Font Style = **Regular**, Size = **12**
18. Click on **OK**.
19. Press **Enter** two times.
20. Click on **Format**.
21. Click on **Tabs. . .**
22. Click on **Clear All**.
23. Set the following tab stops:
    Tab Stop Position = **1.63**, Alignment = **Right**
    Click on **Set**.
    Tab Stop Position = **2.31**, Alignment = **Right**
    Click on **Set**.
    Tab Stop Position = **3.06**, Alignment = **Right**

Click on **Set**.
Tab Stop Position = **3.81**, Alignment = **Right**
Click on **Set**.
Tab Stop Position = **4.5**, Alignment = **Right**
Click on **Set**.
Tab Stop Position = **5.38**, Alignment = **Right**
Click on **Set**.
Tab Stop Position = **6.44**, Alignment = **Right**
Click on **Set**.

24. Click on **OK**.
25. Type: **Opponent**
26. Press the **Tab** key.
27. Type: **At**
28. Press the **Tab** key.
29. Type: **Hits**
30. Press the **Tab** key.
31. Type: **Walks**
32. Press the **Tab** key.
33. Type: **RBI's**
34. Press the **Tab** key.
35. Type: **Home**
36. Press the **Tab** key.
37. Type: **Runs**
38. Press **Enter**
39. Press the **Tab** key.
40. Type: **Bats**
41. Press the **Tab** key four times.
42. Type: **Runs**
43. Press the **Tab** key.
44. Type: **Scored**
45. Press **Enter** two times.
46. Press the **Delete** key.
47. Press **Enter**.

This is how the Baseball Games file should look:

Maggie's Baseball Stats

Opponent	At	Hits	Walks	RBI's	Home	Runs
	Bats				Runs	Scored

48. Click on **Save** on the Standard toolbar.
49. Type: **baseball** as the file name.
50. Click on **OK** (Word 6) or **Save** (Word 7) to save the file.
51. Click on **File**.

52.   Click on **Close**.

Record the Baseball Macro

Record a macro that will open the baseball games file and position the insertion point at the bottom of the document. Assign this macro to your toolbar, so it will be easy to run. If your toolbar is displayed on the screen, skip to step three. If your toolbar is not displayed, display it now.

1.   Click the right mouse button on a blank spot on the Standard toolbar. The list of available toolbars appears on the screen.
2.   Click on your toolbar name to display it.
3.   Click on **New** on the Standard toolbar.
4.   Double-click on **REC** on the Status Bar to turn on the macro recorder.
5.   Type: **Baseball** for the macro name
6.   Click in the **Description** box at the bottom of the screen to position the insertion point.
7.   Type: **Keep track of baseball game stats** for the description.
8.   Click on **Toolbars** to assign the macro to your toolbar.
9.   Drag the name **Baseball** to your toolbar.
      The Custom Button dialog box appears.
10.   Click on **Edit...** The Button Editor appears.
11.   Create a design for the button face that looks like a baseball diamond. Use this example, or create your own design for the button face.

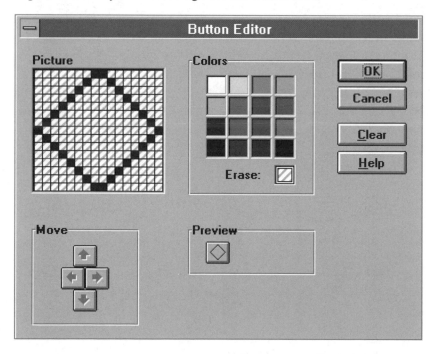

12.   Click on **OK**.
13.   Click on **Close**.
14.   Click on **Open** on the Standard toolbar.

15. Click on **baseball.doc** (Word 6) or **baseball** (Word 7) as the document to open.
16. Click on **OK** (Word 6) or **Open** (Word 7).
17. Press **Ctrl + End** to position the insertion point at the bottom of the document.
18. Click on **Stop** on the Macro Record toolbar.

Check out the Baseball macro to make sure it works.

1. Click on **File**.
2. Click on **Close**.
3. Click on the **Baseball** button on your toolbar to run the macro.
   The baseball games file appears on the screen, with the insertion point at the bottom of the document. The recorded part of the macro is finished.

Design the Baseball Games Dialog Box

Create a dialog box for entering the baseball game information next. Put the baseball games file away before you start designing the dialog box.

1. Click on **File**.
2. Click on **Close**.
3. Click on **Tools**.
4. Click on **Macro. . .**
5. Click on **Baseball** as the macro name.
6. Click on **Edit**.
7. Press **Alt + C** to add comments to the macro. Look at the Status bar at the bottom of the screen as you type the following comments.
   REM ***

REM Macro:	**Baseball**
REM Author:	**Maggie O'Hara**
REM Purpose:	**Keep track of baseball game stats**

   REM ***
8. If you're using Word 7, modify the FileOpen statement to include the exact location of the Baseball file. If you're using Word 6, you can skip this step.
   Type: FileOpen **.Name = "C:\My Documents\baseball.doc"**,
9. Click on the **Dialog Editor** button on the macro toolbar.
   A blank dialog box appears in the Dialog Editor. Change the title of the dialog box.
10. Click on **Edit**.
11. Click on **Info...** The Dialog Information screen appears.
12. Click in the text box to the right of the word "Text$" to position the insertion point.
13. Delete "**Microsoft Word**"
14. Type: **Baseball Games Tracker** as the title of the dialog box.
15. Click on **OK**.
    "Baseball Games Tracker" now appears as the title of the empty dialog box on the screen.

Adding Items to the Dialog Box

This is how the finished dialog box will look. It contains text items, text boxes and command buttons. This dialog box holds a lot of information, so let's begin by expanding the size of the dialog box.

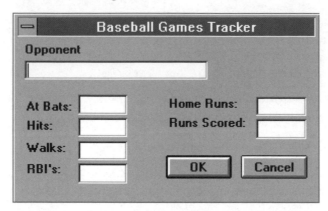

1. Move the mouse pointer to the lower right corner of the dialog box.
    The mouse pointer turns into a double-headed arrow.
2. Click and drag the double-headed arrow down and to the right to expand the size of the dialog box. Make the dialog box wider than it is tall.
3. Release the mouse button when the dialog box is the size you want.

Now that you've got plenty of space to work with, let's add the items to the dialog box.

4. Click on **Item**.
5. Click on **Text**.
6. Type: **Opponent**
    The first field in baseball games file is the name of the opposing team. So, that should be the first field you enter in the dialog box when the macro runs.
7. Click on **Item**.
8. Click on **Text Box**.
    A text box for entering the name of the opposing team appears below the text item.
9. Click on the right edge of the text box and drag it to the right with the double-headed arrow to expand the size of the box.
    Some baseball teams have long names, so make your text box large enough to accommodate them.
10. Double-click on "Edit Text."
11. In the .Field text box, delete .TextBox1 and type **.Opponent**
    "Opponent" is the name of the field that will be used inside the macro when you're referring to the name of the opposing team.
12. Click on **OK**.
13. Click on **Item**.
14. Click on **Text**.
15. Type: **At Bats:**

16. With the four-headed arrow, click and drag **At Bats** down a little, so that is not so close to the edit box above it.
17. Press **Enter**. Another text box is inserted into the dialog box.
18. Type: **Hits:**
19. Press **Enter**.
20. Type: **Walks:**
21. Press **Enter**.
22. Type: **RBI's:**
23. Click on **Item**.
24. Click on **Text Box**.
25. With the four-headed arrow click and drag the text box so that it is across from the text item "At Bats."
26. Double-click on the text box for entering the number of At Bats.
27. In the .Field text box, delete **.TextBox2** and type **.AtBats**
28. Click in the "**Width**" text box at the top of the screen.
29. Type: **65** as the width of the text box
30. Click on **OK** to close the Text Box Information screen.
31. Press **Enter**. The Dialog Editor creates a text box for entering the number of hits in the game.
32. Double-click on the text box for entering the number of hits.
33. In the .Field text box, delete **.TextBox3** and type **.Hits**
34. Click in the "**Width**" text box at the top of the screen.
35. Type: **65** as the width of the text box
    You're making this text box the same size as the one above it.
36. Click on **OK**.
37. Press **Enter**.
38. Double-click on the text box for entering the number of walks.
39. In the .Field text box, delete **.TextBox4** and type **.Walks**
40. In the Width text box, type **65**
41. Click on **OK**.
42. Press **Enter**.
43. Double-click on the text box for entering the number of RBI's.
44. In the .Field text box, delete **.TextBox5** and type **.RBIs**
45. In the Width text box, type **65**
46. Click on **OK**.
47. Click on **Item.**
48. Click on **Text**
49. Type: **Home Runs:**
50. With the four-headed arrow click and drag **Home Runs** to the right of the dialog box, across from the text box for entering the number of At Bats.
51. Press **Enter**
52. Type: **Runs Scored:**
53. Click on **Item**.
54. Click on **Text Box**.

55. With the four-headed arrow click and drag the text box so that it is to the right of the words, "Home Runs." If you need to make your dialog box wider, click on the right edge of the dialog box and drag the two-headed arrow to the right to expand the size of the box.

56. Double-click on the text box for entering the number of home runs.

57. In the .Field text box, delete **.TextBox6** and type **.HomeRuns**

58. In the Width text box, type **65**

59. Click on **OK**.

60. Press **Enter**.

61. Double-click on the text box for entering the number of runs scored.

62. In the .Field text box, delete **.TextBox7** and type **.RunsScored**

63. In the Width text box, type **65**

64. Click on **OK**.

65. Click on **Item**

66. Click on **Button…**

67. Press **Enter** to place an OK button in the dialog box.

68. Press **Enter** to place a Cancel button in the dialog box.

69. Click and drag the OK and Cancel buttons around in the dialog box so that they fit in the blank space below Home Runs and Runs Scored.

70. If you have some extra white space in your dialog box, you can remove it by making the dialog box smaller. To do this, click and drag the edges of the dialog box. Click on the bottom edge of the dialog box and drag the two-headed arrow up to make the dialog box shorter. Click on the right edge of the dialog box and drag the two-headed arrow to the left to make the dialog box narrower.

Copy the Dialog Box Definition Into the Macro

Your dialog box looks terrific! Copy it onto the clipboard, then into the Baseball macro.

1. Click on the title bar of the dialog box to select it.

2. Click on **Edit**.

3. Click on **Copy**.

    The dialog box definition is now on the clipboard.

4. Click on **File**.

5. Click on **Exit** to exit the Dialog Editor and return to the macro-editing window.

6. Position the insertion point on the End Sub statement at the end of the macro.

7. Press **Enter** to insert a blank line into the macro.

8. Press **Ctrl + V** to paste the dialog box definition from the clipboard into the macro.

The dialog box definition should look like the example below. There are seven fields that require your input in the Baseball Games Tracker dialog box. When the macro runs, the insertion point will travel to those seven fields in the order their statements appear in the dialog box definition. The order of Baseball Games Tracker is:

```
Begin Dialog UserDialog 396, 150, "Baseball Games Tracker"
    Text 10, 6, 75, 13, "Opponent", .Text1
    TextBox 10, 22, 243, 18, .Opponent                         1
    Text 11, 58, 61, 13, "At Bats:", .Text2
    Text 11, 77, 36, 13, "Hits:", .Text3
    Text 11, 96, 53, 13, "Walks:", .Text4
    Text 11, 115, 47, 13, "RBI's:", .Text5
    TextBox 80, 54, 65, 18, .AtBats                            2
    TextBox 80, 75, 65, 18, .Hits                              3
    TextBox 80, 96, 65, 18, .Walks                            4
    TextBox 80, 117, 65, 18, .RBIs                            5
    Text 201, 55, 93, 13, "Home Runs:", .Text6
    Text 201, 74, 104, 13, "Runs Scored:", .Text7
    TextBox 318, 55, 65, 18, .HomeRuns                        6
    TextBox 318, 76, 65, 18, .RunsScored                     7
    OKButton 198, 110, 88, 21
    CancelButton 297, 110, 88, 21
End Dialog
```

Define the Dialog Record

To use the Baseball Games Tracker dialog box in the Baseball macro you need to define the dialog record and display the dialog box.

1. Position the insertion point on the **End Sub** statement.
2. Press **Enter** to insert a blank line into the macro.
3. Type: **Dim GamesRecord As UserDialog** in the blank line.
    "GamesRecord" is the name of the dialog record. Any time you refer to a field in the macro, you'll type the record name, "GamesRecord" and then the field name.

Display the Dialog Box

Use the Dialog() function to display the Baseball Game Tracker dialog box.

1. Position the insertion point on the next line after the **Dim** statement.
2. Type: **ButtonChoice = Dialog(GamesRecord)**
    "ButtonChoice" is the name of the variable that will tell the macro how you closed the dialog box. "GamesRecord" is the name of the dialog record for the Baseball Game Tracker dialog box.

Use the Dialog Box Information in the Macro

The last step in completing the Baseball macro is to use the information from the dialog box in the macro. The logic in the Baseball macro is the same as the logic you used in the BasketballCards macro. The macro will:

1. Open the Baseball Games master file.
2. Position the insertion point at the bottom of the file.
3. Display the Baseball Game Tracker dialog box.
4. Check how you closed the dialog box.
5. If you clicked on OK to close the dialog box, update the Baseball.doc file by writing the information you entered in the dialog box to the master file.

6.   If you clicked on Cancel to close the dialog box, go to "Quit" and end the macro.

7.   Ask if you'd like to enter the information about another game.

8.   Check how you answered the question "Do you want to enter the information for another game?"

9.   If you clicked on "Yes" to enter another game, loop back up and display the dialog box again.

10. If you clicked on "No" to enter another game, continue running the macro by executing the next instruction.

11. Ask if you'd like to print and save the file.

12. Check how you answered the question "Do you want to save and print the file?"

13. If you clicked on "Yes" to save and print the file, execute the save and print commands in the macro.

14. If you clicked on "No" to save and print the file, end the macro.

Now let's write the WordBasic statements to make all this happen.

The Baseball macro will contain a loop to allow you to enter the information for more than one game at a time. Type a label statement to tell the macro where to go when it loops.

1.   Position the insertion point on the **Begin Dialog** statement.

2.   Press **Enter** to place a blank line into the macro.

3.   Type: **Continue:** in the blank line.

4.   Position the insertion point on the End Sub statement.

5.   Press **Enter** to insert a blank line into the macro.
     Type the following statements, beginning at the blank line.

6.   Type: **If ButtonChoice = 0 Then   'Check if Cancel button chosen**
     **   GoTo Quit:**
     **   EndIf**

7.   Type: **Insert GamesRecord.Opponent**
     This Insert statement will type the name of the team you played, which was entered in the Baseball Game Tracker dialog box, to the Baseball.doc master file. "GamesRecord" is the name of the dialog record, and "Opponent" is the name of the field within that record.

8.   Type: **Insert Chr$(9)** to press the Tab key in the document window.

9.   Type: **Insert GamesRecord.AtBats**
     This Insert statement will type the number of "at bats" in the baseball.doc master file.

10. Type: **Insert Chr$(9)** to press the Tab key in the document window.

11. Type: **Insert GamesRecord.Hits**
     This Insert statement types the number of hits you made in the baseball game in the baseball.doc master file.

12. Type: **Insert Chr$(9)** to press the Tab key in the document window.

13. Type: **Insert GamesRecord.Walks**
     This Insert statement types the number of walks you made in the baseball game in the baseball.doc master file.

14. Type: **Insert Chr$(9)** to press the Tab key in the document window.

15. Type: **Insert GamesRecord.RBIs**

This Insert statement types the number of RBI's in the baseball.doc master file.

16. Type: **Insert Chr$(9)** to press the Tab key in the document window.

17. Type: **Insert GamesRecord.HomeRuns**

This Insert statement types the number of home runs in the baseball.doc master file.

18. Type: **Insert Chr$(9)** to press the Tab key in the document window.

19. Type: **Insert GamesRecord.RunsScored**

This Insert statement types the number of runs scored in the baseball.doc master file.

20. Type: **InsertPara**

The InsertPara statement moves the insertion point down to the next line in the document window.

21. Type: **Again = MsgBox("Do you want to enter another game?", "Baseball Games Tracker", 36)**

This message box will allow you to choose whether you want to enter the information for another baseball game. You'll click on "Yes" if you want to enter another game, and "No" if you don't want to enter the information for another game.

22. Type: **If Again = - 1 Then'   Check if you want to enter another game**
         GoTo Continue:
      EndIf

If you want to enter the information for another game, the macro will loop back up to the label "Continue" and display the dialog box again. If you don't want to enter the information for another game, the macro will drop down to the next line and execute the statement it finds there.

23. Type: **PrintSave = MsgBox("Do you want to print and save the file?", "Baseball Games Tracker", 36)**

This message box will allow you to choose whether you want to print and save the baseball.doc file.

24. Type: **If PrintSave = - 1 Then   'Check if you want to print and save**
         FileSave
         FilePrint
      EndIf

25. Type: **Quit:**

This label statement is necessary to tell the macro where to go when you click on Cancel to close the Baseball Game Tracker dialog box.

The Baseball macro should look like this:

```
Sub MAIN
REM ********************************************************
REM Macro:     Baseball
REM Author:    Maggie O'Hara
REM Purpose:   Keep track of baseball game stats
REM ********************************************************
```

```
FileOpen .Name = "C:\My Documents\baseball.doc",
.ConfirmConversions = 0, .ReadOnly = 0, .AddToMru = 0,
.PasswordDoc = "", .PasswordDot = "", .Revert = 0,
.WritePasswordDoc = "", .WritePasswordDot = ""
EndOfDocument

Continue:
Begin Dialog UserDialog 396, 150, "Baseball Games Tracker"
    Text 10, 6, 75, 13, "Opponent", .Text1
    TextBox 10, 22, 243, 18, .Opponent
    Text 11, 58, 61, 13, "At Bats:", .Text2
    Text 11, 77, 36, 13, "Hits:", .Text3
    Text 11, 96, 53, 13, "Walks:", .Text4
    Text 11, 115, 47, 13, "RBI's:", .Text5
    TextBox 80, 54, 65, 18, .AtBats
    TextBox 80, 75, 65, 18, .Hits
    TextBox 80, 96, 65, 18, .Walks
    TextBox 80, 117, 65, 18, .RBIs
    Text 201, 55, 93, 13, "Home Runs:", .Text6
    Text 201, 74, 104, 13, "Runs Scored:", .Text7
    TextBox 318, 55, 65, 18, .HomeRuns
    TextBox 318, 76, 65, 18, .RunsScored
    OKButton 198, 110, 88, 21
    CancelButton 297, 110, 88, 21
End Dialog

Dim GamesRecord As UserDialog
ButtonChoice = Dialog(GamesRecord)
If ButtonChoice = 0 Then        'Check if Cancel button chosen
    Goto Quit :
EndIf
Insert GamesRecord.Opponent
Insert Chr$(9)
Insert GamesRecord.AtBats
Insert Chr$(9)
Insert GamesRecord.Hits
Insert Chr$(9)
Insert GamesRecord.Walks
Insert Chr$(9)
Insert GamesRecord.RBIs
Insert Chr$(9)
Insert GamesRecord.HomeRuns
Insert Chr$(9)
Insert GamesRecord.RunsScored
InsertPara

Again = MsgBox("Do you want to enter another game?", "Baseball
Games Tracker", 36)
If Again = -1 Then    'Check if you want to enter another game
    Goto Continue:
EndIf
PrintSave = MsgBox("Do you want to print and save the file?",
"Baseball Games Tracker", 36)
```

```
If PrintSave = -1 Then       'Check if you want to print and save
    FileSave
    FilePrint
EndIf
Quit:
End Sub
```

26. Click on **Save** on the Standard toolbar.
27. Click on **Yes**.

Let's try it out.

If you run your macro for the first time in a new document window and keep the macro-editing window open then you can easily fix any typing errors you may have made when you created the macro. If you get an error, click on Window, Global: Baseball and fix the highlighted statement. Resave the macro, then return to the document window and run the macro again. Make sure you click on File, Close to close the Baseball file before you run the macro again.

1.   Click on **New** on the Standard toolbar.
2.   Click on the **Baseball** button on your toolbar.
     The Baseball file is open in the document window. The Baseball Games Tracker dialog box appears on the screen. The insertion point is in the Opponent field, waiting for you to enter the name of the team you played.
3.   Type: **Astros**
4.   Press the **Tab** key to move to the At Bats field.
5.   Type: **4**   At Bats
6.   Press the **Tab** key to move to the Hits field.
7.   Type: **2**   Hits
8.   Press the **Tab** key to move to the Walks field.
9.   Type: **1**   Walk
10. Press the **Tab** key to move to the RBI's field.
11. Type: **1**   RBI
12. Press the **Tab** key to move to the Home Runs field.
13. Type: **0**   Home Runs
14. Press the **Tab** key to move to the Runs Scored field.
15. Type: **1**   Run Scored
16. Press **Enter** or click on **OK** to close the dialog box.
17. Press **Enter** or click on **Yes** when a message box appears asking if you'd like to enter the information for another game.
18. Type: **Yankees**
19. Press the **Tab** key to move to the At Bats field.
20. Type: **3**   At Bats
21. Press the **Tab** key to move to the Hits field.
22. Type: **2**   Hits
23. Press the **Tab** key to move to the Walks field.
24. Type: **0**   Walks
25. Press the **Tab** key to move to the RBI's field.

26. Type: **0**   RBI's
27. Press the **Tab** key to move to the Home Runs field.
28. Type: **1**   Home Run
29. Press the **Tab** key to move to the Runs Scored field.
30. Type: **1**   Run Scored
31. Press **Enter** or click on **OK** to close the dialog box.
32. Click on **No** when a message box appears asking if you'd like to enter the information for another game.
33. Click on **Yes** when a message box appears asking if you'd like to print and save the file.

   Check out those stats! You're ready for the major league!

34. Click on **File**.
35. Click on **Close**.

   Remember to close the Baseball file when you're done with the Baseball macro.

36. Click on **Window**.
37. Click on **Global: Baseball**.
38. Click on **File, Close** to close the macro-editing window.

In the next chapter, we're going to see how smart macros are in math by making some macro games. You already know how to make your life easier with macros —

Now let's add some fun!

CHAPTER 7

Math, Games, & Other Great Stuff

Computers are fantastic math wizards. One of the main things they did when they were first invented was crunch numbers, and they're still used for that purpose a lot today. In this chapter, we're going to look at some of the things macros can do with numbers. You'll learn things you need to understand to create games and other powerful tools. It will dazzle and amaze you!

Expressions

An expression is made up of numbers that perform a mathematical calculation, like "2 + 4." Expressions in the world of macros are just like the expressions you work with in Math class.

You can use numbers or numeric variables in a WordBasic expression. An expression contains an operator that tells WordBasic which type of mathematical calculation you want to perform (addition, subtraction, multiplication, or division). For example,

87 + 95

> An expression made up of the numbers eighty seven and ninety five, joined by the operator: plus. WordBasic knows to add the two numbers together.

Grade/NumberOfScores

> An expression made up of the numeric variables "Grade" and "NumberOfScores" joined by the division operator. WordBasic knows to take the value of the variable "Grade" and divide it by the value in the variable "NumberOfScores."

You can use any of the standard operators in a macro.

+	Addition
–	Subtraction
*	Multiplication
/	Division

In a WordBasic numeric expression, the result of the calculation, the answer, is placed in a numeric variable. Here are a few examples of WordBasic numeric expressions:

Answer = Factor * 10

> The value of the variable "Factor" will be multiplied by 10 and stored in the variable "Answer."

TotalScore = Test1 + Test2

> The value of the variable "Test1" will be added to the value in the variable "Test2" and stored in the variable "TotalScore."

Decimal = Numerator / Denominator

> The value of the variable "Numerator" will be divided by the value of the variable "Denominator" and stored in the variable "Decimal."

Expressions in Macros

In this chapter, we're going to look at using numeric expressions in macros. This ability to tell a macro to perform mathematical calculations opens up a whole new world of things you can do with Microsoft Word.

When you want to include a numeric expression in a macro, the first thing you need to do is figure out how you would do the calculation yourself. You need to give the macro exact directions, so make sure you are really clear about how the calculation works. A macro will calculate an expression the same way you do, so once you know how to do the calculation manually, all you have to do is write an expression in the macro to do the same thing.

Converting Strings to Numbers

The most common ways to enter information into a macro are through text boxes in a custom dialog box or through InputBox$( ) functions. Both of these methods store the information you enter as text information. In order for WordBasic to perform a mathematical calculation, the variables in the expression must be numeric. WordBasic can't calculate using a string variable, even if there is a number in that string variable. Because of this WordBasic rule, you sometimes need to convert string variables to numeric variables before you calculate an expression.

THE VAL() FUNCTION

The Val( ) function is used to convert string variables to numeric variables so they can be used in mathematical calculations. The syntax of the Val() function is:

Val (a$)

"Val" is the name of the function. It stands for "Value." Using this function tells WordBasic to find the *value* of the string it finds inside the parentheses. "a$" contains the text string that will be converted. For example:

Number$

> Number$ is a string variable that was entered in an Input box. In order to use Number$ in a mathematical calculation, you must convert it to a numeric variable with the Val function. Val(Number$).

DialogRecord.Number$

> DialogRecord.Number$ is a variable that was entered in a text box in a custom dialog box. In order to use DialogRecord.Number$ in a mathematical calculation, you must convert it to a numeric variable with the Val function. Val(DialogRecord.Number$).

You can combine the Val function with a WordBasic expression to perform a calculation with data that was entered in an Input box or a custom dialog box.

GradeAverage = Val(TotalScores$) / Val(NumberOfScores$)
Decimal = Val(FractionRecord.Numerator$) / Val(FractionRecord.Denominator$)

Converting Numbers to Strings

WordBasic is very logical. It gives you a way to convert string values to numeric values, and it also gives you a way to convert numeric values back to string values. Some WordBasic statements and functions accept only string values. The MsgBox statement and the Insert statement are two statements that accept only string values.

THE STR$() FUNCTION

If you want to use a numeric variable in a MsgBox statement or an Insert statement, you need to use the Str$() function to convert the number to a text string.

The syntax of the Str$() function is:

Str$(*n*)

"Str$" is the name of the function. It stands for "String." Using this function tells WordBasic to convert the number it finds inside the parentheses to a *string of characters*. "*n*" contains the number that will be converted. Let's look at an example of the Str$() function in an Insert statement.

Insert Str$(GradeAverage)

This Insert statement types the value of the numeric variable "GradeAverage" in the document window. The Str$() function converts the number in the variable "GradeAverage" to a string of characters that can be printed.

When you're running a macro with a numeric expression, if you encounter the error message "Type Mismatch," it means that you forgot to convert a string variable to a numeric variable, or a numeric variable to a string variable. Word was expecting one "type" of data, and you gave it a different type. This is an easy problem to fix. Just check all your variables and make sure they are numeric variables when you're using them to calculate and string variables when you're displaying them.

Let's put all this stuff together and make a macro.

Fraction-to-Decimal Macro

Let's create a macro that will calculate the decimal value of a fraction. Before you begin writing the macro, think about how you would do the calculation yourself. Remember this section in Math class — divide the numerator by the denominator to get the decimal value of a fraction. You will enter the numerator and denominator in a dialog box, and use Val () functions to convert the text strings into numeric variables. The numeric variables will then be used in a numeric expression to perform the calculation. The last step will be to use Str$() functions to convert the numeric variables to string variables so that the result of the calculation can be printed on the screen.

1. Click on **Tools**.
2. Click on **Macro...**

3. Type: **FractionToDecimal** as the macro name.
4.Click once in the description box to position the insertion point.
5. Type: **Calculate the decimal value of a fraction** as the description.
6. Click on **Create**.
7. Press **Alt + C** to play the Comments macro. Look at the Status bar at the bottom
    of the screen as you type the following comments.
    REM **
    REM Macro: FractionToDecimal (Alt + F)
    REM Author:Gerry Laird
    REM Purpose: Calculate the decimal value of a fraction
    REM **
8. Click on the **Dialog Editor** button on the macro toolbar.
    A blank dialog box appears in the Dialog Editor. Change the title of the dialog
    box.
9. Click on **Edit**.
10. Click on **Info...** The Dialog Information screen appears.
    11.   In the "Text$" box, delete Microsoft Word and type: **Fraction To
    Decimal Converter**
12. Click on **OK**.
    "Fraction To Decimal Converter" now
    appears as the title of the empty dialog
    box on the screen. Now, design the
    dialog box.

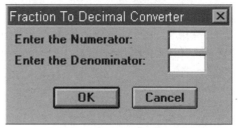

**Enter the numerator and
denominator in a custom dialog box**

13. Click on **Item**.
14. Click on **Text**.
15. Type: **Enter the Numerator:**
16. Press **Enter** to place another text item in
    the dialog box.
17. Type: **Enter the Denominator:**
18. Click on **Item**.
19. Click on **Text Box**.
20. Double-click on the text box.
21. In the .Field text box, delete **.TextBox1** and type **.Numerator$**
22. In the Width text box, type **52** as the width of the box.
23. Click on **OK**.
24. Click and drag the text box for entering the numerator to the right side of the
    dialog box, across from the text, "Enter the Numerator."
25. Press **Enter** to place another text box in the dialog box.
26. Double-click on the text box for entering the denominator.
27. In the .Field text box, delete **.TextBox2** and type **.Denominator$**
28. In the Width text box, type **52** as the width of the box.
29. Click on **OK**.
30. Click on **Item**.
31. Click on **Button...**

32. Press **Enter** to place an OK button in the dialog box.
33. Click and drag the OK button to the bottom left side of the dialog box.
34. Press **Enter** to place a Cancel button in the dialog box.
35. Click and drag the Cancel button to the right of the OK button.
36. If you have too much white space in your dialog box, you can remove it by making the dialog box smaller. Do this by clicking and dragging any edge of the dialog box.

   That should just about do it. Now, copy the dialog box definition into the macro.

37. Click on the title bar of the dialog box to select it.
38. Click on **Edit**.
39. Click on **Copy**.
40. Click on **File**.
41. Click on **Exit**.
42. Position the insertion point on the End Sub statement.
43. Press **Enter** to place a blank line in the macro, then _ to place the insertion point on that blank line.
44. Press **Ctrl + V** to paste the dialog box definition into the macro.
45. Press **Enter** to move the insertion point down to the next line.
   Type the following statements, beginning at the blank line.
46. Type: **Dim FractionRecord As UserDialog**
   The Dim statement defines the dialog record for the Fraction dialog box.
47. Type: **ButtonChoice = Dialog(FractionRecord)**
   "ButtonChoice" is the name of the variable that will tell the macro how you closed the dialog box. "FractionRecord" is the name of the dialog record for the Fraction dialog box.
48. Type: **If ButtonChoice = 0 Then**
   GoTo Quit:
   EndIf
49. Type: **Decimal = Val(FractionRecord.Numerator$) / Val(FractionRecord.Denominator$)**
   The formula for converting a fraction to a decimal is to divide the numerator by the denominator. Division is shown with a slash (/) in a macro expression. The answer will be stored in the numeric variable "Decimal."
50. Type: **Insert FractionRecord.Numerator$ + " / " + FractionRecord.Denominator$ + " = " + Str$(Decimal)**
   This Insert statement types the fraction and its equivalent decimal value on the screen. FractionRecord.Numerator$ and FractionRecord.Denominator$ type the string variables that were entered in the dialog box on the screen. Str$(Decimal) converts the numeric variable, "Decimal" to a string variable, and types it on the screen.
51. Type: **InsertPara**
   The InsertPara statement moves the insertion point down one line, so that if you want to run the macro again, the insertion point will be in the right spot.
52. Type: **Quit:**

This label statement is necessary to tell the macro where to go when you click on Cancel to close the dialog box.

The FractionToDecimal macro should look like this:

```
Sub MAIN
REM***********************************************************
REM Macro:      FractionToDecimal (Alt + F)
REM Author:     Gerry Laird
REM Purpose:    Calculate the decimal value of a fraction
REM***********************************************************
Begin Dialog UserDialog 288, 90, "Fraction To Decimal Converter"
    Text 10, 6, 159, 13, "Enter the Numerator:", .Text1
    Text 10, 25, 176, 13, "Enter the Denominator:", .Text2
    TextBox 213, 5, 52, 18, .Numerator$
    TextBox 213, 26, 52, 18, .Denominator$
    OKButton 61, 58, 88, 21
    CancelButton 163, 58, 88, 21
End Dialog

Dim FractionRecord As UserDialog
ButtonChoice = Dialog(FractionRecord)
If ButtonChoice = 0 Then
    Goto Quit:
EndIf
Decimal = Val(FractionRecord.Numerator$) /
Val(FractionRecord.Denominator$)
Insert FractionRecord.Numerator$ + " / " +
FractionRecord.Denominator$ + " = " + Str$(Decimal)
InsertPara
Quit:
End Sub
```

53. Click on **Save** on the Standard toolbar.
54. Click on **Yes**.

Before you assign this macro to a keyboard shortcut key, its a good idea to test it a few times to make sure it works.

1.   Click on **New** on the Standard toolbar.
2.   Click on **Tools**.
3.   Click on **Macro...**
4.   Click on **FractionToDecimal**.
5.   Click on **Run**.
      The Fraction To Decimal dialog box appears on the screen.
6.   Type: **1** as the numerator.
7.   Press the **Tab** key to move to the denominator text box.
8.   Type: **2** as the denominator.
9.   Press **Enter** or click on **OK** to close the dialog box.
      The macro will calculate the decimal equivalent of the fraction ½ and type "1 / 2 = 0.5" on the screen.

Try another one.
1. Click on **Tools**.
2. Click on **Macro…**
3. Click on **FractionToDecimal**.
4. Click on **Run**.
5. Type: **2** as the numerator.
6. Press the **Tab** key.
7. Type: **5** as the denominator.
8. Press **Enter** or click on **OK** to close the dialog box.
   The macro calculates the decimal and types "2 / 5 = 0.4" on the screen.

Now, assign the macro to the keyboard shortcut key Alt + F (for Fractions).
1. Click on **Tools**.
2. Click on **Customize…**
3. Click on **Keyboard**.
4. Click on **Macros** under Categories.
5. Click on **FractionToDecimal** under Macros
6. Click in the box **Press new shortcut key**.
7. Press **Alt + F**.
   Look below the "Press new shortcut key" box to make sure Alt + F is currently unassigned. If it is already assigned to another function, pick a different shortcut key.
8. Click on **Assign**.
9. Click on **Close**.

Run the FractionToDecimal macro by pressing Alt + F. Use the fractions: 1/4, 3/4 and 3/8. When you get to this section in Math class, you can check your homework with the macro.

More Than One Numeric Expression in a Macro

A macro can have as many numeric expressions as you need to perform the task you have in mind. You now have a macro that will convert any fraction to its decimal equivalent. Wouldn't it be great if the macro could also calculate percent? If you add a numeric expression to the FractionToDecimal macro instructing the macro to multiply the decimal answer by one hundred, you could calculate the percent as well as the decimal value of a fraction. Let's check it out.
1. Click on **Window**.
2. Click on **Global: FractionToDecimal**.
3. Position the insertion point on the Insert statement:
   Insert FractionRecord.Numerator$. . . .
4. Press **Enter** to create a blank line in the macro.
5. Type: **Percent = Decimal * 100** in the blank line.
   The mathematical formula for converting a decimal to a percent is to multiply the decimal by 100. The macro already knows the decimal value of the fraction. It's in the variable "Decimal." You can use the variable "Decimal" to perform the second calculation.

6.   Modify the Insert statement by adding the highlighted text.
     Insert FractionRecord.Numerator$ + " / " + FractionRecord.Denominator$ + "
     = " + Str$(Decimal) + " = " + Str$(Percent) + "%"
7.   Click on **Save** on the Standard toolbar.
8.   Click on **Yes**.
9.   Click on **Window**.
10. Click on the document window.
11. Press **Alt + F** to test the FractionToDecimal macro. Use the fractions: 1/2, 2/5,
     4/5 and 7/8. The macro prints the fraction, then the decimal equivalent, then the
     percentage. Pretty slick!

Creating a Loop With the GoTo Statement

As we saw in the last chapter, the GoTo statement is used to tell the macro to go
to another spot in the macro and continue by executing the instructions it finds there.

**A Go statement can tell a macro to skip a bunch of instructions and
go to the end of the macro.**

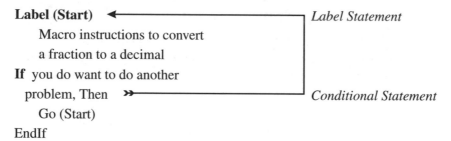

Macro instructions to display a dialog box.
If you clicked on Cancel to
  close the dialog box, Then   *Conditional Statement*
      Go (End)
EndIf
Label (End)   *Label Statement*

**A Go statement can tell a macro to repeat a bunch of instructions
and go to the beginning of the macro.**

Label (Start)   *Label Statement*
    Macro instructions to convert
    a fraction to a decimal
If you do want to do another
    problem, Then   *Conditional Statement*
      Go (Start)
EndIf

In the FractionToDecimal macro, you have to run the macro for each fraction you
want to convert to a decimal. It would save a lot of time if the macro let you do
several problems without having to re-run the macro each time. You can add a loop to
the macro, telling it to start at the top of the macro and perform the instructions again,
as illustrated in the flow chart on the next page..

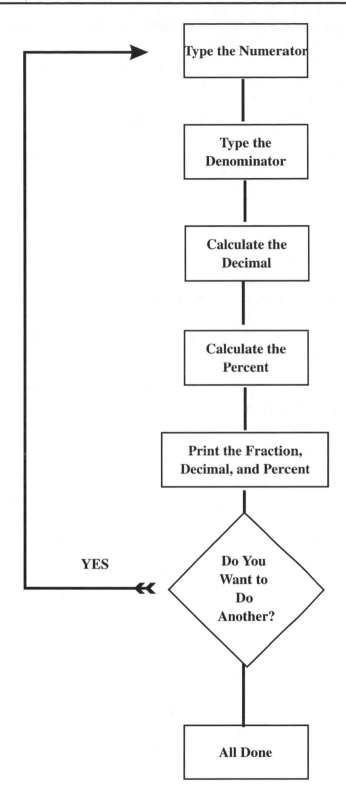

Let's add a GoTo statement and a conditional statement to create a loop in the FractionToDecimal macro.

1.   Click on **Window**.
2.   Click on **Global: FractionToDecimal**.
3.   Position the insertion point on the Begin Dialog statement.
4.   Press **Enter** to insert a blank line into the macro.
5.   Type: **Start:** in the blank line.
     This label identifies where you want the macro to go when it loops.
6.   Position the insertion point on the Quit: statement.
7.   Press **Enter** to insert a blank line into the macro. Type the following MsgBox() function in the blank line.
8.   Type: **Button = MsgBox ("Do you want to do another problem?", "Fraction to Decimal Converter", 4)**
     This MsgBox function will display the question "Do you want to do another?" on the screen. The title of the message box is "Fraction to Decimal Converter." The number four instructs the macro to place yes and no buttons in the message box.
9.   Type: **If Button = - 1 Then   'Check if you want to do another**
                   GoTo Start:
              EndIf
     If you want to do another problem, the macro will go to the label "Start" and display the dialog box for entering the numerator and denominator again. If you don't want to do another problem, the macro will end.

The FractionToDecimal macro should look like this:

```
Sub MAIN
REM*****************************************************************
REM Macro:      FractionToDecimal (Alt + F)
REM Author:     Gerry Laird
REM Purpose:    Calculate the decimal value of a fraction
REM*****************************************************************

Start:
Begin Dialog UserDialog 292, 86, "Fraction To Decimal Converter"
    Text 10, 6, 159, 13, "Enter the Numerator:", .Text1
    Text 10, 25, 176, 13, "Enter the Denominator:", .Text2
    TextBox 220, 5, 52, 18, .Numerator$
    TextBox 220, 26, 52, 18, .Denominator$
    OKButton 45, 54, 88, 21
    CancelButton 149, 54, 88, 21
End Dialog

Dim FractionRecord As UserDialog
ButtonChoice = Dialog(FractionRecord)
If ButtonChoice = 0 Then
    Goto Quit:
EndIf
Decimal = Val(FractionRecord.Numerator$)/
Val(FractionRecord.Denominator$)
```

```
Percent = Decimal * 100
Insert FractionRecord.Numerator$ + " / " +
FractionRecord.Denominator$ + " = " + Str$(Decimal) + " = " +
Str$(Percent) + "%"
InsertPara
Button = MsgBox("Do you want to do another problem?",
"Fraction to Decimal Converter", 4)
If Button = - 1 Then          'Check if you want to do another
    Goto Start:
EndIf
Quit:
End Sub
```

10. Click on **Save** on the Standard toolbar.
11. Click on **Yes**.
12. Click on **Window**.
13. Click on the document window.
14. Press **Alt + F** to run the macro. Type the numerator and denominator and press **Enter** or click on **OK**. Press **Enter** or click on **Yes** to do another problem. Do several problems, answering **Yes** to allow the macro to loop back up to the top and run the macro again. After you've run the macro several times, click on **No** to allow the macro to end.
15. Click on **Window**.
16. Click on **Global: FractionToDecimal**
17. Click on **File, Close** to close the document window.

Spaghetti Programming

In the world of computer programming one of the most frightening conditions is "spaghetti programming." Spaghetti programming occurs when GoTo statements tell a program to go over here and perform some instructions, then go over there and perform some instructions, then go somewhere else and perform some instructions. The program is jumping around all over the place and ends up getting tangled up like a plate of spaghetti. This is not good! You need to be careful, when you use a GoTo statement, that the macro goes to one location and has a definite way to stop, or end the loop. In the FractionToDecimal loop, the loop ends when you answer "no" to the question "Do you want to do another?"

The Endless Loop

An endless loop occurs when a program is stuck in a loop and can't get out. The GoTo statement is a statement that can cause an endless loop, so be careful. When you use a GoTo statement in a macro make doubly sure that you have allowed a way for the macro to end. Your message boxes should always contain two choices, "Yes" and "No" or "OK" and "Cancel." So, you can press "no" or "cancel" as a way out of the loop.

If you ever find yourself in an endless loop, you can press the Esc (Escape) key to end the macro.

Future Date Macro

Let's write another macro that uses a numeric expression to do a mathematical calculation. The FutureDate macro counts the number of days between today and a future date that you enter. This macro comes in handy when you need to figure out how many days there are until a report is due, or until your birthday, or until school is out. You'll enter the date in an Input box and use two WordBasic date functions, Today () and DateValue () to perform the calculation.

THE TODAY() FUNCTION

The Today () function tells you the serial number for today's date according to the computer's system date. A serial date is a date that computers use to perform mathematical calculations. It's really easy for the computer to work with dates in this format, because they are in the form of numbers, like 35103.

THE DATEVALUE() FUNCTION

The DateValue () function converts a date entered as text into a serial number date. For example, if you enter the date December 18, 1997, the serial date would be 35782. To figure out the number of days between two dates, WordBasic just subtracts the two serial numbers. For example, the date December 18, 1997 has a serial date of 35782. Today's date has a serial date of 35715. To figure out the number of days between today and December 18, 1997, WordBasic does a simple subtraction problem: 35782 − 35715. Now, let's create the FutureDate macro and see how all of this works.

1. Click on **Tools**.
2. Click on **Macro...**
3. Type: **FutureDate** as the macro name.
4. Click once in the description box to position the insertion point.
5. Type: **Calculate the number of days between today and a future date**
6. Click on **Create**.
7. Press **Alt + C** to play the Comments macro. Look at the Status bar at the bottom of the screen as you type the following comments.

    REM ***
    REM Macro: **FutureDate (Alt + T)**
    REM Author: **Chris Smith**
    REM Purpose: **Calculate the number of days between today and a**
    REM   **future date**
    REM***

8. Type: **FutureDate$ = InputBox$ ("Enter a future date using the format Month, Day, Year, like August 2, 1998", "A Look Into the Future")**
    When the macro runs, an Input box will appear on the screen asking you to type a date in the future. The date you enter will be stored in the variable "FutureDate$."
9. Type: **SerialFutureDate = DateValue (FutureDate$)**

This statement translates the text date you entered, stored in the string variable FutureDate$, into a serial date and stores it in the numeric variable "SerialFutureDate."

10. Type: **NumDays = SerialFutureDate - Today( )**

This expression calculates the number of days between the date you entered and today. The answer will be stored in the numeric variable "NumDays." SerialFutureDate is the numeric variable that holds the serial date for the date you entered in the Input box. The function "Today ( )" is already in serial date format, so WordBasic can just subtract the two numbers. Internally, the expression might look like this,

$$32 = 36504 - 36472$$

11. Type: **MsgBox "The number of days between today and " + FutureDate$ + " is " + Str$(NumDays), "A Look Into the Future"**

The MsgBox statement displays a message box on the screen. "A Look Into the Future" will appear as the title of the box. The message inside the box will tell you the number of days between the date you entered (stored in thestring variable FutureDate$) and today's date. The Str$() function is used to convert the numeric variable "NumDays" to a string variable that can be displayed in a MsgBox statement.

The FutureDate macro should look like this:

```
Sub MAIN
REM ***************************************************
REM Macro:      FutureDate (Alt + T)
REM Author:     Chris Smith
REM Purpose:    Calculate the number of days between today and a
REM             future date
REM ***************************************************
FutureDate$ = InputBox$("Enter a future date using the format
Month, Day, Year, like August 2, 1998", "A Look Into the
Future")

SerialFutureDate = DateValue(FutureDate$)

NumDays = SerialFutureDate - Today()

MsgBox "The number of days between today and " + FutureDate$ +
" is " + Str$(NumDays), "A Look Into the Future"

End Sub
```

12. Click on **Save** on the Standard toolbar.
13. Click on **Yes**.

Now, test the macro.

1. Click on **Window**.
2. Click on the document window.
3. Click on **Tools**.
4. Click on **Macro...**
5. Click on **FutureDate**.

6.　Click on **Run**.

An Input box appears on the screen asking you to type the date.

7.　Type: *the date of your next birthday* in the format month, day, year.

8.　Click on **OK**.

The macro will calculate the number of days between today and your next birthday.

9.　Click on **OK** to clear the message box from the screen.

Assign the macro to the keyboard shortcut key Alt + T (for Time).

1.　Click on **Tools**.

2.　Click on **Customize...**

3.　Click on **Keyboard**.

4.　Click on **Macros** under Categories.

5.　Click on **FutureDate** under Macros

6.　Click in the box **Press new shortcut key**.

7.　Press **Alt + T**.

Look below the "Press new shortcut key" box to make sure Alt + T is unassigned. If it is already assigned to another function, pick a different shortcut key.

8.　Click on **Assign**.

9.　Click on **Close**.

10.　Run the FutureDate macro by pressing Alt + T. Run it for the date summer vacation begins, two weeks from today and a crazy date in the future.

11.　Click on **Window**.

12.　Click on **Global: FutureDate**.

13.　Click on **File, Close** to close the macro-editing window.

*R*elational *O*perators

Lots of games are based on making comparisons. For example, you check how your answer compares with something in the game. When you want to make comparisons in a macro, use relational operators. Relational operators are symbols that state how values stand in *relation* to each other. Are they the same, is one bigger than the other, is one smaller than the other? How do they compare? The relational operators in the following table are probably familiar to you from Math class.

Relational Operator	Meaning
=	Equal to
<>	Not equal to
>	Greater than
>=	Greater than or equal to (like $\geq$ in Math class)
<	Less than
<=	Less than or equal to (like $\leq$ in Math class)

Word evaluates expressions with relational operators as either true or false. For example,

Expression	Evaluation
4 = 6	False (4 is not equal to 6)
7<> 6	True (7 is not equal to 6)
9>12	False (9 is not greater than 12)
8<= 8	True (8 is equal to 8)
8<=9	True (8 is less than 9)

Word can also evaluate expressions that contain numeric variables. Substitute the variable name for the actual number, and use the same operators. For example,

Expression	Evaluation
MathGrade = 95	True (if the value of the variable "MathGrade" is 95)
MathGrade>80	False (if the value of the variable "MathGrade" is 75)
Count<=Total	True (if the value of the variable "Count" is 6 and the value of the variable "Total" is 6)

Relational Operators in Macro Statements

A macro can use relational operators to make comparisons in the macro. For example, if you enter a number in an Input box, the macro could check the value of the number you entered.

If Val(Number$) = 100

This statement checks to see if the value of the number you entered in an Input box is equal to one hundred. If it is, the macro will perform one set of instructions. If it isn't, the macro will perform another set of instructions.

If Val(Number$) TotalScore

This statement checks to see if the value of the number you entered in an Input box is greater than the value of the number in the numeric variable "TotalScore." If it is, the macro will perform one set of instructions. If it isn't, the macro will perform another set of instructions. We're going to look at several examples of macros that use relational operators to make comparisons. The first example is a game.

The Random Number Game

We're going to write a macro that will play a guessing game. It's called the Random Number Game. This macro will pick a random number and let you guess the number. A random number is any old number that someone (or something) picks. In this case the computer will pick the number. You'll use the Rnd() function, GoTo statements and nested If statements to write this game.

THE RANDOM NUMBER FUNCTION

The Rnd() function is used to generate random numbers. When you write the instruction, you specify the range of numbers you want the number to be selected from. Maybe you want any number between 1 and 50, or any number between 0 and 10. The syntax of the Rnd() function is:

$$\textbf{Int(Rnd() * (}\textit{b - a}\textbf{) + a)}$$

It's not as scary as it looks. "Int" tells the macro that the random number is an integer. Without "Int," the random number would be something like, 11.8645045789321. "Int" turns the number into 11. "Rnd" tells the macro to pick a random number (any old number). The rest of the function tells the macro to pick the random number *between* the numbers you specify in *a* and *b*. "*b*" is the high number of the pair, and "*a*" is the low number. The random number will be greater than or equal to the low number (a) and less than the high number (b). Here's how it works.

$$Number = Int(Rnd() * (51 - 1) + 1$$

"Number" is a numeric variable that will hold the random number. Word will select any number from one to fifty. When you write the Rnd() function, the low number is the number you want to start with, and the high number is one more than the maximum number you want to select.

Guess = Int(Rnd() * (7-1) + 1)   Generates a random number from 1 to 6.
Factor = Int(Rnd() * (13-0) + 0)   Generates a random number from 0 to 12.

NESTED IF'S

Several decisions are necessary in the RandomNumber game, so we'll use nested If statements to make those decisions. In the RandomNumber game, you'll guess a number. The macro will check to see if your number matches the number the computer picked. There are three possibilities for evaluating the guess,

    Your number matches the random number
    Your number is greater than the random number
    Your number is less than the random number

If your guess matches the computer's number, you win and the game is over. If your guess is greater than the computer's number, the macro needs to tell you that, and ask if you want to guess again.

If YourGuess > RandomNumber Then   *The first If statement*
    Your guess was too high. Do you want to guess again?
    If you want to guess again Then   *The second If statement*
        Go back to the top and guess again
    EndIf
EndIf

The first If statement checks to see if your number is greater than the random number. If it is, then the macro evaluates the second If statement asking if you'd like to guess again. This second If statement is known as a nested If because it is *between* the first If and EndIf. The macro will only evaluate the second If statement if the first If statement is true. The macro needs the second If statement because if the macro automatically looped back up to the top of the program when you guessed the wrong number, you could end up in an endless loop.

If you want to guess again, then the program will loop back up to the top of the macro and ask you to enter another number. If you don't want to guess again, the program will end. Notice how each If statement has a matching EndIf statement.

Let's write the RandomNumber game and see how all this fits together.

1.   Click on **Tools**.

2.   Click on **Macro...**

3.   Type: **RandomNumber** as the macro name.

4.   Click once in the description box to position the insertion point.

5.   Type: **Guessing game to guess a random number**

6.   Click on **Create**.

7.   Press **Alt + C** to play the Comments macro. Look at the Status bar at the bottom of the screen as you type the following comments.

REM ***

REM Macro: RandomNumber

REM Author: Frances Eggers

REM Purpose: Guessing game to guess a random number

REM ***

8.   Type: **Title\$ = "Random Number Game"**

This statement creates a string variable named "Title\$" that contains the words "Random Number Game." The Input boxes and Message boxes can use the variable "Title\$" instead of having to type the great big old long title in each statement.

9.   Type: **RandomNumber = Int(Rnd() * (51 - 1) + 1)**

This statement generates a random number between one and fifty and places it in the numeric variable "RandomNumber."

10.   Type: **Guess:**

This Label statement tells the macro where to begin the loop for making guesses at the random number. It is placed after the statement that generates the random number. (Can't have the macro changing the number every time you make a guess).

11.   Type: **Guess\$ = InputBox\$("I am thinking of a number between 1 and 50. Try to guess my number. What is your guess?", Title\$)**

This Input box will ask you to enter a number. The number you type will be stored in the variable "Guess\$."

12.   Type: **If Val (Guess\$) = RandomNumber Then**

MsgBox "My number was " + Str\$(RandomNumber) + "." + Chr\$(32) + Chr\$(32) + "Good Guessing!", Title\$

EndIf

This If statement compares your guess, which is stored in the variable "Guess\$" with the number that the computer picked, which is stored in the variable "RandomNumber." If the numbers are equal a message box will appear on the screen telling you that you guessed the number. If the numbers do not match, the macro will move down to the next instruction and follow the instructions it finds there.

13.   Type: **If Val (Guess$) > RandomNumber Then**

        Button = MsgBox ("Your guess was too high. Do you want to try again?", Title$, 4)

        If Button = -1 Then

            GoTo Guess:

        EndIf

    EndIf

If Word finds that your guess was greater than the random number it chose, then it will display a message box on the screen asking if you want to guess again. If you want to guess again, the macro will loop back up to the top of the macro and display the Input box for entering your guess. If your guess was not greater than the random number, then the macro will skip the second If statement and go down to the next instruction it finds after the last EndIf statement.

14.   Type: **If Val (Guess$) < RandomNumber Then**

        Button = MsgBox ("Your guess was too low. Do you want to try again?", Title$, 4)

        If Button = -1 Then

            GoTo Guess:

        EndIf

    EndIf

If your guess was less than the computer's random number, then a message box will appear on the screen asking if you want to try again. If you do, then the macro will loop back up to the top and display the Input box again. If your guess was not less than the computer's random number (a false condition) then the macro will skip the second If statement and go down to the next instruction it finds after the last EndIf statement. The macro finds the End Sub statement, and the program ends.

The RandomNumber macro should look like this:

```
Sub MAIN
REM **************************************************
REM Macro:      RandomNumber
REM Author:     Frances Eggers
REM Purpose:    Guessing game to guess a random number
REM **************************************************
Title$ = "Random Number Game"
RandomNumber = Int(Rnd() * (51 - 1) + 1)

Guess:
Guess$ = InputBox$("I am thinking of a number between 1 and
50. Try to guess my number. What is your guess?", Title$)

If Val(Guess$) = RandomNumber Then
   MsgBox "My number was" + Str$(RandomNumber) + "." +
   Chr$(32) + Chr$(32) + "Good Guessing!", Title$
EndIf
```

```
If Val(Guess$) > RandomNumber Then
   Button = MsgBox("Your guess was too high. Do you want to
   guess again?", Title$, 4)
   If Button = - 1 Then
      GoTo Guess:
   EndIf
EndIf
If Val(Guess$) < RandomNumber Then
   Button = MsgBox("Your guess was too low. Do you want to
   guess again?", Title$, 4)
   If Button = - 1 Then
      GoTo Guess:
   EndIf
EndIf
EndIf
End Sub
```

15. Click on **Save** on the Standard toolbar.
16. Click on **Yes**.

Test the game a few times in the document window. If you get an error message, click on Window, Global: RandomNumber and fix the highlighted statement. Then, return to the document window and try again. Use your debugging techniques to check for matching parentheses and quotation marks and commas between arguments. Press **F1** to get help on the syntax of a command.

A common bug in macros with variables is misspelled variable names. The macro doesn't give you a syntax error when this happens, it just doesn't work correctly. So, check to make sure your variable names are spelled the same way throughout the macro. Did you type "RandomNumber" one time and "RandonNumber" the next? If your game doesn't work correctly, check the variable names.

1. Click on **Window**.
2. Click on **Document1** (or whatever document window is listed).
   If the RandomNumber macro-editing window is the only window listed, click on **New** on the Standard toolbar to create a blank document window.
3. Press **Alt + E** to erase the screen if it is not blank.
4. Click on **Tools**.
5. Click on **Macro...**
6. Click on **RandomNumber**
7. Click on **Run**.
   An Input box appears on the screen asking you to type a number.
8. Type a number between 1 and 50.
9. Click on **OK**.
   The macro will compare the number you typed with the random number it picked. If the numbers match, a message box will appear on the screen congratulating you. If the numbers don't match, the macro will tell you if your guess was high or low, and let you try again.
10. Click on **Yes** to try again.
11. Type another number, and click on **OK** until you match the computer's number.

Now, assign the macro to your toolbar. Having the toolbar displayed on the screen when you want to play the Random Number game will make it fast and easy to play.

1. Position the mouse pointer on a blank spot on the Standard toolbar.
2. Click the right mouse button to display the list of possible toolbars.
3. Click on your toolbar name to display your toolbar on the screen.
    If your toolbar name is not displayed on the list of possible toolbars, click on **More Toolbars...** and select your toolbar from there.
4. Click on **Tools**.
5. Click on **Customize...**
6. Click on **Toolbars**.
7. Click on **Macros** under Categories.
8. Click on **RandomNumber** under Macros.
9. Click the mouse button and drag the name **RandomNumber** to your toolbar. Make sure the buttons overlap a little. If the Customize dialog box covers up your toolbar and you can't see where to drag the RandomNumber button, click on the title bar of the Customize dialog box and move it down a little on the screen so that you can see your toolbar.
10. Click on the question mark picture in the Custom Button dialog box. It's the picture in the lower right corner of the button choices.
11. Click on **Assign**.
12. Click on **Close**.

Play the RandomNumber game by clicking on the question mark button on your toolbar. Run it several times, answering "yes" to make additional guesses, and answering "no" to stop the game. There is a definite way out of the loop in this macro. Clicking on "no" stops the loop and ends the macro.

Aren't macros fun?

I don't know about you, but when I play a game, I like to keep score. Let's add a counter to the RandomNumber game to count the number of guesses you make each time you play the game. It makes it more exciting to try to beat your record.

Using Counters in a Macro

When you want to keep track of how many times a set of macro instructions is performed, you use a counter. A counter always begins with the value of zero. When you start a counter at zero, you are initializing the counter. That's an important thing to do, because it ensures that the count is accurate each time you run the macro. It's like resetting a stopwatch back to zero before you begin a race. Each time the set of instructions is executed, you add one to the counter. Counters are helpful in tons of macros. Let's add a counter to the RandomNumber macro so that you can keep track of the number of guesses you make each time you play the game.

1. Click on **Window**.
2. Click on **Global: RandomNumber**
3. Position the insertion point on the statement that generates a random number, *RandomNumber = Int(Rnd() * (51 - 1) + 1)*.
4. Press **Enter** to create a blank line in the macro.

5. Type: **Counter = 0** in the blank line.

   The numeric variable "Counter" is going to be used to keep track of the number of guesses you make. This statement initializes the counter to zero. Whenever you use a counter in a macro, you need to initialize it at the beginning of the macro.

6. Position the insertion point on the If statement that checks if your guess matches the random number, *If Val(Guess$) = RandomNumber Then*

7. Press **Enter** to create a blank line in the macro.

8. Type: **Counter = Counter + 1** in the blank line.

   This statement adds one to the counter every time you make a guess. It says, take whatever is in the numeric variable "Counter" and add one to it. This expression is placed right after the InputBox$ function because you need to add to the counter every time you make a guess, regardless of whether you guessed correctly, too high, or too low.

9. Position the insertion point on the following MsgBox statement:
   MsgBox "My number was " + Str$(RandomNumber) + "." + Chr$(32) + Chr$(32) + "Good Guessing!", Title$

10. Modify the MsgBox statement to add the counter. Type:
    MsgBox "My number was " + Str$(RandomNumber) + "." + Chr$(32) + Chr$(32) + **"You made " + Str$(Counter) + " guesses."**, Title$

The RandomNumber macro should look like this:

```
Sub MAIN
REM ****************************************************
REM Macro:      RandomNumber
REM Author:     Frances Eggers
REM Purpose:    Guessing game to guess a random number
REM ****************************************************
Title$ = "Random Number Game"
Counter = 0
RandomNumber = Int(Rnd() * (51 - 1) + 1)

Guess:
Guess$ = InputBox$("I am thinking of a number between 1 and
50. Try to guess my number. What is your guess?", Title$)

Counter = Counter + 1
If Val(Guess$) = RandomNumber Then
   MsgBox "My number was " + Str$(RandomNumber) + "." +
   Chr$(32) + Chr$(32) + "You made " + Str$(Counter) + "
   guesses.", Title$
EndIf

If Val(Guess$) > RandomNumber Then
   Button = MsgBox("Your guess was too high. Do you want to
   guess again?", Title$, 4)
   If Button = - 1 Then
      GoTo Guess:
   EndIf
EndIf
```

```
If Val(Guess$) < RandomNumber Then
   Button = MsgBox("Your guess was too low. Do you want to
   guess again?", Title$, 4)
   If Button = - 1 Then
      GoTo Guess:
   EndIf
EndIf
End Sub
```

11. Click on **Save** on the Standard toolbar.
12. Click on **Yes**.
13. Click on **Window**.
14. Click on the document window.
15. Run the macro a few times by clicking on the Random Number Game button on your toolbar. Try to guess the number in one, two or three guesses. It's not as easy as it sounds!
16. Click on **Window**.
17. Click on **Global: RandomNumber**.
18. Click on **File, Close** to close the macro-editing window.

Loops

A loop statement tells a macro to repeat a group of instructions either a certain number of times or until a condition is met. For example, "Run around the track four times" is an example of a loop that repeats a certain number of times, four times. "Practice your free throws until you make 25" is an example of a loop that repeats until a condition is met. You keep on shooting free throws *until* you reach 25. When you have made 25 free throws, then the condition is met and you can stop and rest.

There are several ways of writing loops in macros. In the Random Number macro you created the simplest type of loop with the GoTo statement. We're going to look at another type of loop, the For...Next loop.

The For...Next Loop

The For...Next loop is used when you want to perform a group of instructions a specific number of times. The syntax of the For...Next loop is:

> **For** *CounterVariable* = *Start* **To** *End* [**Step** *Increment*]
> Series of instructions
> **Next** *CounterVariable*

When a macro sees a For...Next loop, it performs the instructions between the For and Next as many times as it takes for the counter to go from the start value to the end value.

"CounterVariable" is the name of the variable that will keep track of how many times the macro has performed the loop. "Start" is the starting value of the loop. "End" is the ending value of the loop. This is where you tell the macro how many times you want the loop performed. "Step" tells the macro what you're counting by.

It's an optional argument. If you don't include it in the statement, the loop will count by ones.

For counter = 1 To 10 Step 1

This statement tells the macro to start at 1 and loop 10 times, counting by one's. The loop will be performed ten times. You could also write the statement like this:

For counter = 1 Tto 10

When you're counting by ones, and you usually are, you don't have to include the "Step" argument. Here's another example.

For loop = start To finish step size

This statement tells the macro to start at the value it finds in the variable "start" and loop as many times as necessary until it reaches the value in the variable "finish." The macro will be counting by the value in the variable "size." "Loop" is the variable that keeps track of how many times the loop has been performed.

We're going to write a multiplication racetrack macro that will include a For…Next loop. The loop will include statements to generate two random numbers and ask you to multiply them. It will keep track of the number of answers you get right, and tell you the correct answer when you get one wrong. The macro will perform the loop 10 times, so you will be given 10 problems to solve each time the macro runs.

THE MULTRACE MACRO

The first part of the MultRace macro can be recorded. It includes statements for selecting a font, setting tab stops and typing the heading information on the screen. After the recorded part of the macro is done, you can edit the macro and add the loop statements. Add this macro to your toolbar.

1. Press **Alt + E** to erase your screen if it is not blank.
2. Click the right mouse button on a blank section of the Standard toolbar. If your toolbar is already displayed, skip to step number four.
3. Click on your toolbar name to display the toolbar.
4. Double-click on **REC** on the status bar to turn on the macro recorder.
5. Type: **MultRace** for the macro name.
6. Click once in the description box to position the insertion point.
7. Type: **Practice mult facts with For…Next loop** as the description.
8. Click on **Toolbars** to assign the macro to your toolbar.
9. Drag the name **MultRace** to your toolbar. Make sure the buttons overlap a little.
10. Click on the button that looks like a little calculator (second column from the left, second row from the bottom)
11. Click on **Assign**.
12. Click on **Close**.
13. Click on **File**.
14. Click on **Page Setup…**
15. Click on **Margins**.
16. Set the margins: Left Margin = **1**
Right Margin = 1

17. Click on **OK**.
18. Click on **Format, Font...**
19. Select Font = **Courier New**, Font Style = **Bold**, Size = **20**
20. Click on **OK**.
21. Press **Ctrl + E** to turn on centering
22. Type: **Multiplication Racetrack**
23. Press **Enter** two times.
24. Press **Ctrl + L** to turn on left justification.
25. Click on **Format, Font...**
26. Select Font = **Courier New**, Font Style = **Regular**, Size = **14**
27. Click on **OK**.
28. Click on **Format**.
29. Click on **Tabs. . .**
30. Click on **Clear All**.
31. Set the following tab stops:
     Tab Stop Position = **0.75**, Alignment = **Right**
     Click on **Set**.
     Tab Stop Position = **1**, Alignment = **Right**
     Click on **Set**.
     Tab Stop Position = **1.38**, Alignment = **Right**
     Click on **Set**.
     Tab Stop Position = **1.63**, Alignment = **Right**
     Click on **Set**.
     Tab Stop Position = **2.13**, Alignment = **Right**
     Click on **Set**.
     Tab Stop Position = **2.5**, Alignment = **Left**
     Click on **Set**.

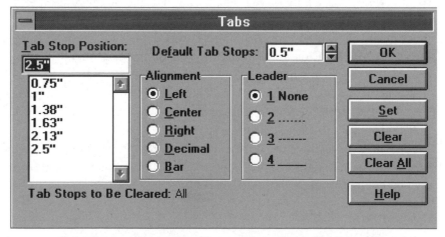

Set tab stops by typing the position, then clicking on Set

32. Click on **OK**.
33. Click on **Stop** on the Macro Record toolbar to turn off the macro recorder.

Now, let's add the statements that cannot be recorded.

1. Click on **Tools**.
2. Click on **Macro...**
3. Click on **MultRace**.
4. Click on **Edit**.
5. Press **Alt + C** to play the Comments macro. Look at the Status bar at the bottom of the screen as you type the following comments.

   REM **

   REM Macro: MultRace

   REM Author: Kelly Walsh

   REM Purpose: Practice mult facts with a For...Next loop

   REM **

6. Position the insertion point on the End Sub statement.
7. Press **Enter** to create a blank line in the macro. Type the following statements beginning at the blank line.
8. Type: **space\$ = Chr\$(32)**

   tab\$ = Chr\$(9)

   counter = 0

   right = 0

   These statements initialize the variables that will be used in the macro and make the macro easier to understand later. The first statement fills the variable "space\$" with the special code for adding a space to a macro statement. In the macro, when you need a space you can type "space\$" instead of "Chr\$(32)." "Tab\$" holds the special code for adding a tab character to a macro statement. "Counter" will be used to keep track of how many times the loop has been performed. "Right" will be used to keep track of how many problems you answered correctly.

9. Type: **For counter = 1 To 10**

   This statement controls the loop (what power). The numeric variable "counter" will keep track of how many times the macro has performed the loop. The macro will start at 1 and loop until the value in the variable "counter" reaches 10. Every time the macro performs the loop, one will be added to the counter.

10. Type: **factor1 = Int(Rnd() * (13 - 0) + 0)**

    factor2 = Int(Rnd() * (13 - 0) + 0)

    The two numeric variables "factor1" and "factor2" will hold random numbers between 0 and 12. Those two numbers will be shown on the screen as a multiplication problem that you'll be asked to solve.

11. Type: **Insert tab\$ + Str\$(factor1) + tab\$ + "*" + tab\$ + Str\$(factor2) + tab\$ + "=" + tab\$**

    This statement displays a multiplication problem on the screen. It will type "*factor1 * factor2 =.*" Of course it will type the numbers that are *in* the variables, not the variable names. You'll then be asked to type the answer. The tab characters are used to line up the numbers on the screen and make the game look good.

12. Type: **Input "What is your answer", Answer**
     This statement will display a question in the status bar asking you to type the
     answer to the problem. After you type your answer, it will be stored in the
     numeric variable "Answer."

13. Type: **Insert Str$(Answer) + tab$**
     This Insert statement will type your answer on the screen and press the Tab key.
     The insertion point is now in the correct spot for the macro to tell you if you
     answered the problem correctly or not.

14. Type: **If Answer = factor1 * factor2 Then**
     > **right = right + 1**
     > **Insert "You are brilliant!"**
     > **InsertPara**

     Else
     > **Insert "The answer is" + space$ + Str$(factor1 * factor2) + "."**
     > **InsertPara**

     EndIf
     Next counter

     This statement (big statement) checks to see if your answer is right or not. If the
     value in the numeric variable "Answer" is equal to the number that the computer
     gets when it multiplies factor1 and factor2, then the If statement is true. (The
     computer always gets the right answer when it multiplies.) When the If
     statement is true, the macro adds one to the variable "right" which is keeping
     track of your score and displays a message on the screen. If the answer is
     wrong, the macro will tell you the correct answer. The "Next" statement is
     always the last statement in a For...Next loop. It signals the end of the loop.
     The macro knows that the loop starts with the word "For" and ends with the
     word "Next."

15. Type: **InsertPara**
     > **Beep**
     > **Insert "Congratulations, smarty! You got" + space$ +Str$(right) +**
     > **space$ + "right!"**

     These last three statements will be executed after the loop ends. They will tell
     you how many problems you answered correctly.

     The MultRace macro should look like this:

```
Sub MAIN
REM ********************************************************
REM Macro:      MultRace
REM Author:     Kelly Walsh
REM Purpose:    Practice mult facts with a For. . .Next loop
REM ********************************************************
FilePageSetup .Tab = "0", .PaperSize = "0", .TopMargin = "1" +
Chr$(34), .BottomMargin = "1" + Chr$(34), .LeftMargin =
"1" + Chr$(34), .RightMargin = "1" + Chr$(34), .Gutter = "0" +
Chr$(34), .PageWidth = "8.5" + Chr$(34), .PageHeight = "11" +
Chr$(34), .Orientation = 0, .FirstPage = 0, .OtherPages = 0,
.VertAlign = 0, .ApplyPropsTo = 4, .FacingPages = 0,
```

```
.HeaderDistance = "0.5" + Chr$(34), .FooterDistance = "0.5" +
Chr$(34), .SectionStart = 2, .OddAndEvenPages = 0,
.DifferentFirstPage = 0, .Endnotes = 0, .LineNum = 0,
.StartingNum = "", .FromText = "", .CountBy = "0", .NumMode = - 1
FormatFont .Points = "20", .Underline = 0, .Color = 0,
.Strikethrough = 0, .Superscript = 0, .Subscript = 0, .Hidden
= 0, .SmallCaps = 0, .AllCaps = 0, .Spacing = "0 pt",
.Position = "0 pt", .Kerning = 0, .KerningMin = "", .Tab =
"0", .Font = "Courier New", .Bold = 1, .Italic = 0
CenterPara
Insert "Multiplication Racetrack"
InsertPara
InsertPara
LeftPara
FormatFont .Points = "14", .Underline = 0, .Color = 0,
.Strikethrough = 0, .Superscript = 0, .Subscript = 0, .Hidden
= 0, .SmallCaps = 0, .AllCaps = 0, .Spacing = "0 pt",
.Position = "0 pt", .Kerning = 0, .KerningMin = "", .Tab =
"0", .Font = "Courier New", .Bold = 0, .Italic = 0
FormatTabs .Position = "", .DefTabs = "0.5" + Chr$(34), .Align
= 0, .Leader = 0, .ClearAll
FormatTabs .Position = "0.75" + Chr$(34), .DefTabs = "0.5" +
Chr$(34), .Align = 2, .Leader = 0, .Set
FormatTabs .Position = "1" + Chr$(34), .DefTabs = "0.5" +
Chr$(34), .Align = 2, .Leader = 0, .Set
FormatTabs .Position = "1.38" + Chr$(34), .DefTabs = "0.5" +
Chr$(34), .Align = 2, .Leader = 0, .Set
FormatTabs .Position = "1.63" + Chr$(34), .DefTabs = "0.5" +
Chr$(34), .Align = 2, .Leader = 0, .Set
FormatTabs .Position = "2.13" + Chr$(34), .DefTabs = "0.5" +
Chr$(34), .Align = 2, .Leader = 0, .Set
FormatTabs .Position = "2.5" + Chr$(34), .DefTabs = "0.5" +
Chr$(34), .Align = 0, .Leader = 0, .Set

space$ = Chr$(32)
tab$ = Chr$(9)
counter = 0
right = 0

For counter = 1 To 10
factor1 = Int(Rnd() * (13 - 0) + 0)
factor2 = Int(Rnd() * (13 - 0) + 0)
Insert tab$ + Str$(factor1) + tab$ + "*" + tab$ +
Str$(factor2) + tab$ + "=" + tab$
Input "What is your answer", Answer
Insert Str$(Answer) + tab$
If answer = factor1 * factor2 Then
    right = right + 1
    Insert "You are brilliant!"
    InsertPara
Else
    Insert "The answer is" + space$ + Str$(factor1 * factor2) + "."
    InsertPara
```

```
EndIf
Next counter
InsertPara
Beep
Insert "Congratulations, smarty! You got" + space$ +
Str$(right) + space$ + "right!"
End Sub
```

16. Click on **Save** on the Standard toolbar.

17. Click on **Yes**.

Let's try it out. If you get an error message the first time you run the macro, click on Window, Global: MultRace and fix the highlighted statement. Then return to the document window and run the macro again.

1. Click on **New** on the Standard toolbar.

2. Click on the calculator button on your toolbar.
    Notice the question in the status bar at the bottom of the screen asking you to type your answer.

3. Type the answer to the problem on the screen and press **Enter**.
    Your answer shows in the status bar at the bottom of the screen.

4. Continue answering multiplication problems and pressing Enter until you have finished all ten problems.

5. Click on **Window**.

6. Click on **Global: MultRace**

7. Click on **File, Close** to close the macro-editing window.

Let's write another macro that uses a For…Next loop, the FontList macro.

THE FONTLIST MACRO

The FontList macro will look deep inside your computer and print an example of every font that will print on your printer. This is a handy macro because sometimes you want to use a different font but have no idea what the different fonts look like.

This macro will use two new functions, CountFonts() and Font$(). CountFonts() tells you the number of fonts available on your computer. The Font$() function tells you the name of the current font from the list of available fonts. We will combine these two functions in a For…Next loop.

The number of times the loop repeats in the FontList macro will be equal to the number of fonts on your computer. The loop might repeat 20 times on your computer and only 10 on mine. That's okay, the macro can handle it regardless of the number of fonts on your computer. The end value in the "For" statement will contain a variable for the number of fonts on your computer instead of an actual number like we saw in the multiplication game.

Let's get started. You can record a little of this macro, so do that part first. Recording even a little of a macro saves time because you can assign the macro at the same time. Assign this macro to the Format menu.

1. Press **Alt + E** to erase the screen.

2. Double-click on **REC** on the status bar to turn on the macro recorder.

3. Type: **FontList** for the macro name.

4. Click once in the description box to position the insertion point.
5. Type: **Prints a list of available fonts** as the description.
6. Click on **Menus** to assign this macro to the Format menu.
7. Click on **F&ormat** (the Format menu) in the Change What Menu box.
8. Click on **Add**.

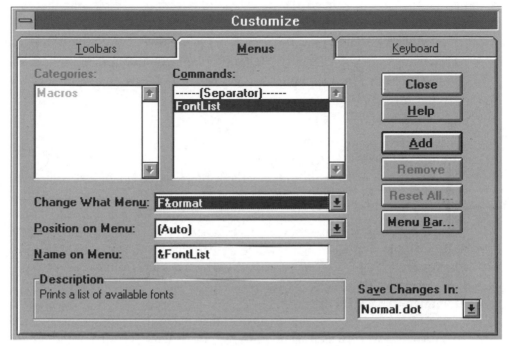

Add the FontList macro to the Format menu

9. Click on **Close**.
10. Type: **Beginning of Font List**
11. Press **Enter** two times.
12. Click on **Stop** on the Macro Record toolbar to turn off the recorder.

Now, let's add the good stuff.

1. Click on **Tools**.
2. Click on **Macro...**
3. Click on **FontList**
4. Click on **Edit**.
5. Press **Alt + C** to play the Comments macro. Look at the Status bar at the bottom of the screen as you type the following comments.

   REM ***

   REM Macro: **FontList**

   REM Author: **Beth Bradley**

   REM Purpose: **Prints a list of available fonts**

   REM **

6. Position the insertion point on the End Sub statement.

7. Press **Enter** to create a blank line in the macro. Type the following statements beginning at the blank line.

8. Type: **OldFont$ = Font$() 'Saves default font**
    This statement saves the default font for your computer in the variable OldFont$. You'll need this font at the end of the macro.

9. Type:

    For LoopCounter = 1 To CountFonts()   **'Loop for the number of fonts**
    FontName$ = Font$(LoopCounter)   **'Places font name in FontName$**
    Font FontName$**   **'Changes font to FontName$
    Insert "This is " + FontName$ + "."   **'Types a sentence**
    InsertPara
    Next LoopCounter

    Okay, let's check out what's going on.

    For LoopCounter = 1 To CountFonts()
    "LoopCounter" is the name of the variable that keeps track of how many times the loop has been performed. Each time the program loops, one will be added to "LoopCounter." "CountFonts()" is a WordBasic function that tells the macro the total number of fonts that are available on your computer with your selected printer. The "For" statement tells the macro to begin at 1 and repeat the loop until it has read every font on your computer.

    FontName$ = Font$(LoopCounter)
    FontName$ is a variable that will hold the name of the current font. "Font$()"is a WordBasic function that tells the macro the name of the current font. So, Font$(LoopCounter) places the name of the font whose position in the list of fonts corresponds to the value of "LoopCounter" into the variable FontName$.

    Font FontName$
    The "Font" statement changes the font in the document window. So, this statement changes the font to the font that is in the variable "FontName$."

    Insert "This is " + FontName$ + "."
    This statement will print an example of the current font on the screen. It will print whatever font is in the variable FontName$.

    InsertPara
    This statement types a blank line in the document.

    Next LoopCounter
    This statement tells the macro that it has reached the end of the loop.

10. Type: **InsertPara**
            InsertPara
    When the loop ends, Word will type two blank lines.

11. Type: **Font OldFont$**   **'Sets font to default font**
            Insert "End of Font List"
    These statements type the words "End of Font List" in the default font for your computer so that you'll know the macro has read every font.

12. Type: **InsertPara**

   Insert Str$(CountFonts()) + Chr$(32) + "fonts were found on your computer."

   The InsertPara statement will move the insertion point down to the next line in the document window and the Insert statement will print the number of fonts that were found on your computer.

   The FontList macro should look like this:

```
Sub MAIN
REM *********************************************************
REM Macro:      Font List
REM Author:     Beth Bradley
REM Purpose:    Prints a list of available fonts
REM *********************************************************
Insert "Beginning of Font List"
InsertPara
InsertPara
OldFont$ = Font$()                    'Saves default font
For LoopCounter = 1 To CountFonts()'Loop for the number of fonts
FontName$ = Font$(LoopCounter)    'Place font name in FontName$
Font FontName$                    'Change font to FontName$
Insert "This is " + FontName$ + "." 'Type a sentence
InsertPara
Next LoopCounter
InsertPara
InsertPara
Font OldFont$                     'Sets font to default font
Insert "End of Font List"
InsertPara
Insert Str$(CountFonts()) + Chr$(32) + "fonts were found on
your computer."
End Sub
```

13. Click on **Save** on the Standard toolbar.
14. Click on **Yes**.

   Now, let's try it out.

1. Click on **New** on the Standard toolbar.
2. Click on **Format**.
3. Click on **FontList**.

   Word prints an example of every font available on your printer.
4. Click on **Print** to print a copy of the font list for future reference.
5. Click on **File, Close, No** to close the document window.

   The macro-editing window appears on the screen.
6. Click on **File, Close** to close the macro-editing window.

Chapter Review — Absolutely, Positively the Most Important Stuff

1. The **Val(a$)** function is used to convert string variables to numeric variables so they can be used in mathematical calculations.
2. The **Str$(*n*)** function is used to convert numeric variables to string variables so they can be printed on the screen.
3. The **Today** () function returns a serial number for today's date according to the computer's system date.
4. The **DateValue** () function converts a date entered as text into a serial number date.
5. The **GoTo** statement tells a macro to loop back up to a certain label statement in the macro, and begin following instructions there.
6. **Int(Rnd() * (*b* - *a*) + a)** is used to generate random numbers.
7. A nested If statement is an If statement within an If statement

    If *first condition* **Then**
        One or more instructions
        If *second condition* **Then**
            One or more instructions
        EndIf
    EndIf

8. A loop statement tells a macro to repeat a group of instructions either a certain number of times or until a condition is met.
9. The For…Next loop is used when you want to perform a group of instructions a specific number of times.

    For *CounterVariable* = *Start* **To** *End* [**Step** *Increment*]
        Series of instructions
    Next *CounterVariable*

10. Before you begin recording or writing a macro that uses loops, nested If's or numeric expressions, carefully plan the steps you want the macro to follow. Do as many of the steps as you can in advance without the macro recorder turned on (like playing with font sizes, margins and tab stops). Do the mathematical calculations on paper to make sure you're absolutely certain how they work.

Projects for Practice

Batting Averages in the Baseball Macro

1. In the last chapter, you created a macro to keep track of your baseball stats. Now that you know how to do mathematical calculations in a macro, let's modify the Baseball macro to figure out your batting average. The formula for figuring out a batting average is:

    BattingAverage = Hits / (AtBats – Walks)

    Let's add this formula to the Baseball macro. First, modify the Baseball Stats master file to include a column for batting averages.

    ◆ Click on **Open** on the Standard toolbar.

    ◆ Click on **baseball.doc** (Word 6) or **baseball** (Word 7).

    ◆ Click on **OK** (Word 6) or **Open** (Word 7).

    ◆ Position the insertion point on *Opponent*

    ◆ Press **End** to move the insertion point to the end of the line.

    ◆ Press the **Tab** key.

    ◆ Type: **Batting**

    ◆ Press ↓ to move the insertion point down to the next line.

    ◆ Press the **Tab** key.

    ◆ Type: **Average**

    ◆ Click on **Save** on the Standard toolbar.

    ◆ Click on **File, Close** to close the Baseball Stats master file.

    Now, modify the Baseball macro.

    ◆ Click on **New** if you need to display the menu bar.

    ◆ Click on **Tools**.

    ◆ Click on **Macro...**

    ◆ Click on **Baseball**.

    ◆ Click on **Edit**.

    ◆ Position the insertion point on the **InsertPara** statement before the statement *Again = MsgBox ("Do you want to enter another game?", "Baseball Games Tracker", 36)*

    ◆ Press **Enter** to place a blank line into the macro.

    Type the following statements beginning at the blank line.

    ◆ Type: **Insert Chr$(9)** to press the Tab key in the document window

◆ Type: **If Val(GamesRecord.Hits) = 0 Then**
                Insert "No Avg"
       Else
                CalcBattingAverage = Val(GamesRecord.Hits) /
                (Val(GamesRecord.AtBats) - Val(GamesRecord.Walks))
                BattingAverage = Int(CalcBattingAverage * 1000)
                Insert Str$(BattingAverage)
       EndIf

If you didn't get any hits in the game, you don't have a batting average. The If statement is necessary because an error will occur in your macro if zero is one of the numbers in a division problem. The Val functions are necessary to convert text information into numeric information. Check this statement carefully. Make sure each left parenthesis has a matching right parenthesis.

The Baseball macro should look like this:

```
Sub MAIN
REM ********************************************************
REM Macro:     Baseball
REM Author:    Maggie O'Hara
REM Purpose:   Keep track of baseball game stats
REM ********************************************************
FileOpen .Name = "BASEBALL.DOC", .ConfirmConversions = 0,
.ReadOnly = 0, .AddToMru = 0, .PasswordDoc = "", .PasswordDot =
"", .Revert = 0, .WritePasswordDoc = "", .WritePasswordDot = ""
EndOfDocument
Continue:
Begin Dialog UserDialog 396, 150, "Baseball Games Tracker"
    Text 10, 6, 75, 13, "Opponent", .Text1
    TextBox 10, 22, 243, 18, .Opponent
    Text 11, 58, 61, 13, "At Bats:", .Text2
    Text 11, 77, 36, 13, "Hits:", .Text3
    Text 11, 96, 53, 13, "Walks:", .Text4
    Text 11, 115, 47, 13, "RBI's:", .Text5
    TextBox 80, 54, 65, 18, .AtBats
    TextBox 80, 75, 65, 18, .Hits
    TextBox 80, 96, 65, 18, .Walks
    TextBox 80, 117, 65, 18, .RBIs
    Text 201, 55, 93, 13, "Home Runs:", .Text6
    Text 201, 74, 104, 13, "Runs Scored:", .Text7
    TextBox 318, 55, 65, 18, .HomeRuns
    TextBox 318, 76, 65, 18, .RunsScored
    OKButton 198, 110, 88, 21
    CancelButton 297, 110, 88, 21
End Dialog

Dim GamesRecord As UserDialog
ButtonChoice = Dialog(GamesRecord)
```

```
If ButtonChoice = 0 Then    'Check if Cancel button chosen
    Goto Quit:
EndIf
Insert GamesRecord.Opponent
Insert Chr$(9)
Insert GamesRecord.AtBats
Insert Chr$(9)
Insert GamesRecord.Hits
Insert Chr$(9)
Insert GamesRecord.Walks
Insert Chr$(9)
Insert GamesRecord.RBIs
Insert Chr$(9)
Insert GamesRecord.HomeRuns
Insert Chr$(9)
Insert GamesRecord.RunsScored
Insert Chr$(9)
If Val(GamesRecord.Hits) = 0 Then
    Insert "No Avg"
Else
    CalcBattingAverage = Val(GamesRecord.Hits) /
    (Val(GamesRecord.AtBats) - Val(GamesRecord.Walks))
    BattingAverage = Int(CalcBattingAverage * 1000)
    Insert Str$(BattingAverage)
EndIf
InsertPara
Again = MsgBox("Do you want to enter another game?", "Baseball
Game Tracker", 36)
If Again = 1 Then        'Check if you want to enter another game
    Goto Continue:
EndIf
PrintSave = MsgBox("Do you want to print and save the file?",
"Baseball Game Tracker", 36)
If PrintSave = - 1 Then     'Check if you want to print and save
    FileSave
    FilePrint
EndIf
Quit:
End Sub
```

- ◆ Click on **Save** on the Standard toolbar.
- ◆ Click on **Yes**
- ◆ Click on **Window.**
- ◆ Click on the document window. If the Baseball macro-editing window is the only window listed, click on New on the Standard toolbar to create a document window.
- ◆ Press **Alt + E** to erase the screen if it is not blank.
- ◆ Click on the Baseball button on your toolbar.
- ◆ Enter the game information and press **Enter** or click on **OK**.

◆ Click on **Yes** when asked if you want to enter another game.

◆ Enter the information for a couple of games and press **Enter** or click on **OK**.

◆ Click on **Yes** to save and print the baseball file.
  Now, you can see your batting average for each game.

◆ Click on **File, Close** to close the Baseball file.

◆ Click on **Window, Global: Baseball**

◆ Click on **File, Close** to close the macro-editing window.

RollTheDice Game

2. Let's write another macro game — a dice game. The object of the game is to roll the dice and get as close to a total of 24 as possible without going over 24. In each game, you can roll as many times as you want to. RollTheDice will use two GoTo statements. The first GoTo statement will loop back up to the part of the macro that rolls the dice when you choose to roll again. The second GoTo statement will loop back to the top of the macro if you choose to play the game again. Part of this macro can be recorded, so we'll do that part first. We're going to include statements for erasing the screen in this macro, so that when you choose to play the game again, the screen will be clean each time. If you don't have anything on your screen now, type "Any old junk."

◆ Double-click on **REC** to turn on the macro recorder.

◆ Type: **RollTheDice** for the macro name.

◆ Click once in the description box to position the insertion point.

◆ Type: **Roll the dice and try to get a total of 24** as the description.

◆ Click on **Toolbars** to assign the macro to your toolbar.

◆ Drag the name **RollTheDice** to your toolbar. Make sure the buttons overlap a little.

◆ Click on **Edit...** to create a button face design.

◆ Create a button face that looks like a die. Use the mouse to set the background color to white, then select black to make the dots.

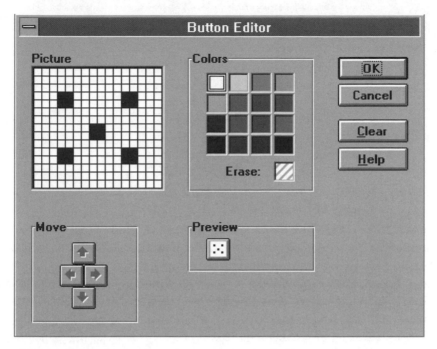

- ◆ Click on **OK** when you get the picture just like you want it.
- ◆ Click on **Close**.
- ◆ Press **Ctrl + Home** to move the insertion point to the top of the document.
- ◆ Press **Shift + Ctrl + End** to highlight the entire document window.
- ◆ Press the **Delete** key to erase the document window.
- ◆ Click on **Format, Font...**
- ◆ Select Font – **Arial**, Font Style = **Regular**, Size = **12**
- ◆ Click on **OK**.
- ◆ Type: **Roll the Dice**
- ◆ Press **Enter** two times.
- ◆ Type: **Try to roll a total of**
- ◆ Press **Enter** four times.
- ◆ Click on **Stop** on the Macro Record toolbar to turn off the macro recorder.

Now, let's add the statements that cannot be recorded.

- ◆ Click on **Tools**.
- ◆ Click on **Macro...**
- ◆ Click on **RollTheDice**.
- ◆ Click on **Edit**.
- ◆ Press **Alt + C** to play the Comments macro. Look at the Status bar at the bottom of the screen as you type the following comments.

```
REM *****************************************************
REM Macro:      RollTheDice
REM Author:     Darren Peters
REM Purpose:    Dice game to try to roll a total of 24
REM *****************************************************
```

◆ Position the insertion point on the line after the last REM statement.

◆ Type: **Start:**
         Total = 0
         FirstDie = 0
         SecondDie = 0
         Goal = 24

These statements are placed at the beginning of the macro, just after the REM statements. The "Start:" statement is a label that the macro will use when it needs to loop back to the top to start another game. "Total" is a numeric variable that will keep track of your total as you roll. "FirstDie" is a numeric variable that will keep track of the first die in the pair of dice. "SecondDie" is a numeric variable that will keep track of the second die in the pair of dice. "Goal" is a numeric variable that will keep track of what the goal is for the game. We've set the goal at 24. Having the goal in a variable makes the macro flexible, because if you want to change the goal to another number, all you have to do is change this one statement that sets the goal. If you want to change the goal each time you play the game, then you could enter the goal in an Input box.

◆ Position the insertion point on the second InsertPara statement after the statement, *Insert "Try to roll a total of"*

```
Insert "Roll the Dice"
InsertPara
InsertPara
Insert "Try to roll a total of "
InsertPara
InsertPara
```

◆ Press **Enter** to add a blank line to the macro.

◆ Type: **Insert Chr$(9) + Str$(Goal)** in the blank line.

The Insert statements in the macro should look like this:

```
Insert "Roll the Dice"
InsertPara
InsertPara
Insert "Try to roll a total of "
InsertPara
Insert Chr$(9) + Str$(Goal)
InsertPara
InsertPara
InsertPara
End Sub
```

◆ Position the insertion point on the End Sub statement.

◆ Press **Enter** to insert a blank line into the macro. Type the following macro statements starting at the blank line.

◆ Type: **RollAgain:**

This label statement tells the macro where to loop when you want to roll the dice again.

◆ Type: **FirstDie = Int(Rnd() * (7 - 1) + 1)**

    SecondDie = Int(Rnd() * (7 - 1) + 1)

These statements generate random numbers between one and six. The roll of the first die is stored in the numeric variable "FirstDie" and the roll of the second die is stored in the numeric variable "SecondDie." The numbers one through six are the numbers that are possible when you roll dice, so the random numbers will be picked between the numbers one and six.

◆ Type: **Total = Total + FirstDie + SecondDie**

This statement adds your current roll to the total.

◆ Type: **Insert "You rolled a " + Str$(FirstDie) + " and a " + Str$(SecondDie)**

This statement shows you what your last roll was.

◆ Type: **InsertPara**

This statement types a blank line in the document.

◆ Type: **Button = MsgBox ("Do you want to roll again?", "Roll the Dice", 4)**

This statement displays a message box on the screen asking if you'd like to roll again.

◆ Type: **If Button = -1 Then**

        GoTo RollAgain:

    EndIf

This If statement checks to see how you answered the question in the message box asking if you want to roll again. If you do want to roll again, the macro will loop back up to the label statement "RollAgain." If you don't want to roll again, the macro will continue with the next statement.

◆ Type: **If Total = Goal Then**

        Beep

        Beep

        Insert "Fantastic! You did it!"

    EndIf

This If statement checks to see if the total you rolled is equal to the goal. If it is, a message will appear on the screen, congratulating you for winning the game.

◆ Type: **If Total > Goal Then**

        Insert "You went over the goal of " + Str$(Goal)

    EndIf

This If statement checks to see if your total is greater than the goal of the game. If it is, a message will be displayed on the screen telling you that you went over the goal.

◆ Type: **If Total < Goal Then**
                   Insert "You were under the goal of " + Str$(Goal)
            EndIf

This If statement checks to see if your total is less than the goal of the game. If it is, a message will be displayed on the screen telling you that you were under the goal.

◆ Type: **InsertPara**
            Insert "Your total was " + Str$(Total)

These statements show you the total for all of your rolls.

◆ Type: **Button2 = MsgBox ("Do you want to play another game?", "Roll the Dice", 4)**

This statement displays a message box on the screen asking if you'd like to play the game again. Your answer will be stored in the variable "Button2."

◆ Type: **If Button2 = –1 Then**
                   GoTo Start:
            EndIf

This If statement checks to see if you want to play the game again. If you do, the macro loops back up to the label "Start." If you don't, the macro ends.

The RollTheDice macro has two loops. The first loop goes to RollAgain, so you can keep rolling, trying to get twenty-four. The second loop goes to Start, so you can play a whole new game.

The RollTheDice macro should look like this:

```
Sub MAIN
REM ******************************************************
REM Macro:      RollTheDice
REM Author:     Darren Peters
REM Purpose:    Dice game to try to roll a total of 24
REM ******************************************************
Start:
Total = 0
FirstDie = 0
SecondDie = 0
Goal = 24

StartOfDocument
EndOfDocument 1
EditClear

FormatFont .Points = "12", .Underline = 0, .Color = 0,
.Strikethrough = 0, .Superscript = 0, .Subscript = 0, .Hidden
= 0, .SmallCaps = 0, .AllCaps = 0, .Spacing = "0 pt",
.Position = "0 pt", .Kerning = 0, .KerningMin = "", .Tab =
"0", .Font = "Arial", .Bold = 0, .Italic = 0
Insert "Roll the Dice"
InsertPara
InsertPara
Insert "Try to roll a total of"
InsertPara
```

```
Insert Chr$(9) + Str$(Goal)
InsertPara
InsertPara
InsertPara

RollAgain:
FirstDie = Int(Rnd() * (7 - 1) + 1)
SecondDie = Int(Rnd() * (7 - 1) + 1)
Total = Total + FirstDie + SecondDie

Insert "You rolled a " + Str$(FirstDie) + " and a " +
Str$(SecondDie)
InsertPara
Button = MsgBox("Do you want to roll again?", "Roll the Dice", 4)
If Button = - 1 Then
   GoTo RollAgain:
EndIf

If Total - Goal Then
   Beep
   Beep
   Insert "Fantastic! You did it!"
EndIf

If Total > Goal Then
   Insert "You went over the goal of " + Str$(Goal)
EndIf

If Total < Goal Then
   Insert "You were under the goal of " + Str$(Goal)
EndIf
InsertPara
Insert "Your total was " + Str$(Total)

Button2 = MsgBox("Do you want to play another game?", "Roll
the Dice", 4)
If Button2 = - 1 Then
   GoTo Start:
EndIf
End Sub
```

◆ Click on **Save** on the Standard toolbar.

◆ Click on **Yes**.

Now, let's play.

◆ Click on **Window**.

◆ Click on the document window.

◆ Roll the Dice by clicking on the cool-looking die on your toolbar.
A message appears on the screen telling you what you rolled. A message box asks if you want to roll again.

◆ Click on **Yes** or press **Enter** to keep rolling.
If you get an error the first time you run this macro, click on Window, Global: RollTheDice to return to the macro-editing window and fix the highlighted

statement. Then click on Window, Document1 to return to the document window to play the game again.

◆ After each roll, the macro will ask you if you want to roll again. Keep rolling until you think your total is equal to twenty four.

◆ After you click on "no" to stop rolling, the macro will tell you if you matched the number twenty four, went over twenty four or were under. It will then ask if you want to play another game.

◆ Click on **Yes** to play again.

◆ To end the game, click on **No** you don't want to roll again and click on **No** you don't want to play again.

Did you get 24? Outstanding! Now that you know the macro works, close the macro-editing window.

◆ Click on **Window**.

◆ Click on **Global: RollTheDice**.

◆ Click on **File**.

◆ Click on **Close**.

The Jobs Macro

3. You really, really, really want a new CD Player. The one you want is too expensive for your parents to handle, so they've told you that if you can earn $100, they will chip in the rest. You have thought of four ways of making money: mowing grass, babysitting, washing cars and walking dogs. The Jobs macro will let you keep track of how much money you've earned so far, and how much more you need to reach your $100 goal. This macro will include a custom dialog box for entering the amount of work you did. It will perform mathematical calculations to figure out if you've reached your goal.

Step 1 — Create the Jobs macro

1. Click on **Tools**.

2. Click on **Macro. . .**

3. Type: **Jobs** as the macro name.

4. Click once in the description box to position the insertion point.

5. Type: **Calculate part time job earnings** as the description.

6. Click on **Create**.

7. Press **Alt + C** to play the Comments macro. Look at the Status bar at the bottom of the screen as you type the following comments.

```
REM **************************************************
REM Macro:      Jobs
REM Author:     Charlotte George
REM Purpose:    Calculate part-time job earnings
REM **************************************************
```

Step 2 — Create the Dialog Box

1. Click on the **Dialog Editor** button on the macro toolbar.
2. Click on **Edit**.
3. Click on **Info...**
4. In the "Text$" box, delete "**Microsoft Word**" and type **Jobs**
5. Click on **OK**.
   This is how the finished dialog box will look. It contains text items, text boxes, command buttons, check boxes and a group box.

6. Move the mouse pointer to the lower right corner of the dialog box.
7. Click and drag the double-headed arrow down and to the right to expand the size of the dialog box. Make the dialog box taller than it is wide.
8. Click on **Item**.
9. Click on **Text**.
10. Type: **Goal**
    You might be saving for a stereo this month, and a computer game the next. Entering your goal in the dialog box will allow you to save for different amounts.
11. Click on **Item**.
12. Click on **Text Box**.
13. Click on the right edge of the text box and drag it to the left with the double-headed arrow to make the text box for entering the goal smaller.
14. Double-click on the text box for entering the goal.
15. In the ".Field" text box, delete **.TextBox1** and type **.Goal**
16. Click on **OK**.
17. Click on **Item**.
18. Click on **Group Box**.
19. Type: **Jobs**
20. Click on **Item**.
21. Click on **Button...**
22. Click on **Check Box**.
23. Click on **OK**.
24. Type: **Mow Grass**
25. Double-click on "Mow Grass"
26. In the **.Field** text box, delete **.CheckBox1** and type **.MowGrass**

27. Click on **OK**.
28. Press **Enter**.
29. Type: **Baby-Sit**
30. Double-click on "Baby-Sit"
31. In the **.Field** text box, delete **.CheckBox2** and type **.BabySit**
32. Click on **OK**.
33. Press **Enter**.
34. Type:**Walk Dogs** (two words)
35. Double-click on "Walk Dogs"
36. In the **.Field** text box, delete **.CheckBox3** and type **.WalkDogs** (one word)
37. Click on **OK**.
38. Press **Enter**.
39. Type: **Wash Cars** (two words)
40. Double-click on "Wash Cars"
41. In the **.Field** text box, delete **.CheckBox4** and type **.WashCars** (one word)
42. Click on **OK**.
43. Click in the group box to select it.
44. Click and drag the lower right corner of the group box up and to the left to make the group box smaller.
45. Click in a blank portion of the dialog box to *un*-select the group box.
46. Click on **Item**.
47. Click on **Text**.
48. Type: **Number of Jobs**
49. With the four-headed arrow, click and drag "Number of Jobs" up and to the right side of the dialog box (look at the dialog box picture for the exact location).
50. Click on **Item**.
51. Click on **Text Box**.
52. With the two-headed arrow, click and drag the right side of the text box to the left to shorten the size of the box.
53. With the four-headed arrow, click and drag the text box so that it is just to the right of the check box "Mow Grass."
54. Double-click on the text box.
55. In the **.Field** text box, delete **.TextBox2** and type **.NumYards**
     Make a note of the width parameter at the top of the Text Box Information dialog box. The other three text boxes for entering amounts — babysitting amounts, dog walking amounts and car washing amounts, need to be the same size as this one. For each of the three text boxes, change the width parameter on the Text Box Information screen when you're entering the field names.
56. Click on **OK** to close the Text Box Information screen.
57. Press **Enter**.
58. Double-click on the text box for entering the number of hours you spent babysitting.
59. In the **.Field** text box, delete **.TextBox3** and type **.NumHours**
60. Click in the "**Width**" box at the top of the screen.

61. Delete **160**
62. Type the width of the Mow Grass text box.
63. Click on **OK**.
64. Press **Enter**.
65. Double-click on the text box for entering the number of dogs you walked.
66. In the **.Field** text box, delete **.TextBox4** and type **.NumDogs**
67. Change the "**Width**" box at the top of the screen to the width of the Mow Grass text box.
68. Click on **OK**.
69. Press **Enter**.
70. Double-click on the text box for entering the number of cars you washed.
71. In the **.Field** text box, delete **.TextBox5** type **.NumCars**
72. Change the "**Width**" box at the top of the screen to the width of the Mow Grass text box.
73. Click on **OK**.
74. Click on **Item**.
75. Click on **Button...**
76. Press **Enter** to place an OK button in the dialog box.
77. Click and drag the OK button to the lower left corner of the dialog box, below the check boxes.
78. Press **Enter** to place a Cancel button in the dialog box.
79. Click and drag the Cancel button to the lower right corner of the dialog box, below the text boxes.
80. Now that the Jobs dialog box has all the pieces, click and drag the items around inside the box if you need to fine-tune its appearance. Click and drag any side of the dialog box to make the dialog box larger or smaller, depending on how much white space you have showing on the screen.

Step 3 — Copy the Dialog Box Definition Into the Macro

1. Click on the title bar of the dialog box to select it.
2. Click on **Edit**.
3. Click on **Copy**.
4. Click on **File**.
5. Click on **Exit** to exit the Dialog Editor and return to the macro-editing window.
6. Position the insertion point on the line after the last REM statement.
7. Press **Ctrl + V** to paste the dialog box definition from the clipboard into the macro.

Step 4 — Write the Remaining WordBasic Statements

1. Position the insertion point on the **End Sub** statement.
2. Press **Enter** to insert a blank line into the macro.
3. Type the following WordBasic statements beginning at the blank line. Remember, place one statement on each line.
4. Type: **Dim JobsRecord As UserDialog**   'Create the dialog record
5. Type: **ButtonChoice = Dialog(JobsRecord)**   'Display the dialog box

6. Type: **If ButtonChoice = 0 Then   'Check if Cancel button chosen**
           GoTo Quit:
           EndIf

If you clicked on OK to close the dialog box, then the macro will continue by executing the next statement in the macro. If you clicked on Cancel, then macro will go to the label "Quit" and end.

Create an If statement for each check box to see if it was selected or not. If the check box was selected, then calculate the amount of money you earned doing that type of work.

7. Type: **If JobsRecord.MowGrass = 1 Then**
           MowGrassTotal = Val(JobsRecord.NumYards) * 25
           EndIf

If you checked the Mow Grass box, this calculation multiplies the number of yards mowed by 25 (which is what you charge for mowing grass).

8. Type: **If JobsRecord.BabySit = 1 Then**
           BabySitTotal = Val(JobsRecord.NumHours) * 2
           EndIf

This calculation multiplies the number of hours you spent babysitting by 2 (which is your hourly rate for babysitting).

9. Type: **If JobsRecord.WalkDogs = 1 Then**
           DogWalkTotal = Val(JobsRecord.NumDogs) * 5
           EndIf

This calculation multiplies the number of dogs you walked by 5 (which is what you charge for your dog walking service).

10. Type: **If JobsRecord.WashCars = 1 Then**
           WashCarsTotal = Val(JobsRecord.NumCars) * 5
           EndIf

This calculation multiplies the number of cars you washed by 5 (which is what you charge for your car washing service).

11. Type: **GrandTotal = MowGrassTotal + BabySitTotal + WashCarsTotal + DogWalkTotal**

This statement calculates the total amount of money you earned.

12. Type: **If GrandTotal >= Val(JobsRecord.Goal) Then**
           Insert "You have reached your goal by earning " + "$" + Str$(GrandTotal)
           Else
           Remaining = Val(JobsRecord.Goal) - GrandTotal
           Insert "You have earned " + "$" + Str$(GrandTotal)
           InsertPara
           InsertPara
           Insert "You need " + "$" + Str$(Remaining) + " to reach your " + "$" + JobsRecord.Goal + " goal."
           EndIf

This If statement compares the amount of money you earned, stored in the variable "GrandTotal" with the goal, stored in the variable "JobsRecord.Goal." If you've reached your goal a message will appear on the screen showing you how much you've earned. If you haven't reached your goal, the macro will calculate how much more you need to earn and show you that amount.

13. Type: **Quit:**

This label statement is necessary to tell the macro where to go when you click on Cancel to close the dialog box.

The Jobs macro should look like this:

```
Sub MAIN
REM *******************************************************
REM Macro:     Jobs
REM Author:    Charlotte George
REM Purpose:   Calculate part time job earnings
REM *******************************************************
Begin Dialog UserDialog 254, 180, "Jobs"
   Text 10, 6, 36, 13, "Goal", .Text1
   TextBox 10, 22, 94, 18, .Goal
   GroupBox 10, 46, 128, 83, "Jobs"
   CheckBox 20, 58, 112, 16, "Mow Grass", .MowGrass
   CheckBox 20, 75, 92, 16, "Baby-Sit", .BabySit
   CheckBox 20, 92, 112, 16, "Walk Dogs", .WalkDogs
   CheckBox 20, 109, 111, 16, "Wash Cars", .WashCars
   TextBox 156, 51, 85, 18, .NumYards
   TextBox 156, 72, 85, 18, .NumHours
   TextBox 156, 93, 85, 18, .NumDogs
   TextBox 156, 114, 85, 18, .NumCars
   OKButton 11, 144, 88, 21
   CancelButton 155, 144, 88, 21
End Dialog
Dim JobsRecord As UserDialog          'Create dialog record
ButtonChoice = Dialog(JobsRecord)     'Display the dialog box
If ButtonChoice = 0 Then        'Check if Cancel button chosen
   Goto Quit:
EndIf

If JobsRecord.MowGrass = 1 Then
   MowGrassTotal = Val(JobsRecord.NumYards) * 25
EndIf

If JobsRecord.BabySit = 1 Then
   BabySitTotal = Val(JobsRecord.NumHours) * 2
EndIf

If JobsRecord.WalkDogs = 1 Then
   DogWalkTotal = Val(JobsRecord.NumDogs) * 5
EndIf

If JobsRecord.WashCars = 1 Then
   WashCarsTotal = Val(JobsRecord.NumCars) * 5
EndIf
```

```
GrandTotal = MowGrassTotal + BabySitTotal + WashCarsTotal +
DogWalkTotal

If GrandTotal >= Val(JobsRecord.Goal) Then
    Insert "You have reached your goal by earning " + "$" +
    Str$(GrandTotal)
Else
    Remaining = Val(JobsRecord.Goal) - GrandTotal
    Insert "You have earned " + "$" + Str$(GrandTotal)
    InsertPara
    InsertPara
    Insert "You need " + "$" + Str$(Remaining) + " to reach
    your " + "$" + JobsRecord.Goal + " goal."
EndIf
Quit:
End Sub
```

14.   Click on **Save** on the Standard toolbar.
15.   Click on **Yes**.

Run the Jobs macro and check it out. If you get an error the first time you run the macro, click on Window, Global: Jobs and fix the highlighted statement. Resave the macro, then click on Window, Document1 and run the macro again.

1.   Click on **Window**.
2.   Click on the document window.
3.   Press **Alt + E** to erase the document window if it is not blank.
4.   Click on **Tools**.
5.   Click on **Macro...**
6.   Click on **Jobs**.
7.   Click on **Run**.
       The Jobs dialog box appears with the insertion point in the Goal field, waiting for you to enter your goal.
8.   Type: **100**
9.   Click on the following Check boxes:
       Mow Grass
       Walk Dogs
       Wash Cars
10.   Click the mouse button in the text box for entering the number of yards you mowed (the text box across from the check box "Mow Grass").
11.   Type: **2**
12.   Press the **Tab** key two times to move to the walking dogs text box.
13.   Type: **1**
14.   Press the **Tab** key to move to the washing cars text box.
15.   Type: **3**
16.   Press **Enter** or click on **OK** to close the dialog box.
       The jobs macro calculates the amount of money you've earned as follows:

Mowing Grass	2 yards at $25.00 a yard	=	$50.00
Walking Dogs	1 dog at $5.00	=	5.00

| Washing Cars | 3 cars at $5.00 each | = | 15.00 |
| Total Amount Earned | | = | $70.00 |

You need $30 to reach your $100 goal.

Step 5 — Assign the Jobs macro to the Tools menu.

1. Click on **Tools**.
2. Click on **Customize...**
2. Click on **Menus**.
4. Click on **Macros** under Categories.
5. Click on **Jobs** under Macros.
6. Click on **&Tools** under Change What Menu.
7. Click on **Add**.
8. Click on **Close**.
9. Press **Alt + E** to erase the screen.
10. Click on **Tools**.
11. Click on **Jobs** to run the Jobs macro.
12. Type a goal in the Goal text box.
13. Click on each type of work you did.
14. Type the number of jobs you did for each type of work
15. Click on **OK**.

Did you reach your goal? Are you on your way to the CD store?

Run the macro a few more times experimenting with different goals and different combinations of work performed. Check the boxes to indicate which jobs you did, then type the amounts in the text boxes beside each check box.

16. Click on **Window**.
17. Click on **Global: Jobs**
18. Click on **File, Close** to close the macro-editing window.

Universal Programming Truths

The techniques you've used in writing Word macros are the same techniques you'd use in writing programs in any computer programming language. The actual command names may vary, but the logic is the same. An If statement is an If statement in any language. A loop is a loop. If you want to learn another programming language, apply the logic you've learned here to the particulars of the language you want to learn. It's really cool, because once you learn one language, it's easy to learn others.

Congratulations!

You've mastered the art of making macros. There are millions and millions of ways to use macros to make your life easier. The examples in this book are just a sample. If you want to learn more about macros, experiment on your own and make macros. The more you use macros, the more you'll find ways to use them. At the end of this book, in the Appendix, you'll find some macros that are yours to keep. Feel free to use them as they are or modify them to work better for you.

Congratulations!
You're a
Macro Magic
Wizard

CHAPTER 8

Some Word Macros

To create the following macros, record as many of the statements as possible. Then edit the macros and add the statements that cannot be recorded.

Shape Inserter Macro

Record macros that will insert various shapes into a document by turning on the macro recorder and clicking on **Insert, Symbol...** Click on the shape you want, click on **Insert, Close** and then turn off the macro recorder. Assign the macros to keyboard shortcut keys, and you'll be able to place the shape into your document with one quick keystroke. Here are a few of the shapes that you might want to have recorded in macros:

The Symbol macro contains one statement, InsertSymbol. The "CharNum" argument is different for each symbol.

```
Sub MAIN
InsertSymbol .Font = "Symbol", .CharNum = "183"
End Sub
```

Transposes Two Characters Macro

Do your fingers sometimes mess up when you're typing? This macro fixes that problem by transposing two characters, so if you type "fro" the macro changes it to "for." To run this macro, place the insertion point to the right of the two characters you want to switch, like: fro|

```
Sub MAIN
REM **********************************************************
REM Macro:      Transpose
REM Purpose:    Transposes two characters
REM **********************************************************
CharLeft 1, 1   'Moves the insertion pt left 1 and selects the
                character
EditCut          'Removes the character & places it on the
                clipboard
CharLeft 1       'Moves the insertion point left 1
EditPaste        'Inserts the character from the clipboard
CharRight 1      'Moves the insertion point right 1
End Sub
```

Word Count Macro

Do you ever use the same word over and over again in a paper? With this macro, you can enter the word and the macro will count how many times the word is used in your document.

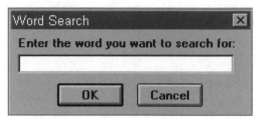

**Type the word you want to search
for in a dialog box**

```
Sub MAIN
REM ***********************************************************
REM Macro:      CountWords
REM Purpose:    Count number of times a word is in a document
REM ***********************************************************
Begin Dialog UserDialog 320, 78, "Word Search"
Text 10, 6, 292, 13, "Enter the word you want to search for:",
.Text1
TextBox 10, 22, 288, 18, .Word$
OKButton 62, 50, 88, 21
CancelButton 167, 50, 88, 21
End Dialog
Dim WordCntRecord As UserDialog        'Define dialog record
ButtonChoice = Dialog(WordCntRecord)   'Display dialog box
If ButtonChoice = 0 Then               'Check how dialog box closed
   Goto Quit:
EndIf
StartOfDocument       'Places insertion pt at top of doc
Count = 0          'Initializes counter
quotes$ = Chr$(34)
Title$ = "Word Search"
EditFind .Find = WordCntRecord.Word$
While EditFindFound() = - 1   'Searches until word not found
   Count = Count + 1
   RepeatFind
Wend
If Count = 0 Then
   MsgBox(quotes$ + WordCntRecord.Word$ + quotes$ + " was not
   found.", Title$)
EndIf
If Count = 1 Then
   MsgBox(quotes$ + WordCntRecord.Word$ + quotes$ + " was
   found once.", Title$)
EndIf
```

```
If Count > 1 Then
    MsgBox(quotes$ + WordCntRecord.Word$ + quotes$ + " was
    found " + Str$(Count) + " times.", Title$)
EndIf
Quit:
End Sub
```

Multiplication Macro

Ever forget any of those pesky multiplication facts? This macro creates a table of the multiplication facts from 1 to 12.

Multiplication Facts

1	2	3	4	5	6	7	8	9	10	11	12
2	4	6	8	10	12	14	16	18	20	22	24
3	6	9	12	15	18	21	24	27	30	33	36
4	8	12	16	20	24	28	32	36	40	44	48
5	10	15	20	25	30	35	40	45	50	55	60
6	12	18	24	30	36	42	48	54	60	66	72
7	14	21	28	35	42	49	56	63	70	77	84
8	16	24	32	40	48	56	64	72	80	88	96
9	18	27	36	45	54	63	72	81	90	99	108
10	20	30	40	50	60	70	80	90	100	110	120
11	22	33	44	55	66	77	88	99	110	121	132
12	24	36	48	60	72	84	96	108	120	132	144

```
Sub MAIN

REM ***********************************************************

REM Macro:     Multiply

REM Purpose:   Print multiplications facts from 1 to 12

REM ***********************************************************

FilePageSetup .Tab = "0", .PaperSize = "0", .TopMargin = "1" +
Chr$(34), .BottomMargin = "1" + Chr$(34), .LeftMargin = "1" +
Chr$(34), .RightMargin = "1" + Chr$(34), .Gutter = "0" +
Chr$(34), .PageWidth = "8.5" + Chr$(34), .PageHeight = "11" +
Chr$(34), .Orientation = 0, .FirstPage = 0, .OtherPages = 0,
.VertAlign = 0, .ApplyPropsTo = 4, .FacingPages = 0,
.HeaderDistance = "0.5" + Chr$(34), .FooterDistance = "0.5" +
Chr$(34), .SectionStart = 2, .OddAndEvenPages = 0,
.DifferentFirstPage = 0, .Endnotes = 0, .LineNum = 0,
.StartingNum = "", .FromText = "", .CountBy = "0", .NumMode = - 1

FormatFont .Points = "18", .Underline = 0, .Color = 0,
.Strikethrough = 0, .Superscript = 0, .Subscript = 0, .Hidden
= 0, .SmallCaps = 0, .AllCaps = 0, .Spacing = "0 pt",
.Position = "0 pt", .Kerning = 0, .KerningMin = "", .Tab =
"0", .Font = "Arial", .Bold = 1, .Italic = 0

CenterPara

Insert "Multiplication Facts"

InsertPara

InsertPara

LeftPara

TableInsertTable .ConvertFrom = "", .NumColumns = "12",
.NumRows = "12", .InitialColWidth = "Auto", .Format = "20",
.Apply = "167"

TableSelectTable

TableRowHeight .RulerStyle = "0", .LineSpacingRule = 2,
.LineSpacing = "30 pt", .LeftIndent = "0" + Chr$(34),
.Alignment = 0, .AllowRowSplit = 1

FormatFont .Points = "14", .Underline = - 1, .Color = - 1,
.Strikethrough = - 1, .Superscript = - 1, .Subscript = - 1,
.Hidden = - 1, .SmallCaps = - 1, .AllCaps = - 1, .Spacing =
"", .Position = "", .Kerning = - 1, .KerningMin = "", .Tab =
"0", .Font = "Arial", .Bold = 1, .Italic = 0

For Factor1 = 1 To 12              'Loop for printing facts

   For Factor2 = 1 To 12

      Insert Str$(Factor1 * Factor2)

      NextCell

   Next Factor2

Next Factor1

TableDeleteCells .ShiftCells = 2

End Sub
```

Thank You Notes

Write your thank you notes in half the time! The Thank You Notes macro creates custom made, fill in the blanks thank you notes that are good looking and easy to make. Follow the Party Invitation macro example (p. 109) to see the steps necessary to write this macro.

The Thank You Notes dialog box

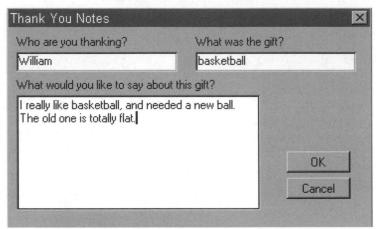

Dear William,

Thank you very much for the basketball. I really like basketball, and needed a new ball. The old one is totally flat. It was great having you at my party. Thanks for everything.

Your friend,

Sandy

```
Sub MAIN
REM ********************************************************
REM Macro:      Thanks
REM Purpose:    Create fill in the blanks thank you notes
REM ********************************************************
Begin Dialog UserDialog 484, 186, "Thank You Notes"
   Text 10, 6, 177, 13, "Who are you thanking?", .Text1
   TextBox 10, 22, 216, 18, .Name$
   Text 250, 6, 144, 13, "What was the gift?", .Text2
   TextBox 250, 22, 227, 18, .Gift$
   Text 10, 46, 324, 13, "What would you like to say about
   this gift?", .Text3
   TextBox 10, 62, 325, 105, .Comment$, 1
   OKButton 376, 108, 88, 21
   CancelButton 374, 134, 88, 21
End Dialog
```

```
Dim ThanksRecord As UserDialog        'Define the dialog record
ButtonChoice = Dialog(ThanksRecord) 'Display the dialog box
If ButtonChoice = 0 Then              'Check if Cancel button chosen
    Goto Quit:
EndIf
FilePageSetup .Tab = "0", .PaperSize = "0", .TopMargin = "1.3" +
Chr$(34), .BottomMargin = "1.3" + Chr$(34), .LeftMargin = "1.5" +
Chr$(34), .RightMargin = "1.5" + Chr$(34), .Gutter = "0" +
Chr$(34), .PageWidth = "8.5" + Chr$(34), .PageHeight = "11" +
Chr$(34), .Orientation = 0, .FirstPage = 0, .OtherPages = 0,
.VertAlign = 0, .ApplyPropsTo = 4, .FacingPages = 0,
.HeaderDistance = "0.5" + Chr$(34), .FooterDistance = "0.5" +
Chr$(34), .SectionStart = 2, .OddAndEvenPages = 0,
.DifferentFirstPage = 0, .Endnotes = 0, .LineNum = 0,
.StartingNum = "", .FromText = "", .CountBy = "0", .NumMode = - 1
ViewPage
InsertFrame
FormatFrame .Wrap = 1, .WidthRule = 1, .FixedWidth = "6" +
Chr$(34), .HeightRule = 2, .FixedHeight = "1.5" + Chr$(34),
.PositionHorz = "Center", .PositionHorzRel = 1, .DistFromText
= "0.13" + Chr$(34), .PositionVert = "Top", .PositionVertRel =
0, .DistVertFromText = "0" + Chr$(34), .MoveWithText = 0,
.LockAnchor = 0
InsertPicture .Name = "C:\WINWORD\CLIPART\DIVIDER1.WMF",
.LinkToFile = "0"
FormatFont .Points = "22", .Underline = 0, .Color = 0,
.Strikethrough = 0, .Superscript = 0, .Subscript = 0, .Hidden
= 0, .SmallCaps = 0, .AllCaps = 0, .Spacing = "0 pt",
.Position = "0 pt", .Kerning = 0, .KerningMin = "", .Tab =
"0", .Font = "Times New Roman", .Bold = 0, .Italic = 0
InsertPara
Insert "Dear" + Chr$(32) + ThanksRecord.Name$ + ","
SpacePara2
InsertPara
Insert Chr$(9) + "Thank you very much for the" + Chr$(32) +
ThanksRecord.Gift$ ¡ "."
Insert Chr$(32) + Chr$(32)
Insert ThanksRecord.Comment$ + Chr$(32) + Chr$(32)
Insert "It was great having you at my party. Thanks for
everything."
InsertPara
Insert "Your friend,"
InsertPara
InsertPara
Insert "Sandy"
SpacePara1
InsertPara
InsertFrame
FormatFrame .Wrap = 1, .WidthRule = 1, .FixedWidth = "6" +
Chr$(34), .HeightRule = 2, .FixedHeight = "1.5" + Chr$(34),
.PositionHorz = "Center", .PositionHorzRel = 1, .DistFromText
= "0.13" + Chr$(34), .PositionVert = "Bottom",
```

```
.PositionVertRel = 0, .DistVertFromText = "0" + Chr$(34),
.MoveWithText = 0, .LockAnchor = 0
 InsertPicture .Name = "C:\WINWORD\CLIPART\DIVIDER1.WMF",
.LinkToFile = "0"
 Button = MsgBox("Do you want to print the thank you note?", 4)
 If Button = - 1 Then FilePrint
    Quit:
 End Sub
```

Average Grades

With this macro, you'll always know where you stand in school. The Average Grades macro allows you to enter your grades and it will average them for you.

```
Sub MAIN
REM ***********************************************************
REM Macro:      AverageGrades
REM Purpose:    This macro averages your grades
REM ***********************************************************
Counter = Val(InputBox$("How many scores do you wish to
average?", "Average Grades"))
For Loop = 1 To Counter        'Loop to add grades together
Score = Val(InputBox$("Enter your test score please.",
"Average Grades"))
Total = Total + Score
Next Loop
Average = Total / Counter      'Calculate grade average
MsgBox "Your Grade Average is: " + Str$(Average), "Average
Grades"
End Sub
```

Area Macro

The Area macro is one of those cool math macros. It calculates the area of a square, rectangle, triangle, or circle.

The Area dialog box

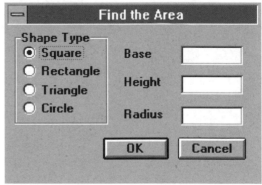

```
Sub MAIN
REM ***********************************************************
REM Macro:      Area
REM Purpose:    Find the area of a square, rectangle, triangle
REM             and circle
REM ***********************************************************
```

```
Begin Dialog UserDialog 330, 144, "Find the Area"
   GroupBox 10, 6, 123, 87, "Shape Type"
   OptionGroup .ShapeType
      OptionButton 20, 18, 83, 16, "Square", .Square
      OptionButton 20, 35, 107, 16, "Rectangle", .Rectangle
      OptionButton 20, 52, 91, 16, "Triangle", .Triangle
      OptionButton 20, 69, 72, 16, "Circle", .Circle
   Text 154, 21, 39, 13, "Base", .Text1
   TextBox 229, 19, 80, 18, .Base
   Text 154, 46, 51, 13, "Height", .Text2
   TextBox 229, 46, 80, 18, .Height
   Text 154, 76, 53, 13, "Radius", .Text3
   TextBox 229, 75, 80, 18, .Radius
   OKButton 125, 103, 88, 21
   CancelButton 226, 103, 88, 21
End Dialog
Dim AreaRecord As UserDialog      'Define dialog record
ButtonChoice = Dialog(AreaRecord)   'Display the dialog box
If ButtonChoice = - 1 Then        'Check which button chosen
   Goto Calculate:
Else
   Goto Quit:
EndIf

Calculate:
If AreaRecord.ShapeType = 0 Then
   Area = Val(AreaRecord.Base) * Val(AreaRecord.Base)
   Insert "The area of your square is " + AreaRecord.Base +
   " * " + AreaRecord.Base + " = " + Str$(Area)
   InsertPara
EndIf
If AreaRecord.ShapeType = 1 Then
   Area = Val(AreaRecord.Base) * Val(AreaRecord.Height)
   Insert "The area of your rectangle is " + AreaRecord.Base +
   " * " + AreaRecord.Height + " = " + Str$(Area)
   InsertPara
EndIf
If AreaRecord.ShapeType = 2 Then
   Area = 0.5 * Val(AreaRecord.Base) * Val(AreaRecord.Height)
   Insert "The area of your triangle is " + "½ * " +
   AreaRecord.Base + " * " + AreaRecord.Height + " = " +
   Str$(Area)
   InsertPara
EndIf
If AreaRecord.ShapeType = 3 Then
   Area = Val(AreaRecord.Radius) * Val(AreaRecord.Radius) * 3.14
   Insert "The area of your circle is " + "3.14 * " +
   AreaRecord.Radius + " * " + AreaRecord.Radius + " = " +
   Str$(Area)
   InsertPara
EndIf
```

```
Quit:
End Sub
```

Name and Address Macro

This macro creates a two column name and address file. You enter the information in one easy-to-use dialog box, and the macro adds the information to a name and address master file. This macro can be modified to format anything that needs to be shown in columns, such as a school newspaper or a program.

The Name and Address dialog box

Name and Address File

Susan Smith
3456 Whiteway Avenue
Memphis, TN 70008
(901) 889-3983

Ben Jones
2359 Rainwater Drive
Houston, TX 77339
(713) 435-9086

Jenny Yerger
8907 Halpern Street
Apt. 502
West Orange, NJ 90012
(413) 293-9843

```
Sub MAIN
REM  *******************************************************
REM Macro:      Address
REM Purpose:    Keep a name and address file of my friends
REM  *******************************************************
CenterPara
Insert "Name and Address File"
InsertPara
```

```
InsertPara
InsertPara
InsertBreak .Type = 3
LeftPara
FormatColumns .Columns = "2", .ColumnNo = "1", .ColumnWidth =
"2.75" + Chr$(34), .ColumnSpacing = "0.5" + Chr$(34),
.EvenlySpaced = 1, .ApplyColsTo = 4, .ColLine = 0,
.StartNewCol = - 1
Continue:
Begin Dialog UserDialog 320, 192, "Address File"
    Text 10, 6, 44, 13, "Name", .Text1
    TextBox 10, 22, 294, 18, .Name
    Text 10, 46, 61, 13, "Address", .Text2
    TextBox 10, 63, 295, 64, .Address, 1
    Text 10, 136, 112, 15, "Phone Number", .Text3
    TextBox 10, 152, 178, 18, .PhoneNumber
    OKButton 221, 136, 88, 21
    CancelButton 221, 160, 88, 21
End Dialog
Dim AddressRecord As UserDialog      'Define the dialog record
ButtonChoice = Dialog(AddressRecord) 'Display the dialog box
If ButtonChoice = 0 Then         'Check if Cancel button chosen
    Goto Quit:
EndIf
Insert AddressRecord.Name
InsertPara
Insert AddressRecord.Address
InsertPara
Insert AddressRecord.PhoneNumber
InsertPara
InsertPara
Again = MsgBox("Do you want to enter another address?", "Name
and Address File", 36)
If Again = - 1 Then
    Goto Continue:
EndIf
Quit:
End Sub
```

Changeable Business Card Macro

This macro creates cool looking business cards. You choose which jobs to include on the card (babysitting, mowing grass, or whatever) and enter them in a custom dialog box, shown on the next page. You can also choose the price and rate for each job.

```
Sub MAIN
REM********************************************************
REM Macro:      BusinessCards
REM Purpose:    Create custom made business cards
REM********************************************************
```

Fill in the blanks to create changeable business cards

Henry's Helpers

- **Mow Grass**   **$25.00**   **per yard**
- **Baby Sit**   **$2.00**   **per hour**
- **Walk Dogs**   **$5.00**   **per dog**
- **Wash Cars**   **$5.00**   **per car**

```
Begin Dialog UserDialog 532, 148, "Business Cards"
    Text 10, 8, 28, 13, "Job", .Text1
    Text 215, 8, 40, 13, "Price", .Text2
    Text 352, 8, 37, 13, "Rate", .Text3
    TextBox 10, 26, 160, 18, .JobType1
    TextBox 215, 26, 100, 18, .JobPrice1
    TextBox 352, 26, 160, 18, .JobRate1
    TextBox 10, 47, 160, 18, .JobType2
    TextBox 215, 47, 100, 18, .JobPrice2
    TextBox 352, 47, 160, 18, .JobRate2
    TextBox 10, 68, 160, 18, .JobType3
    TextBox 215, 68, 100, 18, .JobPrice3
    TextBox 352, 68, 160, 18, .JobRate3
    TextBox 10, 89, 160, 18, .JobType4
```

```
        TextBox 215, 89, 100, 18, .JobPrice4
        TextBox 352, 89, 160, 18, .JobRate4
        OKButton 230, 116, 88, 21
        CancelButton 352, 116, 88, 21
    End Dialog
    Dim BusinessRecord As UserDialog 'Define dialog record
    BusinessRecord.JobPrice1 = "$"    'Assign default values
    BusinessRecord.JobRate1 = "per "
    ButtonChoice = Dialog(BusinessRecord)'Display the dialog box
    If ButtonChoice = 0 Then    'Check if Cancel button chosen
        Goto Quit:
    EndIf
    ViewPage          'Create the business card
    ViewZoom .FullPage
    InsertFrame
    FormatFrame .Wrap = 1, .WidthRule = 1, .FixedWidth = "5" +
    Chr$(34), .HeightRule = 2, .FixedHeight = "3.5" + Chr$(34),
    .PositionHorz = "Center", .PositionHorzRel = 1, .DistFromText
    = "0" + Chr$(34), .PositionVert = "2" + Chr$(34),
    .PositionVertRel = 1, .DistVertFromText = "0" + Chr$(34),
    .MoveWithText = 0, .LockAnchor = 0
    InsertPicture .Name = "C:\WINWORD\CLIPART\HDECOBOX.WMF",
    .LinkToFile = "0"
    DrawTextbox
    FormatDrawingObject .Tab = "2", .FillColor = "1", .LineColor =
    "", .FillPatternColor = "8", .FillPattern = "0", .LineType =
    0, .LineStyle = - 1, .LineWeight = "", .ArrowStyle = - 1,
    .ArrowWidth = - 1, .ArrowLength = - 1, .Shadow = 0,
    .RoundCorners = 0, .HorizontalPos = "0.85" + Chr$(34),
    .HorizontalFrom = 0, .VerticalPos = "1.10" + Chr$(34),
    .VerticalFrom = 0, .LockAnchor = 0, .Height = "3.2" +
    Chr$(34), .Width = "4.3" + Chr$(34), .InternalMargin = "1
    pt"
    CenterPara
    FormatFont .Points = "36", .Underline = 0, .Color = 0,
    .Strikethrough = 0, .Superscript = 0, .Subscript = 0, .Hidden
    = 0, .SmallCaps = 0, .AllCaps = 0, .Spacing = "0 pt",
    .Position = "0 pt", .Kerning = 0, .KerningMin = "", .Tab =
    "0", .Font = "Times New Roman", .Bold = 1, .Italic = 0
    Insert "Henry's Helpers"
    InsertPara
    LeftPara
    FormatFont .Points = "16", .Underline = 0, .Color = 0,
    .Strikethrough = 0, .Superscript = 0, .Subscript = 0,
    .Hidden = 0, .SmallCaps = 0, .AllCaps = 0, .Spacing = "0 pt",
    .Position = "0 pt", .Kerning = 0, .KerningMin = "", .Tab =
    "0", .Font = "Times New Roman", .Bold = 1, .Italic = 0
    FormatTabs .Position = "", .DefTabs = "0.5" + Chr$(34), .Align
    = 0, .Leader = 0, .ClearAll
    FormatTabs .Position = "0.3" + Chr$(34), .DefTabs = "0.5" +
    Chr$(34), .Align = 0, .Leader = 0, .Set
```

```
FormatTabs .Position = "0.5" + Chr$(34), .DefTabs = "0.5" +
Chr$(34), .Align = 0, .Leader = 0, .Set
FormatTabs .Position = "3.2" + Chr$(34), .DefTabs = "0.5" +
Chr$(34), .Align = 2, .Leader = 0, .Set
FormatTabs .Position = "3.32" + Chr$(34), .DefTabs = "0.5" +
Chr$(34), .Align = 0, .Leader = 0, .Set
InsertPara
SpacePara2
Insert Chr$(9)
InsertSymbol .Font = "Symbol", .CharNum = "183"
Insert Chr$(9) + BusinessRecord.JobType1 + Chr$(9) +
BusinessRecord.JobPrice1 + Chr$(9) + BusinessRecord.JobRate1
InsertPara
Insert Chr$(9)
InsertSymbol .Font = "Symbol", .CharNum = "183"
Insert Chr$(9) + BusinessRecord.JobType2 + Chr$(9) +
BusinessRecord.JobPrice2 + Chr$(9) + BusinessRecord.JobRate2
InsertPara
Insert Chr$(9)
InsertSymbol .Font = "Symbol", .CharNum = "183"
Insert Chr$(9) + BusinessRecord.JobType3 + Chr$(9) +
BusinessRecord.JobPrice3 + Chr$(9) + BusinessRecord.JobRate3
InsertPara
Insert Chr$(9)
InsertSymbol .Font = "Symbol", .CharNum = "183"
Insert Chr$(9) + BusinessRecord.JobType4 + Chr$(9) +
BusinessRecord.JobPrice4 + Chr$(9) + BusinessRecord.JobRate4
Quit:
End Sub
```

Bibliography Macro

Ever have trouble typing a bibliography? Those days are gone forever with this spiffy macro. Bibliography Helper lets you enter your research data in one easy to use dialog box, and it types the information in its proper format in a bibliography.

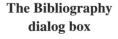

**The Bibliography
dialog box**

Bibliography Helper

Author

Laura Edge

Book Title

Macro Magic in Microsoft Word 6 & 7

Publisher

Rhache Publishers, Ltd.

Date

1997   OK   Cancel

Bibliography

Laura Edge, *Macro Magic in Microsoft Word 6 & 7*, Rhache Publishers, Ltd., 1997

Laura Edge, *Macro Magic in WordPerfect 6.1 & 7*, Rhache Publishers, Ltd., 1997

```
Sub MAIN
REM ************************************************************
REM Macro:      Bibliography
REM Purpose:    Format bibliography for reports
REM ************************************************************
FileOpen .Name = "C:\My Documents\BIBLIOG.DOC",
.ConfirmConversions = 0, .ReadOnly = 0, .AddToMru = 0,
.PasswordDoc = "", .PasswordDot = "", .Revert = 0,
.WritePasswordDoc = "", .WritePasswordDot = ""
EndOfDocument
Continue:
Begin Dialog UserDialog 456, 206, "Bibliography Helper"
    Text 10, 6, 51, 13, "Author", .Text1
    TextBox 10, 22, 431, 18, .Author
    Text 10, 46, 79, 13, "Book Title", .Text2
    TextBox 10, 62, 429, 18, .Title
    Text 11, 91, 71, 13, "Publisher", .Text3
    TextBox 10, 108, 431, 37, .Publisher, 1
    Text 10, 152, 37, 13, "Date", .Text4
    TextBox 10, 170, 118, 18, .Date
    OKButton 201, 172, 88, 21
    CancelButton 319, 172, 88, 21
End Dialog
Dim BibRecord As UserDialog       'Define the dialog record
ButtonChoice = Dialog(BibRecord)     'Display the dialog box
If ButtonChoice = 0 Then      'Check if Cancel button chosen
    Goto Quit:
EndIf
Insert BibRecord.Author + ", "
Italic
Insert BibRecord.Title
Italic
Insert ", " + BibRecord.Publisher +
", " + BibRecord.Date
InsertPara
InsertPara
Again = MsgBox("Do you want to enter
another?", "Bibliography Helper", 36)
If Again = - 1 Then
    Goto Continue:
EndIf
Quit:
End Sub
```

The End